FOR THE COMMUNION
OF THE CHURCHES

FOR THE COMMUNION
OF THE CHURCHES

The Contribution of the
Groupe des Dombes

Edited by

Catherine E. Clifford

WILLIAM B. EERDMANS PUBLISHING COMPANY
GRAND RAPIDS, MICHIGAN / CAMBRIDGE, U.K.

Wm. B. Eerdmans Publishing Co.

2140 Oak Industrial Drive N.E., Grand Rapids, Michigan 49505 /

P.O. Box 163, Cambridge CB3 9PU U.K.

Printed in the United States of America

16 15 14 13 12 11 10   7 6 5 4 3 2 1

Library of Congress Cataloging-in-Publication Data

For the communion of the churches: the contribution of the Groupe des Dombes /
edited by Catherine E. Clifford.

p.   cm.

ISBN 978-0-8028-6532-8 (pbk.: alk. paper)

1. Groupe des Dombes. 2. Christian union. 3. Catholic Church —
Relations — Protestant churches. 4. Protestant churches — Relations —
Catholic Church.   I. Clifford, Catherine E., 1958-   II. Groupe des Dombes.

BX6.G76F67   2010

262.001′1 — dc22

2010037834

www.eerdmans.com

Contents

⸻⟨ʘ∕ʘ∕ʘ⟩⸻

Acknowledgments

—◦◦◦—

I am grateful for the encouragement and support of Norman J. Hjelm and William G. Rusch, who first suggested the publication of this anthology. I also wish to express my gratitude to William B. Eerdmans for his generous support and commitment to publishing works such as this that serve as important resources for expanding ecumenical scholarship and conversation. Ronald MacRae was most helpful in proofreading substantial sections of this volume. This book has been published with the financial support of the Publication Grants Program of Saint Paul University, Ottawa.

I am grateful for permission granted to reprint the following:

Groupes des Dombes. "Towards a Common Eucharistic Faith." Translated by Pamela Gaughan in *Modern Eucharistic Agreement*, edited by H. R. McAdoo, 51-78. London: SPCK, 1973. Original French version: *Vers une même foi eucharistique?* Taizé: Les Presses de Taizé, 1972. Reprinted in *Pour la communion des Églises. L'apport du Groupe des Dombes 1937-1987*. Paris: Centurion, 1988.

Groupes des Dombes. "Towards a Reconciliation of Ministries." Translated by Pamela Gaughan in *Modern Ecumenical Documents on the Ministry*, edited by H. R. McAdoo, 89-107. London: SPCK, 1975. Original French version: *Pour une réconciliation des ministères*. Taizé: Les Presses de Taizé, 1972. Reprinted in *Pour la communion des Églises. L'apport du Groupe des Dombes 1937-1987*. Paris: Centurion, 1988.

Groupes des Dombes. "The Episcopal Ministry: Reflections and Proposals

vii

Concerning the Ministry of Vigilance in the Particular Church." *One in Christ* 14 (1978): 267-88. Original French version: *Le ministère episcopal. Réflexions sur le ministère de vigilance et d'unité dans l'Église particulière.* Taizé: Les Presses de Taizé, 1976. Reprinted in *Pour la communion des Églises. L'apport du Groupe des Dombes 1937-1987.* Paris: Centurion, 1988.

Groupes des Dombes. "The Holy Spirit, the Church and the Sacraments." *One in Christ* 16 (1980): 234-64. Original French version: *L'Esprit Saint, l'Église et les sacraments.* Taisé: Les presses de Taizé, 1979. Reprinted in *Pour la communion des Églises. L'apport du Groupe des Dombes 1937-1987.* Paris: Centurion, 1988.

Groupes des Dombes. "The Ministry of Communion in the Universal Church." Translated by Catherine E. Clifford. Original French version: *Le ministère de communion dans l'Église universelle.* Paris: Centurion, 1986. Reprinted in *Pour la communion des Églises. L'apport du Groupe des Dombes 1937-1987.* Paris: Centurion, 1988.

Groupe des Dombes. *For the Conversion of the Churches.* Translated by James Grieg. Geneva: WCC, 1993. Original French version: *Pour la communion des Églises: Identité et changement dans la dynamique de la conversion.* Paris: Centurion, 1991. Reprinted in *Pour la communion des Églises. L'apport du Groupe des Dombes 1937-1987.* Paris: Centurion, 1988.

Editor's Introduction

——◦◦◦◦——

This book gathers together a number of documents that reflect a significant chapter in the history of ecumenism spanning three decades of doctrinal dialogue by a dedicated and pioneering team of Protestant and Catholic theologians, the Groupe des Dombes. Founded in 1937 by Abbé Paul Couturier, the Groupe des Dombes gathers together Catholic, Reformed, and Lutheran pastors and theologians from across French-speaking Europe. Elsewhere, I have provided an extensive survey of the history of the Groupe des Dombes, giving an account of both its contribution towards theological consensus and the evolution of its rather unique methodology.[1] In these few brief lines, I would like to draw the reader's attention to the context for each of the documents and highlight some of their salient features.

Until now, most of these documents have not been not readily accessible to English-language readers and have not appeared in the standard collections of texts from the international bilateral dialogues.[2] The first four docu-

1. Catherine E. Clifford, *The Groupe des Dombes: A Dialogue of Conversion*, American University Studies, Series VII: Theology and Religion, Vol. 231 (New York: Peter Lang, 2005). See also the important study by Jorge A. Scampini, *La Conversion de las Iglesias, una Necesidad y una Urgencia de la Fe: La Experiencia del Groupe des Dombes Como Desarrollo de un Método Ecuménico Eclesial (1937-1997)*, Ökumenische Beihefte, 42 (Fribourg: Editions Universitaires, 2003).

2. See, for example, Harding Meyer and Lukas Vischer, eds., *Growth in Agreement: Reports and Agreed Statements of Ecumenical Conversations on a World Level* (New York:

ments, on eucharist, ministry, *episcopē*, and the sacraments, appeared in more modest collections of agreed statements[3] or in ecumenical journals.[4] The former have long been out of print. The latter might be read by theologians and specialists, but would not likely have found their way into the resource libraries of the local ecumenical office. The fifth document, one of the earliest ecumenical studies on the vexing issue of papal primacy, has not been translated into English until now.[5] It is my hope that this translation will enable English-language readers to continue seeking, as Pope John Paul II stated it, "the forms in which this ministry may accomplish a service of love recognized by all concerned."[6] The last text included in this anthology, "For the Conversion of the Churches,"[7] sparked great interest and was more widely disseminated. It continues to be a key reference for anyone who seeks to understand the trajectory, not only of the Groupe des Dombes, but of the whole ecumenical movement. It provides significant insights into the task of doctrinal dialogue and the challenge of reception.

The Groupe of "les Dombes" takes its name from the Abbey of Notre Dame des Dombes, a Trappist monastery near Ars-sur-Formans, France, which became its meeting place from 1937 until 1998. Since that time the

---

Paulist, 1984); Jeffrey Gros, Harding Meyer, and William C. Rusch, eds., *Growth in Agreement II: Reports and Agreed Statements of Ecumenical Conversations on a World Level, 1982-1998* (Geneva: WCC / Grand Rapids: Eerdmans, 2000); Jeffery Gros, Thomas F. Best, and Lorelei F. Fuchs, eds., *Growth in Agreement III: International Dialogue Texts and Agreed Statements, 1998-2005* (Geneva: WCC / Grand Rapids: Eerdmans, 2007).

3. "Towards a Common Eucharistic Faith" first appeared in *Modern Eucharistic Agreement,* ed. H. R. McAdoo (London: SPCK, 1973), pp. 53-78; original French version: *Vers une même foi eucharistique?* (Taizé: Les Presses de Taizé, 1972). The English translation of "Towards a Reconciliation of Ministries" was first published in *Modern Ecumenical Documents on the Ministry,* ed. H. R. McAdoo (London: SPCK, 1975), pp. 89-107. Original French version: *Pour une réconciliation des ministères* (Taizé: Les Presses de Taizé, 1972).

4. "The Episcopal Ministry: Reflections and Proposals Concerning the Ministry of Vigilance in the Particular Church," *One in Christ* 14 (1978): 267-88; "The Holy Spirit, the Church and the Sacraments," *One in Christ* 16 (1980): 234-64. Original French version: *Le Ministère épiscopal. Réflexions sur le ministère de vigilance et d'unité dans l'Église particulière* (Taizé: Les presses de Taizé, 1976).

5. *Le ministère de communion dans l'Église universelle* (Paris: Centurion, 1986). All five of the documents cited in notes 3-5 are collected and reprinted in *Pour la Communion des Églises. L'apport du Groupe des Dombes 1937-1987* (Paris: Centurion, 1988).

6. John Paul II, *On Commitment to Ecumenism (Ut Unum Sint)* (Ottawa: CCCB, 1995), no. 95.

7. *For the Conversion of the Churches,* trans. James Grieg (Geneva: WCC, 1993). Original French version: *Pour la conversion des Églises* (Paris: Centurion, 1991).

Cistercian Community has left the Abbey, entrusting it to the care of the Chemin Neuf Community. The dialogue continues to gather regularly at the Benedictine monastery of Les Pradines. Meeting almost without interruption since 1937 (it was not always possible to gather during the Second World War), this is perhaps the longest-standing forum for Protestant-Catholic theological dialogue in the world. Such longevity — including the long tenure of some members — provides a unique context for a sustained conversation that has the capacity to take a long view of the broader ecumenical scene.

While not an officially mandated dialogue commission, the members of the Groupe des Dombes are highly respected pastors and theologians who strive to speak in fidelity to their respective ecclesial traditions. The "unofficial" character of their work means that the documents produced by the Groupe des Dombes have no recognized authority other than the moral weight of the sincere and loyal witness of those who seek the truth in love. This aspect of the Groupe des Dombes' work, far from being felt as a limitation, may be what has given this distinctive band of ecumenists more freedom than others. It has often enabled them to be at the forefront of Protestant-Catholic dialogue, taking up some of the more challenging theological and pastoral issues confronting the churches on the road to Christian unity. For this reason, the influence of their work on other bilateral and multilateral dialogues has been considerable.

The Groupe des Dombes toiled largely in obscurity for over three decades until the full engagement of the Catholic Church in the wider ecumenical movement. In effect, the Catholic Church adopted many features of the ethic of dialogue that were painstakingly developed in this early laboratory. Abbé Couturier's "spiritual ecumenism" was espoused by the teaching of the Second Vatican Council as the "soul of the ecumenical movement."[8] The practice of spiritual ecumenism combines commitment to the cultivation of a climate of common prayer with a spirit of repentance and humble self-critique, and the search for a shared understanding of the truth of the gospel beyond differing expressions of faith. For Paul Couturier — as for the Groupe des Dombes today — the inner renewal of the Spirit, nourished by prayer, leads not only to the conversion of individual hearts. Ultimately, it must awaken a renewal in the theology, life, and practice of the churches and lead to a veritable conversion or transformation in the concrete form of their proclamation and witness to the gospel.

---

8. Second Vatican Council, Decree on Ecumenism *(Unitatis Redintegratio)*, 8.

Pope John Paul II captured this fundamental intuition in his encyclical letter on commitment to ecumenism, *Ut Unum Sint*: "In the teaching of the Second Vatican Council there is a clear connection between renewal, conversion and reform. The Council states that 'Christ summons the church, as she goes her pilgrim way, to that continual reformation of which she always has need, insofar as she is an institution of human beings here on earth. Therefore, if the influence of events or of the times had led to deficiencies . . . these should be appropriately rectified at the proper moment' (*UR* 6). No Christian community can exempt itself from this call."[9]

The members of the Groupe des Dombes took the council's exhortation to heart. Before it became fashionable for other ecumenists to use such language, the Groupe des Dombes regularly sought not only to identify important areas of theological agreement but also to lay out the necessary path of conversion, renewal, and reform in the practical life of the churches. The reader will find a set of proposals urging "the conversion of the churches" at the conclusion of each text. Before the term had been coined, the Groupe des Dombes was deeply engaged in a "dialogue of conversion."[10]

The first document included in this study is the 1971 text, "Towards a Common Eucharistic Faith." It was closely followed in 1972 by "Towards a Reconciliation of Ministries." These agreed statements were prepared by years of painstaking dialogue on intercommunion, apostolic succession, the priestly ministry of Christ and of the church, and pneumatology.[11] They coincided with the publication of similar agreements, notably the Windsor statement of the Anglican–Roman Catholic International Commission,[12] and an agreement reached by the Lutheran–Roman Catholic dialogue in the United States,[13] as well as the draft statements for what was to become the groundbreaking statement of the World Council of Churches' Commission on Faith and Order, *Baptism, Eucharist and Ministry*.[14]

9. John Paul II, *Ut Unum Sint*, no. 16.
10. John Paul II, *Ut Unum Sint*, no. 35.
11. Points of agreement on these questions were summed up in a series of "theses" that were first published in 1964. An English translation of this first series appeared in *Ecumenical Dialogue in Europe: The Ecumenical Conversation at les Dombes*, trans. W. Fletcher Fleet (London: Lutterworth, 1966). The theses of 1965 to 1970 appeared together with the early French versions of the agreed statements on eucharist and ministry. See note 1.
12. Anglican-Roman Catholic International Commission [ARCIC], "Eucharistic Doctrine (Windsor, 1971)," in *the Final Report* (London: SPCK / Catholic Truth Society), pp. 11-16.
13. "The Eucharist as Sacrifice," in *Lutherans and Catholics in Dialogue I-III*, ed. Paul C. Empie and T. Austin Murphy (Minneapolis: Augsburg, 1967), pp. 187-99.
14. Faith and Order *Baptism, Eucharist and Ministry* (Geneva: WCC, 1982).

4

It is remarkable today to look back and see the flurry of theological activity and of agreed statements that appeared in quick succession in this period of the ecumenical movement. The Second Vatican Council marked the official entry of the Catholic Church into the wider ecumenical movement. In the years immediately following the council, bilateral dialogue commissions were established and set about addressing these questions, many of which had been in the air and had been carefully studied by biblical scholars, historians, liturgists, and theologians for decades. New theological insights, now shared by scholars in the different Christian churches, informed the teaching of the council and were waiting to be received more widely in the years immediately following. The new reality of open and formally mandated dialogue commissions provided a space where much of this pent-up energy could flow, now that the logjam of mutual fear and resistance had broken. The Groupe des Dombes' discreet work in the years preceding the council helped to prepare the way for this new engagement. Thanks to its long experience, the Groupe des Dombes was uniquely placed to influence the work that was beginning in the new bilateral commissions.

"Towards a Common Eucharistic Faith" builds on the growing consensus reflected in the draft statement of the Faith and Order Commission meeting at Bristol in 1967.[15] In a manner similar to the other agreed statements that emerged in this period, the document points to a level of "substantial agreement" on eucharistic doctrine. This agreement aims at overcoming contentious disputes and misunderstandings relating to the presence of Christ in the eucharistic bread and wine and the sacrificial character of the eucharist in relation to the unique and unrepeatable nature of Christ's sacrifice. A shared recovery of the biblical notion of anamnesis sheds new light on the eucharistic memorial as a participation and re-presentation of the one sacrifice of Christ. Similarly, a recovery of the epicletic character of the eucharistic liturgy enables Catholic and Protestant perspectives to find a new balance in the shared understanding of the efficacious character of the sacrament.

The unique style of the Groupe des Dombes document is apparent in the second part of the text, which focuses on pastoral or practical concerns, as it explores the conditions for possible eucharistic sharing — a practice that was very new to all the churches in the 1970s. The dialogue was motivated, in part, by an urgent appeal to redress the scandal of division at the table of the Lord made by young people gathering at Taizé in

15. See *New Directions in Faith and Order, Bristol 1967* (Geneva: WCC, 1968).

this period. This text also reflects, for the first time, the hallmark concern for the conversion of the churches. René Girault, a member of the Groupe des Dombes for many years, has written that a new awareness of the group's vocation to foster the conversion of the churches emerged at its meeting in 1970. The conversation seemed to be going in circles. Hébert Roux spoke of the need to get beyond the complacency of the churches and to engage in a "reciprocal confessional *metanoia*":

> One Catholic asked, "We are not sufficiently committed to the goal of ecclesial conversion!" A protestant continued, "Unity is worth the pain of sacrifice. We must reflect on our *metanoia*." The second president formalized the state of the question: "We must pass from platonic considerations to the point of view of life changes. We must leave these theses to pronounce vows in favor of an ecclesial *metanoia*." No one contested this. From then on, it became clear.[16]

A new invitation to ecclesial conversion is evident in "Towards a Reconciliation of Ministries." After outlining an important consensus on the theology of ministry, rooted in an understanding of the apostolic nature of the whole church and of the church's instrumentality in relation to the unique ministry of Christ, the Dombes theologians proposed steps towards a possible mutual recognition of ministries. This mutual recognition would be celebrated liturgically in a mutual laying on of hands. It would be conducted in a spirit of repentance and would invoke the healing grace of God. The dialogue also called for those Protestant churches that have not maintained the office of bishop to consider restoring a personal ministry of *episcopē* as a sign of the apostolic character of the church.

This last proposal met with considerable resistance. Nonetheless, this and the later study of Faith and Order on Ministry[17] prompted important studies that led to a reconsideration of the exercise of *episcopē* as an essential and constitutive element of the church.[18] Before the question had fully

16. René Girault, "Fifty Years of Ecumenical Dialogue: The Groupe des Dombes," *Ecumenical Trends* 24 (1989): 26-30, at 26.

17. The "Ministry" section of *Baptism, Eucharist and Ministry* invited those churches that have not maintained the threefold model of ministry (deacons, presbyters, and bishops) to consider this pattern as normative for the structuring of ministries in the church (M25).

18. See, for example, *Episkope and Episcopate in Ecumenical Perspective* (Geneva: WCC, 1980); and Alan T. Falconer and Peter C. Bouteneff, eds., *Episkope and Episcopacy and the Quest for Visible Unity: Two Consultations* (Geneva: WCC, 1999).

emerged in wider ecumenical discussion, in 1976 the Groupe des Dombes produced one of the earliest studies, "The Episcopal Ministry: Reflections and Proposals for the Ministry of Vigilance in the Particular Church." An interesting feature of this document is that it avoids the use of the term "bishop." This opens the possibility of recognizing the presence of a ministry of oversight that is truly "episcopal" in those churches that have not retained an office of "bishop." "Superintendents," "moderators," and collegial groups of persons have continued to exercise a significant ministry of oversight in the "non-episcopal" churches of the Reformation. Without seeking uniformity of church polities, the Groupe des Dombes renews its invitation for Reformation churches to recover a personal ministry of oversight, while recognizing that Catholics, for their part, must strengthen the dimension of collegiality in the exercise of oversight.

As if to deepen the ground for the consensus identified in the preceding agreed statements, "The Holy Spirit, the Church, and the Sacraments" (1979) provides an important theological reflection on the relationship between the work of God's Spirit and the sacramental actions of the church. Earlier agreements on eucharistic doctrine and on ministry were at times greeted with the suspicion that they had not sufficiently addressed what many considered to be irreconcilable differences in Protestant and Catholic notions of sacramentality. Here, the Groupe des Dombes set out to provide a shared theology of sacramentality rooted in the understanding of the role of the Spirit in the life of the church.

This study also makes an important contribution to ecumenical reflection on ecclesiology. André Birmelé has recognized the enduring value of "The Holy Spirit, the Church and the Sacraments," commenting, "the Groupe des Dombes was first to clear the ground and bring to light the fact that the underlying question of the dialogue is the understanding of the church, the manner in which it is understood as an instrument of God for the salvation of humanity."[19] Indeed, it was only in the decade of the 1990s that the wider ecumenical movement, through the agency of Faith and Order, would turn its attention more fully to questions of ecclesiology.[20] This early study by the Groupe des Dombes stands as an important resource for addressing some of the very issues that continue to be de-

19. André Birmelé, "Un travail de pionnier," *Unité des Chrétiens* 67 (1987): 28.

20. In 1993 the Faith and Order Commission undertook a study of the notion of *koinonia*. Further Faith and Order studies have given rise to *The Nature and Mission of the Church: A Stage on the Way to a Common Statement,* Faith and Order Paper No. 198 (Geneva: WCC, 2005).

bated, including the sacramentality of the church and the efficacy of the sacraments and of the ministry of the church. Few other dialogues have attended sufficiently to the role of the Spirit in their effort to overcome differences in these matters.

"The Ministry of Communion in the Universal Church" is one of the first more comprehensive treatments of papal primacy by an ecumenical dialogue.[21] It also marks an important methodological shift in the work of the Groupe des Dombes.[22] Readers will note that it is considerably longer than the previous agreed statements. Rather than focus simply on affirming a consensus of faith and outlining concrete implications for the life and practice of the church, this more robust study includes an overview of significant historical developments in the life of the churches that have determined the shape of the papacy and resulted in serious differences concerning the understanding of its mission and authority. Only after this reconciling exercise of rereading history together, to arrive at a common understanding of the churches' various positions and biases, does the Groupe des Dombes return to the source of Sacred Scripture. This allows the retrieval of a number of perspectives that might have been obscured by confessional interests in the past. This rather unique manner of studying Scripture and tradition together — reversing the somewhat classical order and treating the biblical sources after considering this historical trajectory of the tradition — is the method followed in all subsequent studies by the Group des Dombes.

A common rereading of Scripture and tradition suggests that the reform of the papacy ought to be guided by a concern to recover a proper balance between the personal, collegial, and communal dimension of the ministry of communion in the universal church. As part of this program for conversion to a more ecumenically receivable form and exercise of papal primacy, the Dombes theologians point to the necessity of clearly distinguishing the role of the Bishop of Rome as Patriarch of the West from his ministry of communion within the universal church. They suggest that these roles have been unfortunately confused in the course of history. This confusion, an "abnormal development," has added to a growing centraliza-

---

21. Among the other early agreed statements on papal primacy, see Paul C. Empie and T. Austin Murphy, eds., *Papal Primacy and the Universal Church*, Lutherans and Catholics in Dialogue V (Minneapolis: Augsburg, 1974); and Anglican-Roman Catholic International Commission [ARCIC], "Authority in the Church I and II," in *The Final Report*, pp. 52-98.

22. I have described the nature of this shift in greater detail in *The Groupe des Dombes: A Dialogue of Conversion*, pp. 196-97 and 245-61.

tion of authority in the papacy and eclipsed the local churches and their bishops.[23]

In 2006, the *Annuario Pontificio* was published by the Vatican with the omission of the title "Patriarch of the West" from among the titles traditionally accorded to the Bishop of Rome. Cardinal Walter Kasper, president of the Pontifical Council for the Promotion of Christian Unity, provided a clarification for this decision.[24] According to the press release, this title was removed because its meaning and the geographical limits of the patriarchal territory of the West have been unclear since the days it first appeared. It can only be applicable to the Latin church, which now extends around the globe. The title "Patriarch of the West" has become "obsolete" and it makes no sense to continue its use.

This Vatican action appears almost as a preemptive strike aimed at heading off further debate of the matter raised by the Groupe des Dombes and other ecclesiologists. Where Rome sees disuse and obsolescence, the Groupe des Dombes sees a possible way forward for reimagining the ministry of the Bishop of Rome in the model of its exercise in the first millennium. The Dombes theologians suggest that, instead of abandoning this ancient title, the church retrieve this ancient form of exercising the ministry of communion where the exercise of authority is more decentralized and a greater autonomy and diversity of the local churches are respected. The question is no less relevant today than when it was first raised. By proposing that the ministry of communion to the whole of the universal church be more adequately distinguished from the Bishop of Rome's presiding over the daily affairs of the church within a circumscribed territory, and allowing for a greater devolution of powers to other territorial patriarchates, the Groupe des Dombes invites a reconsideration of the parameters of the jurisdiction of the Bishop of Rome, a matter that is at the crux of the hesitation on the part of other churches to receive this ministry as it is presently exercised by the pope. This pertinent proposal ought not to be set aside too quickly, as it has not yet received the serious consideration it merits.

The final document included in this anthology is the 1991 text, "For the Conversion of the Churches: Identity and Change in the Dynamic of

23. See "The Ministry of Communion in the Universal Church," nos. 29 and 142-45.

24. The original French text of the press release, "*Communiqué concernant la suppression du titre 'Patriarche d'Occident' dans l'Annuaire pontifical 2006*," can be found at http://www.vatican.va/roman_curia/pontifical_councils/chrstuni/general-docs/rc_pc_chrstuni_doc_20060322_patriarca-occidente_fr.html.

Communion." It was produced after an extended self-reflection on the vocation of the Groupe des Dombes. In 1987, to mark the fiftieth anniversary of their founding, the Groupe des Dombes invited a number of church leaders and dignitaries to a celebration of their contribution to ecumenical reflection. Some of those invited sought to understand more deeply the nature of the "conversion" it was asking of the churches. These questions as well as a number of responses to the work of the dialogue through the years prompted the Dombes theologians to develop a text that would state more clearly the ecclesiological presuppositions that underlie the entire corpus of their work. "For the Conversion of the Churches" provides a foundational reflection on the nature of ecclesial reform and on the indispensable work of renewal that must take place as the churches grow together in unity.

"For the Conversion of the Churches" speaks to the challenge posed by the increasing tension that emerged in the 1980s and continues to our day, between the desire to reassert clear and distinctive denominational or confessional identities, and the need for ongoing reform and change in the life of the churches. Its distinction between Christian, ecclesial, and confessional identities is helpful in understanding that the goal of the ecumenical movement — a goal envisioned by the Groupe des Dombes' own proposals for the conversion of the churches — is not the disappearance of the rich diversity of ecclesial traditions represented by the confessional churches, but their realignment with a common understanding of that which is constitutive of ecclesial identity, or of the church as such. The end is that each church may become more fully church. Such growth is understood as the only path through which the churches can come to recognize one another as churches in the fullest sense of the word. It is the path to their living in greater communion with one another while safeguarding the rich diversity of gifts in each.

Two other substantial documents have been published by the Groupe des Dombes in recent years, though their length and comprehensive nature precludes their inclusion in this volume. The first is an important study on Marian doctrine and devotional practice that appeared in 1999, *Mary in the Plan of God and the Communion of Saints*.[25] This book makes an important contribution to mutual understanding between Catholics

---

25. Groupe des Dombes, *Mary in the Plan of God and the Communion of the Saints*, trans. Matthew J. O'Connell (New York: Paulist, 2002); original French version: *Marie dans le dessein de Dieu et la communion des saints* (Paris: Bayard, 1999).

and Protestants in regard to Marian theology and devotion and serves not only as a resource for ecumenists, but as a helpful resource for adult catechetical instruction. Finally, in 2005, the Groupe des Dombes produced a comprehensive study on teaching authority in the churches, *One Teacher: Doctrinal Authority in the Church.*[26] The Groupe des Dombes does not shy away from the complex nature of this issue, and develops a useful analysis of the ways in which doctrinal authority is vested in texts as well as individuals and groups of persons entrusted with authority in the life of the church. The concluding proposals for the conversion of the churches lay out what will likely be the agenda of the ecumenical movement for decades to come.

It is my hope that the present volume will serve as a resource for students and teachers of ecumenism, of sacramental theology and ecclesiology. It can also be an important sourcebook for many who are engaged in ecumenical ministries and study groups. The Groupe des Dombes continues to make a significant contribution to Protestant-Catholic mutual understanding. Its calls for conversion point out the "growing edges" of the churches. Readers of these works will be rewarded with a deeper knowledge and understanding of both the Protestant and Catholic traditions. They will discover not only an honest and loyal appraisal of what stands in need of renewal,[27] but a profound appreciation for the riches that can be harvested from the Christian tradition as the churches attempt to reimagine a common future in full visible communion.

26. Groupe des Dombes, *One Teacher: Doctrinal Authority in the Church,* trans. Catherine E. Clifford (Grand Rapids: Eerdmans, 2010); original French version: *Un seul maître: L'autorité doctrinale dans l'Église* (Paris: Bayard, 2005).

27. This is one of the principal tasks of those who engage in ecumenical dialogue, according to the Second Vatican Council's Decree on Ecumenism *(Unitatis Redintegratio),* no. 4.

Towards a Common Eucharistic Faith (1971)

DOCTRINAL AGREEMENT ON THE EUCHARIST

—⟨∾⟩—

1. Today, when Christians celebrate the eucharist and proclaim the gospel, they feel themselves increasingly to be brothers in the midst of their fellow-men, with a mission and an eagerness to bear witness together to the same Christ, by word and deed and by their eucharistic celebration. That is why, for some years past, the Group meeting at Les Dombes has been scrutinizing the significance of mutual eucharistic hospitality and joint celebration and the conditions on which they depend.

2. One particularly important condition of this sharing of the Lord's table is substantial agreement on what it is, despite theological diversities.

3. The Group takes over the text of the Faith and Order agreement (1968),[1] seeking to clarify, adapt, and amplify it in the light of the interconfessional situation in France today.

I. The Eucharist: The Lord's Supper

4. The eucharist is the sacramental meal, the new paschal meal of God's people, which Christ, having loved his disciples unto the end, gave them

---

1. *Editor's note:* This is a reference to the work of Faith and Order at Bristol, which would become the basis of the text for *Baptism, Eucharist and Ministry* (Geneva: WCC, 1982). See *New Directions in Faith and Order, Bristol 1967* (Geneva: WCC, 1968).

before his death that they might celebrate it in the light of the resurrection until his coming.

5. This meal is the effective sign of the gift that Christ made of himself as the bread of life, through the sacrifice of his life and his death and by his resurrection.

6. In the eucharist, Christ fulfills in a surpassing manner his promise to be amongst those who gather together in his name.

II. The Eucharist: Act of Thanksgiving to the Father

7. The eucharist is the great act of thanksgiving to the Father for all that he has accomplished in the creation and redemption of the world, for all that he is now accomplishing in the church and in the world, despite our sin, and for all that he is seeking to accomplish through the coming of his kingdom. Thus, the eucharist is the blessing *(berakah)* whereby the church expresses gratitude to God for all his benefits.

8. The eucharist is the great sacrifice of praise in which the church speaks in the name of all creation. For the world that God reconciled with himself in Christ is present at each eucharist: in the bread and the wine, in the persons of the faithful, and in the prayers they offer for all mankind. Thus the eucharist opens up to the world the way to its transfiguration.

III. The Eucharist: Memorial of Christ

9. Christ instituted the eucharist as a memorial *(anamnesis)* of his whole life and above all of his cross and resurrection. Christ, with everything he has accomplished for us and for all creation, is present himself in this memorial, which is also a foretaste of his kingdom. The memorial, in which Christ acts through the joyful celebration of his church, implies this representation and this anticipation. Therefore it is not only a matter of recalling to mind a past event or even its significance. The memorial is the effective proclamation by the church of the great work of God. By its communion with Christ, the church participates in this reality from which it draws its life.

10. The memorial, being at once re-presentation and anticipation, is lived out in thanksgiving and intercession. Making the memorial of the passion, resurrection, and ascension of Christ, our High Priest and Mediator, the church presents to the Father the one perfect sacrifice of his Son and asks him to accord every person the benefit of the great work of redemption it proclaims.

11. Thus, united to our Lord, who offers himself to his Father, and in communion with the universal church in heaven and on earth, we are renewed in the covenant sealed with the blood of Christ and we offer ourselves as a living and holy sacrifice that must be expressed in the whole of our daily life.

12. The memorial of Christ is the essential content of the Word proclaimed, as it is of the eucharist. The celebration of the eucharist and the proclamation of the Word go hand in hand, for the ministry of the Word is directed towards the eucharist and the eucharist in turn implies and fulfills the Word.

IV. The Eucharist: Gift of the Spirit

13. The memorial, in the deep sense that we have given to it, implies the invocation of the Spirit *(epiclesis)*. Christ, in his heavenly intercession, asks the Father to send his Spirit to his children. And so the church, living in the new covenant, prays with confidence for the Spirit, in order to be renewed and sanctified by the bread of life, led in truth and strengthened to fulfill its mission in the world.

14. It is the Spirit which, invoked over the congregation, over the bread and wine, makes Christ really present to us, gives him to us and enables us to perceive him. The memorial and the invocation of the Spirit *(anamnesis and epiclesis)*, directed towards our union with Christ, cannot be accomplished independently of the communion.

15. The gift of the Holy Spirit in the eucharist is a foretaste of the kingdom of God: the church receives the life of the new creation and the assurance of our Lord's return.

16. We recognize that the eucharistic prayer as a whole has the character of an *epiclesis.*

V. The Sacramental Presence of Christ

17. The act of the eucharist is the gift of Christ's person. The Lord said: "Take, eat, this is my body which is given for you." "Drink ye all of this, for this is my blood of the new covenant, which is shed for you and for many for the remission of sins." We accordingly confess unanimously the real, living, and effective presence of Christ in this sacrament.

18. To discern the body and blood of Christ requires faith. However, the presence of Christ revealed to his church in the eucharist does not depend on the faith of the individual, for it is Christ who binds himself in his words and in the Spirit to the sacramental act, the sign of his presence given.

19. Christ's act being the gift of his body and blood, that is to say, of himself, the reality given in the signs of the bread and wine is his body and his blood.[2] It is by virtue of Christ's creative word and by the power of the Holy Spirit that the bread and wine are made a sacrament and hence a "sharing of the body and blood of Christ" (1 Cor. 10:16). They are henceforth, in their ultimate truth, beneath the outward sign, the given reality, and so they remain, since their purpose is to be consumed. What is given as the body and blood of Christ remains given as his body and blood and requires to be treated as such.

20. Noting the diversity of practice among Christian denominations[3] and at the same time drawing from the preceding agreement the necessary conclusions regarding the change of heart *(metanoia)* on the part of the churches that is seen to be essential, we ask that:

> i. On the Roman Catholic side it be pointed out, in particular by catechists and preachers, that the primary purpose of reserving the eucharist is for its distribution to the sick and the absent;[4]

> ii. On the Protestant side the best means should be adopted of showing the respect due to the elements that have served for the celebration of

2. This does not mean that Christ is localized in the bread and wine or that these latter undergo any physico-chemical change. Cf. St Thomas, *ST* III, 76, 3-5; III, 77, 5-8; Calvin, *Institutes* I, 11, 13; IV, 14, 18.

3. Certain Eastern churches (e.g., the Copts) do not reserve the eucharist.

4. See Instruction *Eucharisticum mysterium* (25 May 1967), nos. 49 and 50.

the eucharist, which is to consume them subsequently, without precluding their use for the communion of the sick.

VI. The Eucharist: Communion in the Body of Christ

21. By giving himself to the communicants, Christ unites them in his body. It is in this sense that one can say: if the church makes the eucharist, the eucharist makes the church. The sharing of the one bread and the one cup in a given place makes the communicants one with the whole Christ, with one another, and with all other communicants at all times and in all places. By sharing the one bread they manifest their membership of the church in its universality, the mystery of the redemption is revealed to their eyes, and the whole body grows in grace. The communion is thus the source and strength of all community life among Christians.

22. By his cross, Christ has broken down all the barriers that separate men. We cannot communicate with him in truth, therefore, unless we labor, in the midst of the conflict in which we are involved, to do away with the barriers in the church that separate races, nationalities, languages, classes, and denominations.

23. According to Christ's promise, every believer and member of his body receives in the eucharist the remission of sins and everlasting life and is fed with the food of faith, hope, and love.

24. Fellowship in the eucharistic communion in the body of Christ *(agape)* and the attentions that Christians have for one another and for the world should find a means of expression in the liturgy: by the mutual forgiveness of sins, the kiss of peace, the offering of gifts to be used for community meals or for distribution to brothers in need, and the brotherly welcome extended to all regardless of political, social, or cultural differences.

VII. The Eucharist: A Mission in the World

25. The mission of the church does not simply stem from the eucharist. Whenever the church is really the church, its mission is part of its life. In the eucharist the church is fully itself and is united with Christ in his mission.

26. The world is already present in the act of thanksgiving to the Father, in which the church speaks in the name of all creation; in the memorial where, united with Christ the Redeemer and Mediator, the church prays for the world: in the invocation of the Spirit, in which it hopes for sanctification and the new creation.

27. Reconciled in the eucharist, the members of the body of Christ become the servants of reconciliation among men and witnesses of the joy of the resurrection. Their presence in the world implies fellowship in suffering and hope with all men, among whom they are called upon to bear witness to the love of Christ in service and in combat. The celebration of the eucharist, the breaking of a bread that is necessary to life, is an incitement not to accept conditions in which men are deprived of bread, justice, and peace.

28. The eucharist is also the feast of the perpetual apostolic harvest, in which the church rejoices for the gifts received in the world.

VIII. The Eucharist: Banquet of the Kingdom[5]

29. Our Lord instituted the eucharist for the time from his ascension until his coming again. This is the time of hope, and that is why the eucharist directs our thoughts to the Lord's coming and brings it near to us. It is a joyful anticipation of the heavenly banquet, when redemption shall be fully accomplished and all creation shall be delivered from bondage.

30. Thus, by giving the eucharist to his church, which in its weakness will live to the last in the midst of suffering and strife, our Lord enables it to take new heart and to persevere.

31. This church that Christ feeds throughout its pilgrimage perceives, above and beyond the divisions that still persist, that the eschatological meeting-place is an ecumenical meeting-place, where Israel and all the nations will be gathered together into one people.

5. See *La Cène du Seigneur,* a text adopted by the French Lutheran and Reformed churches.

18

IX. The Presidency of the Eucharist

32. Christ, in the eucharist, gathers together and feeds his church at a meal over which he presides.

33. The sign of Christ's presidency is given in the presiding minister, whom he has called and sent. The mission of ministers has its roots in and is modeled on that of the apostles, and is transmitted to the church by the imposition of hands accompanied by the invocation of the Holy Spirit. This transmission implies the continuity of the ministry, fidelity to apostolic teaching, and a life lived according to the gospel.[6]

34. The minister shows that the congregation is not proprietor of the action it is performing, that it is not the master of the eucharist but receives it from Another, Christ living in his church. While remaining a member of the congregation, the minister is at the same time the man sent to signify God's action and the link between the local community and the other communities in the universal church.

35. In their mutual relations, the eucharistic gathering and its president live their dependence on the one Lord and great High Priest. In its relation to the minister, the congregation is exercising its royal priesthood conferred on it by Christ, the priest. In his relation to the congregation, the minister is living his presidency as the servant of Christ, the pastor.

X. Conclusion

36. At this stage in our quest we give thanks that the major difficulties concerning the eucharistic faith have been removed.

37. We realize, however, that some clarification is still required in regard to the permanence of the sacramental presence and the precise place of the apostolic succession in the ministry. It seems to us that any joint participation in the eucharist demands a real effort to overcome these difficulties and, if need be, on both sides, the abandonment of everything that is marked by controversy within our various denominational positions.

6. Cf. Thesis No. 2 (1968). In Groupe des Dombes, *Pour la communion des Églises. L'apport du Groupe des Dombes 1937-87* (Paris: Centurion, 1988), pp. 29-30.

38. The pursuance of our quest is bound to enrich us still further with the complementary spiritual values among which we live. We can never exhaust the understanding of a mystery which is beyond all understanding and calls us unceasingly to come out of ourselves in order to live in thanksgiving and wonder at this supreme gift of Christ to his church.

XI. Recommendation

39. It is often asked today what degree of concordance of belief is required for a Christian to be received by another church at its communion table. Without claiming to solve here the other questions raised by the different cases of eucharistic hospitality, we think that access to communion should not be refused for reasons of eucharistic belief to Christians of another denomination whose own faith is that professed above.[7]

40. That is why we ask the authorities of our respective churches to consider carefully the new situation created by this agreement on the eucharist when they are weighing up the requests for hospitality addressed to them.

PASTORAL AGREEMENT
The Meaning of the Eucharist

I. The Eucharist: The Lord's Supper

Jesus, on the eve of his death, at a meal he was sharing with his disciples, took the bread and, having said grace, broke it and distributed it among them, saying: "Take, eat, this is my body which is given for you. Do this in remembrance of me." Then, taking a cup of wine, he gave thanks and passed it around, saying: "Drink this, all of you; for this is my blood of the new covenant which is shed for you and for many for the remission of sins. Do this in remembrance of me."

With these words he invited his disciples to repeat his action and Christians to respond to that invitation by coming together to celebrate the eucharist.

7. These Christians are not thereby relieved of the obligation to consider whether their request is a legitimate one, having regard to the justice of their motives and the discipline of their own church.

II. Meeting with Christ in His Death and Resurrection

It is around Christ that we gather to meet him. He makes us live again his death and resurrection in the hope of his coming again, in joy and thankfulness to God. In this way the decisive events whereby we are reconciled with God and with one another are made present and real to us, although they are not repeated. Christ, who prays to his Father and offers himself up for all men, embraces us in his offering and commits us to the love and service of our brothers.

III. The Reality of Christ's Presence in the Sacrament

By sharing and consuming the bread and wine of the eucharist, we receive, according to the life-giving Word of the Lord, his body that is given, his blood that is shed, his whole person. This bread and this wine are thus the body and blood of Christ, given by him to his church.

Fed by Christ, who welcomes us to his table, we all share his life as the Son of God and the brother of all. This life that we received at our baptism, the eucharist feeds and tends in its growth and prepares for its fulfillment in our resurrection.

IV. Invocation and Action of the Spirit

We celebrate the eucharist in the Holy Spirit — the light, love, and strength of God in the hearts of men. By it we move forward, from the coming of Jesus Christ among us until his last coming, towards the freedom and glory to which God calls us. This movement is going on in the church today, thanks to the eucharist.

In the eucharistic prayer the church asks for the promised coming of the Holy Spirit in order to receive and discern the presence of our Lord and to draw life from his death and resurrection.

V. The Minister of the Eucharist

As Christ once chose the apostles, so today he still chooses ministers to gather his church together in prayer and to guide it in its mission.

The presence of one of these ministers, the servant of the Word and of the sacrament, in the midst of the eucharistic gathering, means that Christ himself is presiding at the meal where he gives his body to be eaten.

This service of presiding also expresses the communion our Lord creates between all the members of the congregation and between the individual local churches in the bosom of the universal church.

VI. The Eucharist: A Force for the Liberation of Humanity

By the action of the Spirit and the ministry of the church, Christ carries on the work for which he died and rose again: the work of freeing and reconciling all creation, in the first place by revealing the true face of God. When we accept his invitation to his table, we are taking up his mission in his footsteps by our witness of faith and hope, by our fight against the forces of oppression, destruction, and death, in order to reconcile all things and offer everything to God.

Communicating in the sacrament with the life, the death, and the victory of Jesus, we must also live that communion in our daily lives in society, by our options and our actions, in the face of suffering and failure. We cannot allow conditions to endure in which millions of men are deprived of bread, justice, and peace.

VII. The Eucharist: Source of Unity

Since they commit themselves jointly to uniting and freeing mankind, Christians are called upon to live with one another, in full communion, in the one Lord. In the state of separation in which they still find themselves, the eucharist underlines the scandal of their confessional differences and at the same time their inability to overcome them of their own accord.

But when Christ gives himself to us in the eucharist, he is leading us towards union, in his body, with all communicants at all times and in all places. Thereby he revives our hope of reaching it and strengthens our will to strive for it.

As Christ intended it, the gift of the eucharist overrides our divisions, not by denying or concealing them, but by giving us today the pledge and effective sign of the unity he is always asking of his Father: "May they all be one . . . so that the world may believe."

We hope that we have given expression to the content of Scripture and the traditional faith of the church. We thank God who has enabled us to confess this faith together and we pray that he may hasten the day when we shall receive at the same table the body and blood of his Son.

SIGNATORIES OF THE AGREEMENT

Roman Catholic
Paul Aymard, OSB
Joseph de Baciocchi, SM
René Beaupère, OP
Edmond Chavaz
Marc Clément
Robert Clément, SJ
Jacques Desseaux
André Fabre
Claude Gerest, OP
René Girault
Etienne Goutagny, OCR
Maurice Jourjon
Marie Leblanc, OSB
Pierre Michalon, PSS
André Perroux
Jean Roche, SJ
Bernard Sesboüé, SJ
Maurice Villain, SM

Protestant
Georges Appia
Claude Asmussen
Georges Besse
Henry Bruston
Edouard Diserens
Maurice Ferrier-Welti
Jean-Claude Ill
Michel Leplay
Louis Lévrier
Marc Lods
Hébert Roux
Brother Max Thurian of Taizé
André Veimert
Gaston Westphal

Towards a Reconciliation of Ministries (1972)

POINTS OF AGREEMENT BETWEEN
ROMAN CATHOLICS AND PROTESTANTS

—⸺⟨ഗഗ⟩⸺—

Introduction

1. In pouring out his liberating love, God chose a people called to bear witness, through its history, to a promise given to all people everywhere. This servant-people is called to be at all times and in all places a sign of hope along the path trodden by man. This mission makes God's people one with all mankind, and we are still the beneficiaries today of that *prophetic call.*

2. Into the midst of this people God sends his Son, to be the servant of his fellow-men and to reveal to us the reality of salvation. Jesus Christ is thus the one Lord and Savior who, by giving his life for humans, calls them, through his service, to discover the meaning of their existence and the fullness of a new humanity.

3. The power of his resurrection is manifested from generation to generation by the action of the Holy Spirit, who inspires the church, calls it together in thanksgiving, and sends it forth on the mission entrusted to it. This mission commits the whole of God's people to service that demands fidelity, perseverance, and effectiveness.

4. This is why, listening with renewed attention to the apostolic message and its promise for mankind, we are endeavoring today to discern the call of the Holy Spirit. In ecumenical research, in particular where the ministry of the

25

church and ministries within the church are concerned, the fundamental criterion must be apostolicity, seen as both source and mission. This research not only concerns and sheds light on the internal life of the church, but prepares and qualifies the church for the fulfillment of Christ's mission.

PART ONE

Points of Agreement Regarding the Ministry

I. Christ, Lord and Servant, Unique Minister of His Church

5. It is impossible to speak of the ministry of the church and in the church without first speaking of the ministry of Jesus Christ himself. The ministry he exercised by his life and death, the risen Christ is still carrying on in and for his church today, so that it may serve him among the people of our time.

6. The ministry of Christ is the norm of all doctrine and all practice of the Christian ministry — a ministry that, in all its variety of institutional forms, demands a constantly renewed fidelity to Christ's example. "Yet here I am among you as one who serves," says Jesus (Luke 22:27); "I have given you an example so that you may copy what I have done to you" (John 13:15); and again: "If anyone serves me, he must follow me; wherever I am my servant will be there too" (John 12:26).

7. Jesus Christ himself, mysteriously present to his church, challenges it constantly through his word and his Spirit to examine itself and remain faithful to its vocation and mission. To "follow" Christ and become like him is also an integral part of the apostolic succession.

II. The Church of Christ: Church of the Apostles

8. The church, body of Christ, is apostolic in its very essence, because Christ, sent by the Father, sends the church in turn into the world in the power of the Spirit.

9. The whole church, summoned by Christ, is sent to summon all people to the eschatological assembly of salvation. This means that the whole church has a mission and therefore a ministry. So that the church may fulfill this

mission, Christ has given it, in the person of the apostles, the ministerial sign that it is he who is calling. This is why the apostolic character of the church comprises two inseparable aspects:

10. The apostolicity of the church is founded on Christ's fidelity to his promise to be always with his people, and on the presence and action of the Holy Spirit, who is building it up day by day. There is, therefore, an apostolic succession of the whole church.

11. But within that apostolic succession, in order to manifest his initiative of grace, to guarantee the transcendence of the apostolic message, and to ensure the fulfillment of the church's mission, Christ sent his apostles as his envoys, thanks to the gift of the Holy Spirit. In the wake of the apostles, the apostolic ministry is still being carried on in the church on the foundation they constituted, and it must remain entirely faithful to the message they have transmitted. This ministry — a gift of God for the service of the whole church — forms part of the church's structure. There is, therefore, an apostolic succession in the ministry instituted by our Lord.

12. The fullness of the apostolic succession of the whole church implies continuity in the essential features of the church of the apostles: witness to the faith, fraternal communion, sacramental life, service to man, dialogue with the world, and the sharing of the gifts that God has given to each member.

13. The fullness of the apostolic succession in the ministry implies continuity in the transmission of the ministerial function, fidelity in preaching to the teaching of the apostles, and a life in keeping with the gospel and the demands of mission. These three features are usually inseparable.

This succession, in fact, as a ministerial sign, bears witness to the apostolic character of the church and prepares the community for the coming and the action of our Lord himself.

III. The Ministry of the Whole Church and the Diversity of Ministries within the Church

14. The common mission of the church, attested by the gospels, is entrusted to each Christian by baptism with water and the Holy Spirit and by his or her participation in the eucharist.

15. All members of the body of Christ are called and empowered to live their faith and bear witness to it among their fellows by serving love and justice and by radiating hope. Thus the Christian community in each place bears witness to the reconciliation whereby it lives and calls on all people to be reconciled with God and with one another.

16. At all times and in all places, the church, God's people, is, despite its unworthiness, a "chosen race, a royal priesthood, a consecrated nation, a people set apart to sing the praises of God," who called them "into his wonderful light" (1 Pet. 2:9).

17. Preaching the gospel, the church's service to the world, and the building up of the community all require very different activities, permanent or temporary, spontaneous or institutionalized.

18. Thus, the Holy Spirit calls men and women from among God's people to take on different and complementary ministries that all bear witness to Christ's fidelity to his promises and to the richness of his gifts.

19. From this it can be seen that witness and service in the cause of Christ are not the monopoly of a few but the co-responsibility of all Christians.

IV. Pastoral Ministry and Community: Their Dependence on Christ

20. Whatever the diversity of charisms and functions in a Christian community, the mark of the pastoral ministry[1] is to ensure and signify the church's dependence on Christ, the source of its mission and foundation of its unity.

21. Though he is himself a member of the Christian community, a minister is at the same time to be recognized as an envoy whom that community receives from Christ. The minister's functions bring out the priority in the

---

1. We shall henceforth designate as "pastoral ministry," using this term in the strongest sense, the ministry whose foundation was described in paragraph 11 above and of which it is said that "there is an apostolic succession in the ministry instituted by our Lord." The term "pastoral ministry" covers the whole variety of ordained ministries.

life of the church of divine initiative and authority, the continuity of the mission in the world, and the bond of communion established by the Spirit in the different communities in the unity of the church.

This implies the minister's membership, with ministers of other times and other places, is of the same "college,"[2] deriving from the apostles.

22. This relationship of dependence on the one Lord and Savior is expressed and lived out in the dependence of the community and the minister on one another. Their mutual dependence shows that the church is not in a position of mastery over the word and sacraments, nor is it the source of its own faith, hope, and unity; and it shows that the minister, for his part, does not exist by or for himself, nor can he dispose as he wishes of the Christian community.

Thus, the Christian life and ministry are received from Another — Christ living in his church. They are animated by his Spirit and subject to his judgment.

23. The pastoral ministry, which will endure until Christ's parousia, is also a prophetic ministry: its apostolic origin and its foundation on the authority of our Lord, far from justifying a possessive, inward-looking attitude, oblige it to turn towards the future, which it heralds.

24. The relationships that establish themselves between the ministry and the community in the unity of the church reflect those between the persons of the Trinity in the divine unity: ministry and community find their source of authority in the person of the Father, of their service in the person of the Son, and of their freedom and communion in the person of the Holy Spirit.

V. The Exercise of Pastoral Ministry

25. The essential functions of the pastoral ministry, which inherits the transmissible features of the apostolic function, are indissolubly bound up with one another: proclamation of the Word, celebration of the sacraments, and calling together of the community.

---

2. The term "college" is not to be understood here in its legal or clerical sense but as the expression of "ministerial communion."

26. By the ministry of the Word, Christ feeds the church with the gospel whereby it lives and constantly reveals its riches so that they may be passed on to all people.

This ministry does not stop short at repeating what has already been said long ago; it interprets it and makes it real, guided in this by the Holy Spirit in the communion of the whole church. It also endeavors to identify the points where the message of Jesus Christ and the problems, situations, and culture of the modern world meet one another or, on the contrary, set up tensions.

27. By the ministry of the sacraments, Christ passes on the gift of his person and of his life. In celebrating the sacraments, the minister signifies that it is Christ himself who presides and gives them the efficacy he has promised. He demonstrates too that the word of the gospel is at work in the sacrament, fulfilling what it has announced. By this means the communion of the church with the Holy Spirit, its life as the body of Christ, and its fidelity to God are established and renewed.

28. Through the ministry of calling together the community, Christ is constantly restoring and building up his people's unity in their progress towards the kingdom. This ministry is exercised with respect for the freedom of the Holy Spirit and recognition of the real common responsibility of all Christians.

29. The pastoral ministry, in its three functions, derives its authority from the fact that it is the service of Christ who, as Lord and Head of his body, sets it up in the power of the Spirit.

30. In these three functions of the ministry, the relationship of authority is still present in brotherly love and the shared responsibility of Christian people sent forth into the world by Christ. Thus the faithful and their ministers are bound one to another in different relationships of interdependence and reciprocity.

By dialogue and by prayer, those who celebrate in different contexts the same sacrament are one in opening their hearts to the Holy Spirit.

The questions raised by the life of Christian people, their witness, and their understanding of the message of the gospel, educate the ministers of the word, and clarify for them the meaning of the faith, whose servants they are.

31. Within the priesthood of the baptized, Christ gives his church its structure, thanks to the pastoral ministry through which he leads his disciples to spiritual sacrifice, witness, and service along many roads that, as it were, meet and cross in the eucharist. It is in this sense that the ministry is said to be sacerdotal.

32. God expresses his fidelity to his church by the support he gives to the ministry, though he does not restrict his action to the acts of his ministers. They, for their part, must show their fidelity to God by serving their brethren as good stewards of the mysteries of God (cf. 1 Cor. 4:1-2).

VI. The Ordination of Ministers for Pastoral Work

33. The pastoral ministry, because it expresses the apostolic character of the church, is conferred in the Christian community by the action of ministers already members of the apostolic community, signifying thereby the action of Christ, who is constantly sending servants of the gospel to his church; that is what ordination means.

34. The risen Lord is he who calls to the ministry, ordains, and confers the gift. The ordination of ministers comprises the prayer asking for the gifts of the Holy Spirit and the laying on of hands which signifies them.[3] It proclaims that the church is bound up with the acts of Jesus Christ and his apostles.

35. The ordination of ministers is at once:

(a) an invocation of God to grant the gifts of the Holy Spirit for the needs of the ministry;
(b) the sacramental sign of the answering of this prayer by our Lord, who confers the necessary charisms;

---

3. "As regards the laying on of hands, which is practiced to initiate true priests and ministers of the church into their office, I have no objection to its being received as a sacrament, for in it there is a ceremony first taken from Scripture, then one that Paul testifies not to be empty or superficial but a faithful token of spiritual grace (1 Tim 4:14). However, I have not put it as number three among the sacraments because it is not ordinary or common with all believers but is a special rite for a particular office" (Calvin, *Institutes* IV, 19). Research still needs to be done on the subject of the sacramental nature of ordination, since this point looms large in ecumenical dialogue.

(c) the welcome extended ʋy the whole church to the new servant and his reception into the college of ministers;

(d) the commitment of the minister to the ministry with which he is entrusted.

36. The ordained ministry is definitive in its fundamental reality of serving the gospel, the sacraments, and the community. Its form may vary according to the needs of the church and the mission entrusted to its ministers. The exercise of the pastoral ministry may be suspended for quite a long time without a new ordination being required if it is taken up again. Ordination, the sign of a difference of charisms between the pastoral ministry and the priesthood of the baptized, far from separating ministers from God's people and making them into a clerical caste, identifies them more fully with the life of the church.

37. The foregoing text shows a fundamental agreement between us on the nature and significance of the pastoral ministry in the mystery of the church. Difficulties remain, of which the chief ones seem to fall into two categories.

The first and most important difficulty lies in a different interpretation and appreciation of the concrete and historic shapes assumed by the apostolic succession in the ministry, owing to the separation of the churches.

The second derives from the great differences in the present organization and allocation of ministries on both sides.

These difficulties do not necessarily seem to us an obstacle to a future reconciliation of the ministries on the basis of the agreement reached.

PART TWO
Proposal for a Recognition and Reconciliation of Ministries

I. Introduction

38. The question of the ministries being a major obstacle to unity, it is on this point that the change of heart *(metanoia)* of the churches ought primarily to concentrate. We do not feel that a purely theological agreement can suffice to carry the churches the rest of the way towards unity. Our doctrinal agreement on the pastoral ministry already constitutes a reconciliation in faith; if it is accepted, the reconciliation will still need to be in-

timated by acts on the part of the churches. These might well create a new situation where problems relating to joint celebration would be solved because they would have ceased to exist. The reconciliation of the ministries would then take on a significant character in the eyes of our communities and of the world, in an effort to give the church a new image.

39. Up to the present, a critical examination on each side, undertaken and accepted as a call to reform the church, has enabled us to discern what, on our own side, is in conflict with our mutual beliefs about the ministry and what, on the other, is a sign and reminder of ecclesial value. We have been discovering in each other complementary virtues demanding to be practiced in unity, for we have need one of another in order to be church more perfectly.

From now on, the efforts of the churches in the direction of conversion must tend toward and culminate in a word of mutual recognition, as well as in decisions in regard to themselves that will make possible an act of reconciliation of sacramental and ecclesial significance. Recognition and reconciliation each imply and call for the other.

The points on which a change of heart is necessary in order to achieve full reconciliation are the following:[4]

II. On the Catholic Side

40. We propose that the substantial reality of the ministry that has emerged from the churches born of the Reformation be recognized; because of the defects and deviations that had come about in the exercise of the traditional ministries, and despite the shared sin of separation, God, ever faithful to his church, gave these communities that continued living in an apostolic succession of faith a ministry of the word and sacraments, whose value is manifested by its fruits.[5] This ministry, which arose outside the episcopal succession, can in some cases claim to rest at least on the sign of a presbyteral succession.[6]

Consequently, to complete this recognition and give this ministry au-

4. They are formulated in the case of each confessional family in its own language.

5. Second Vatican Council, Decree on Ecumenism *(Unitatis Redintegratio)*, nos. 3, 20-23.

6. By this we mean that Roman Catholic priests who went over to the Reformed churches ordained pastors. They were able to justify their action in doing so on the basis of one of the theological concepts of the day.

thority in the eyes of their people, the bishops would need to join it to the normal sign of the episcopal succession that is indispensable, in Catholic doctrine, to the fullness of the ministry perfectly signified. Reality and sign complement one another in the mystery of the church. They would thereby affirm the necessary docility of the church to the free initiatives of the Spirit.

41. We propose that a more collegial pattern be adopted for the exercise of the hierarchical ministry at the universal and local levels, so as to show more visibly the ties of reciprocity that exist between the ministers and God's people and, similarly, between priests and bishops.

42. In this same spirit, we propose that more value be attached in the life of the church to the various ministries or charisms founded on the priesthood of the laity and on Christian responsibility deriving from reception of baptism, confirmation, and the eucharist.

III. On the Protestant Side

43. We propose that all the people of our churches should recognize the reality of a ministry of the word and of the sacraments in the Catholic Church. It would accordingly be for the authorities of our churches, on the basis of an agreement as to the nature of the ministry, to confer authority on Catholic ministers to minister to their people.

By reason of the situation created by the rupture in the sixteenth century, we recognize that we are deprived, not of the apostolic succession, but of the fullness of the sign of this succession. The result is a splintering off to form various national churches and the loss of a sense of the unity of the church in time and in space. With a view to the unity of the church and its ministries we recognize the necessity to return to the fullness of the sign of the apostolic succession.

44. We propose that a new value should be set on the significance of the "episcopal" ministry, in particular in regard to its pastoral character, and that the sense of its personalization as a sign of unity should be revived.

45. We propose a review of the practice in certain Reformed churches of delegating authority to people who are not ordained to preach and to cele-

brate the Lord's Supper, so that the difference in charisms between the or-dained ministry and the priesthood of the laity shall no longer be ob-scured. We believe that the significance of ordination would be more clearly brought out by diversified ordinations.

46. On the basis of this mutual change of heart, the reconciliation of min-istries could take the form of a reciprocal laying on of hands,[7] a traditional apostolic gesture that expresses the action of Christ and of the Spirit in the visible body of the church. Its several levels of meaning would enable it to signify a penitential act of reconciliation in which each side would recog-nize before the other where it was deficient and, at the same time, would be accompanied by the invocation of the Holy Spirit and directed towards a sending out into the world. It would give a wider and fuller investiture in the eyes of the churches concerned.

47. We are also aware that the reconciliation of the ministries we desire will raise the question of the ministry of the unity of the universal church in a more immediate fashion. We propose to place this matter on our agenda for our future meetings, if possible with the participation of our brothers of the Orthodox churches.

IV. Questions

48. Might not the foregoing proposal contribute to a positive and ecclesially demanding solution of the urgent pastoral problems with which we are at present faced (certain chaplaincies, scattered communities, pas-toral ministry to interchurch families, ecumenical groups, etc.)? A recon-ciliation of ministries might be envisaged in certain cases where serious ecumenical work at pastoral and community levels has brought to light a fundamental agreement in faith that makes it unequivocally possible. This might be done in the name of the legitimate initiative and discretion left to local churches.[8]

---

7. The laying on of hands should take place with the participation of officially qualified ministers.

8. By this is meant, on the Catholic side, the dioceses and, on the Protestant side, the ec-clesiastical regions. To be legitimate, an initiative of this sort presupposes the obedience of each communion to its own discipline.

That is the spirit in which we have been working. We submit this question to the authorities of our respective churches.

PARTICIPANTS

Roman Catholic	*Protestant*
Fr Jean-Noël Aletti	Pastor Georges Appia
Fr Paul Aymard	Pastor Jacky Argaud
Fr Joseph de Baciocchi	Pastor Daniel Atger
Fr René Beaupère	Pastor André Benoit
Fr Edmond Chavaz	Pastor Alain Blancy
Fr Marc Clément	Pastor Henry Bruston
Fr Irénée H. Dalmais	Pastor Edouard Diserens
Fr Jacques Desseaux	Pastor M. Ferrier-Welti
Fr André Fabre	Pastor Jean-Claude Ill
Fr Claude Gerest	Pastor Jean Jundt
Fr René Girault	Pastor Jean Kaltenmark
Fr Etienne Goutagny	Pastor Michel Leplay
Fr Maurice Jourjon	Pastor Louis Lévrier
Fr Marie Leblanc	Pastor Marc Lods
Fr Gustave Martelet	Pastor Alain Martin
Fr Pierre Michalon	Pastor André Morel
Fr André Perroux	Pastor Hébert Roux
Fr Jean Roche	Brother Max Thurian of Taizé
Fr Bernard Sesboüé	Pastor André Vermeil
Fr Robert Stalder	Pastor Gaston Westphal
Fr Maurice Villain	

The Episcopal Ministry (1976)

REFLECTIONS AND PROPOSALS CONCERNING THE MINISTRY OF VIGILANCE AND UNITY IN THE PARTICULAR CHURCH[1]

—⟨೦⁄೦⟩—

Introduction

1. In 1972 the Groupe des Dombes published some points of agreement under the title: "Towards a Reconciliation of Ministries." It now puts forward a further document, on the subject of the ministry of vigilance, animation, and unity in a broader ecclesial gathering than that of the parish. We shall speak of this ministry as *episcopē*, a Greek term whose meaning is not fully brought out in the French equivalent of "surveillance." This study extends and puts into sharper focus our work of 1972 on the pastoral ministry. It tries to take account of criticisms that were directed at the previous document.[2]

---

1. *Translator's note:* Scriptural quotations are taken from the Jerusalem Bible; quotations from Clement of Rome and Ignatius in nos. 23-29 from *Early Christian Writings*, trans. Maxwell Staniforth (Harmondsworth: Penguin, 1987). The latter will be abbreviated as *ECW.*

2. Here follow some clarifications of terms used, which it will be helpful to keep in mind while reading the text:

    1. *episcopē:* the whole charge of pastoral vigilance and unity.

    2. *episcopos:* a minister who is chiefly responsible for carrying out this charge. We have chosen to use this New Testament term in order to avoid necessarily identifying this minister with any particular historical manifestation (bishop, superintendent, president, etc.). [*Translator's note:* the French text uses the term "l'épiscope"; for the sake of simplicity in English and on analogy with the original, this has been left in the Greek form.]

2. The ministry of *episcopē* concretized quite quickly in the person of the bishop as known in the Catholic and Orthodox churches, in the Anglican Communion, and in a number of churches that stem from the Reformation. The way in which this ministry functioned in fifteenth- and sixteenth-century Catholicism led most of the Reformation churches to try to find other types of institutions in which the ministry of *episcopē* could nonetheless operate: in France, for example, the presbyterian-synodical system.[3] Their failure to find enough evidence in the New Testament for a detailed description of the bishop's ministry also explains why a certain number of Protestants do not feel justified in establishing this ministry in their churches.

3. These different attitudes towards the function of *episcopē* constitute one of the basic obstacles to Christian unity. Today they also bring about a mutual questioning between episcopal and non-episcopal churches. This questioning impels both parties to test the scriptural foundations of their doctrine and practice in order to direct themselves, if necessary, to a structure more in harmony with Christ's purpose in founding the church and more open to the freedom of the Spirit.

---

3. *bishop:* the *episcopos* in Catholic and Orthodox ecclesial tradition, and in other traditions that are close to them.

4. *episcopate:* the collegial body of bishops.

5. *episcopal:* depending on the context, the adjective refers to *episcopē, episcopos,* or bishop.

6. *episcopalian:* is used in the text in a more general sense than its current confessional application: it describes the churches that have bishops.

7. *metanoia:* a New Testament term currently translated by "conversion" or "repentance." We use it to indicate a change affecting not just interior dispositions and personal behavior, but also the manner in which ecclesial institutions function, and even, if necessary, their structure.

8. *college:* we do not restrict this term to the particular sense it has been given in the documents of Vatican II, where it is used to refer to the college of bishops. We give it a broader application to refer also to a group of ministers within the framework of a particular church who, though ultimately distinct, share the same responsibilities in solidarity with one another. A college usually has a president to ensure its unity.

3. Most of the Reformed churches have adopted the mode of government called "presbyteral-synodical," which brings together at different levels of the life of these churches the authority of *elected assemblies* (synods) and of the ministers (pastors and elders) who compose them. This form of government steers between episcopal government and congregationalist government (the practical autonomy of the communities).

A certain lack of vigor in the way in which ecclesial institutions are functioning also calls for a fresh look at their forms.

4. On the Catholic side, the exercise of the episcopate, despite some measure of renewal, is coming up against some serious difficulties that bear especially upon:

- the proclaiming of the Good News in a comprehensible and stimulating language, at the heart of the problems of our time;
- the range of ecclesial contacts in which the bishop, for lack of diocesan organs fitted for dialogue, and sharing in decision-making, is often without a real grasp of the various situations that exist;
- clarity in the dealings between the episcopates of different countries when they want to present a common front on issues that concern them all.

5. The Reformation churches, at least in France, are also experiencing some weaknesses in the way the presbyterian-synodical system functions:

- misuse of parliamentary government that affects church assemblies;
- difficulty in living out pluralism within unity;
- lack of continuity in church government;
- gaps in the concrete expression of concern for the unity and universality of the church.

6. Moreover, the episcopate, by virtue of its nature and purpose, is the subject of a careful study by the Faith and Order Commission of the World Council of Churches. In a document published by the Commission in 1974[4] they say: ". . . these new insights are enabling churches without the historic episcopate to appreciate it as a sign of the continuity and unity of the church. More and more churches, including those in church union negotiations, are expressing willingness to see episcopacy as a pre-eminent sign of the apostolic succession of the whole church in faith, life and doctrine, and, as such, something that ought to be striven for if absent. The only thing they hold as incompatible with contemporary historical and theological research is the notion that the episcopal succession is identical with and comprehends the apostolicity of the whole church."

4. *One Baptism, One Eucharist and a Mutually Recognised Ministry,* Faith and Order Paper 73 (Geneva: WCC, 1975), p. 39, no. 37.

7. This varied data is of an ecumenical significance insofar as it confronts all Christ's disciples with the same demands: to make the life and presence of the churches as transparent as possible to the gospel they preach.

8. This is why the question of *episcopē* and of the episcopate cannot be studied, in our opinion, on a purely doctrinal level. The ideas that are formed about them and the reactions that are made to them are always bound up with the actual, familiar working model. Progress towards reconciliation therefore requires not just the necessary doctrinal clarifications, but the taking into account of the situations in which we each find ourselves. It is from these that we have to set out on the journey in a spirit of conversion *(metanoia)*.

This document therefore falls into two parts: one of doctrinal reflection, and one of proposals for a way of getting beyond the existing situations.

Part One: Doctrinal Reflection

9. A church is born and grows in a place where people turn to the gospel under the influence of the Holy Spirit and are gathered together into communities.

For such a gathering to correspond to what we term the "particular church"[5] in which *episcopē* is exercised in a specific place over a group of parishes and communities, it would need to show the following characteristics:

- it unites men of all ages, origins, and ways of life in order to make one people of them, as a witness to the gospel in the world that surrounds them;
- all the functions of the church are operative in it, primarily the preaching of the Word of God and the celebration of worship and the sacraments;
- it receives the ministries it needs for the building up and mission of the church;

5. From now on we shall use the term "particular church" in the sense of and to replace "local church," an expression used in the points of agreement published in "Towards a Reconciliation of Ministries (1972)," no. 48 and note 8. This latter term in fact leads to misunderstanding.

- it is given new ministers by the Holy Spirit who are ordained within itself;
- it lives in visible communion with the other churches.

10. Our study follows a line that moves from *episcopē*, a necessary function acknowledged by every church, to the way in which it is expressed in specific persons, something that is still a problem today in the ecumenical dialogue.

(A) Consideration of the Data of the New Testament and the Primitive Tradition

(I) Jesus Christ, episcopos of His Church

11. God's plan, to which biblical revelation (the Old Testament) bears witness, stresses the Lord's *episcopē* over his people. The Lord frees and gathers his people together in view of their universal mission; he visits them, and he feeds and guides them.

12. In the New Covenant, Jesus Christ, whom the Father has sent, carries out this *episcopē*. He is forever the one who gathers together, the shepherd and guardian of his church, who restores her by his call and defends her at the cost of his own life (cf. John 10:11-18; 11:51-52); he is also the gate through which must pass the sheep and the true shepherds who are capable of guiding them towards life and in freedom (cf. John 10:1-10; 1 Pet. 5:1-4).

13. Jesus Christ has sealed the new covenant in his blood and keeps it strong and vital through his Spirit. Every minister who is solicitous to maintain this covenant in a particular church will act by the power of the Spirit, on the model of Paul, by faithfully fulfilling the charism he has received. This is how the risen Christ never leaves alone those whom he sends: he gives them the Spirit.

14. The points of agreement reached in 1972 therefore apply to *episcopē*, in particular when they deal with the relation of the church's ministries to the ministry of Christ (nos. 5-7 and 20-24).[6]

---

6. See "Towards a Reconciliation of Ministries (1972)." On the basis of these texts, which we find of continuing value, we would like to clarify some points that were indicated there as

(II) The New Testament Outline of episcopē

15. Faith is aroused and the church is founded by the preaching of the gospel (Rom. 10:17). As he gathers the church together, Christ the "chief Shepherd" (1 Pet. 5:4) gives her a ministry of vigilance to ensure that the proclamation of the Word, the celebration of the sacraments, the *diaconia*, and the other functions of the Body of Christ have coherence and unity.

16. According to the varied witness of the New Testament, the ministry of *episcopē* is exercised on the model of Christ "the *episcopos* of our souls" (1 Pet. 2:25) and of the apostles, insofar as their charge was capable of being handed on. It consists in guiding the flock, watching over it, warning and encouraging it (Acts 20:28-31), censuring it (1 Cor. 5:3-5), and animating the community to respond to its universal mission. This ministry of direction and of presidency does not exist simply for the internal service of the communities: it directs the whole assembly of the faithful in its openness to the world and its advance towards the kingdom.

17. A number of other biblical texts help to define this form of ministry: the transmission and guarding of the deposit (of faith) (Titus 2:1, 7-8; 2 Tim. 1:14 and 2:2), presidency over the communities (1 Tim. 5:17), visiting and coordinating the communities (Acts 15:36), and the discernment of spiritual gifts (1 Pet. 4:10).

(III) The Ministry of episcopē and the Community in the New Testament

18. The function of watching over the community was carried out by specific persons whom the Lord established for the service of the people of the

---

still causing difficulty, and to propose some possible lines of growing convergence between our churches in the spirit of reflections already begun.

We recognized two categories of difficulties that still existed: first, "a different interpretation and appreciation of the concrete and historic shapes assumed by the apostolic succession in the ministry, owing to the separation of the churches"; and second, "the great differences in the present organization and allocation of ministries on both sides" (no. 37).

On the Catholic side, we proposed "that a more collegial pattern be adopted for the exercise of the hierarchical ministry" (no. 41); on the Protestant side, we proposed "that a new value should be set on the significance of the 'episcopal' ministry, in particular in regard to its pastoral character" (no. 44).

New Covenant. Their authority is of a spiritual sort. It is a gift of the Spirit who creates and frees. These ministers are thus called in their own freedom and responsibility to awaken freedom and responsibility in their brothers (cf. Acts 15:28).

19. The ministry of vigilance is then a service and is exercised in a spirit of service in the midst of the people of God, and not in the way in which "the rulers of the pagans lord it over them, and their great men make their authority felt" (Mark 10:42). In the likeness of Christ who "did not come to be served but to serve" (Mark 10:45), those who pasture the flock must not wield a power that dominates, but an authority of communion. The ministry they have received is a call to become examples for the flock (1 Pet. 5:2-4).

20. The Christian community is urged to obey God in receiving Christ, whom he has sent, and those whom Christ sends (Matt. 10:40). By listening to their pastors in the obedience of the faith, the faithful will be behaving as followers of Christ (Phil. 2:29; 4:9; Heb. 13:17).

(IV) The Ministry of episcopē and Collegiality in the New Testament

21. The New Testament refers to the *collegial* character of ministries. This collegiality operates on two levels:

(a) Within a single church, the pastoral ministry is undertaken in its diversity by a group of persons who act as a college (Acts 14:23; 1 Tim. 4:14). The terms *episcopos* and presbyter, which describe these persons, are thus equivalent. But one member of the college was probably appointed as president, according to the custom of the synagogue.

(b) Pastors belonging to different churches carry out their ministry in solidarity. The New Testament alludes to fraternal visits they make (Acts 21:17-18; Gal. 2:1-10), to the exchange of letters (Col. 4:16), to the sending of ministers to newly formed communities (Acts 11:19-26; 13:1-3), to collections organized for the relief of hard-pressed churches (2 Cor. 8-9), and to meetings that enabled joint decisions to be taken (Acts 15:1-35). This network of contacts, which lets us see the emergence of a ministerial body, expresses the unity among particular churches within the universal church.

22. We consider that the New Testament associates with this collegial exercise of *episcopē* a *presidency* expressed in individual persons at different levels of the church:

(a) In the Jerusalem church the figure of a president in the midst of a college of presbyters first becomes visible in the person of James (Acts 15:13-21).

(b) Paul exercises as an apostle, in presence or from a distance, a personal pastoral authority among his fellow workers over the churches he has founded.

(c) The pastoral epistles witness that Paul entrusted the *episcopē* to his fellow workers Titus and Timothy.

(d) For the churches of the apostolic age the person of Peter among the Twelve remained a rallying point and a symbol of the ministry of *episcopē* even after the original college had disappeared (Matt. 16:18-19; Luke 22:32; Gal. 1:18).[7]

23. At the time when the New Testament was sketching out the ministry of *episcopē*, the apostolic writings had not been defined as Scripture any more than *episcopē* had been defined as a ministry. Yet it was the churches presided over by *episcopoi* who gradually received the canon of Scripture. To say this is to acknowledge that the churches that referred themselves in a definitive way to Scripture were right in considering that this was the basis of the ministry of their *episcopoi*. The Christian communities of the first centuries lived in accordance with the belief indicated by Clement of Rome in these words: "when the Apostles appointed *episcopoi* and deacons for the believers of the future . . . this was in no way an innovation, for *episcopoi* and deacons had already been spoken of in Scripture long before that" (*To the Corinthians* 42; *ECW*, p. 45).

---

7. We decided not to develop this paragraph further. For example, some exegetes think that the angels of the seven churches of the Apocalypse are the symbolic designations of the presidents of those churches (Rev. 2–3).

(V) The Ministry of episcopē after the Apostolic Era

24. Some New Testament evidence presents the apostles as establishing presbyter-*episcopoi* in the churches by the laying on of hands (Acts 14:23; Titus 1:5-7) and entrusting to these reliable men the tradition of evangelical instruction (1 Tim. 1:3-7; 2 Tim. 4:1-5).

25. Once the apostles had disappeared, the Christian communities, striving to deal with the dangers of heresies and schisms, looked on those reliable men as the guardians of the apostolic tradition and recognized in them a decision-making authority. The episcopate exercised by one person became widespread during the second century and soon became a rule for all the churches.

26. Between the year 95 (Clement of Rome) and the year 180 (Irenaeus of Lyons), the ministry of *episcopē* as a sign of God's faithfulness to his purpose became the subject of a threefold theological reflection:

27. (a) The *theology of mission* holds that the overriding reference for the person or persons exercising this ministry is the sending of Christ by his Father. Clement: "Christ received his commission from God, and the Apostles theirs from Christ. . . . [I]n view of this, we cannot think it right for these men . . . after being commissioned by the Apostles . . . now to be ejected from their ministry" (*To the Corinthians,* 42 and 44; *ECW,* pp. 45, 46). Ignatius of Antioch: "When someone is sent by the master of a house to manage his household for him, it is our duty to give him the same kind of reception as we should give to the sender; and therefore it is clear that we must regard a bishop *(episcopos)* as the Lord himself" (*To the Ephesians,* 6; *ECW,* p. 77).

28. (b) The *theology of types* looks at the church as the image of those whom Jesus grouped around himself to keep them in unity. It sees in the presbyters the image of the apostles, and in the *episcopos* the image of Christ or of the Father. In other words, not even Ignatius concentrates all the ministry in the *episcopos* alone: "Hold the deacons in as great respect as Jesus Christ; just as you should also look on the *episcopos* as a type of the Father, and the clergy as the apostolic circle forming his council" (*To the Trallians,* 3; *ECW,* pp. 95-96).

29. (c) The *theology of succession* is the third aspect of the reflection on *episcopē*. As early as Clement it is affirmed that the Apostles laid it down "as a rule" that after the deaths of the first community leaders whom they had appointed "other accredited persons should succeed them in their office" (*To the Corinthians*, 44; *ECW*, p. 46). Irenaeus: "We recall the tradition which comes from the Apostles and is preserved in the churches by the succession of presbyters"[8] (*Against the Heresies* 3, 2, 2). "It is our duty to obey those presbyters who are in the church, who have their succession from the Apostles . . . who with their succession in the episcopate have received the sure spiritual gift of truth according to the pleasures of the Father" (*Against the Heresies,* 4, 26, 2).

30. These three theologies show a convergence towards a ministry of *episcopē* carried out by one person and considered as a gift of God to his church, but in no way destroying the collegiality attested previously.

(B) Theological Statement for Today

31. Through the experience of the first Christian communities that Scripture describes, we have tried to take hold once more of what Christ intended with regard to the nature of *episcopē* in the structure of his church. This *episcopē* brings together both collegiality and the presidency of individuals.

Faithfulness to what Christ intended consists in respecting this structure without trying to draw from the New Testament any one normative model of organization. *A fortiori,* we must not set up as norms certain confessional positions that have come about through the vicissitudes of history; nor must we let the constituents of the church's visible nature be dictated to us by any contemporary sociological influences.

(I) The Church and Her episcopē in Relation to Christ

32. In docility to the Holy Spirit, fidelity to Christ, and obedience to the Father, all Christians exercise their charisms and their functions in solidarity for the good of the body of the church and of her mission.

8. Irenaeus still keeps the term "presbyter" as equivalent to the term *"episcopos."*

33. Within the church, the *episcopos* and the presbyters live out the same ministerial and sacramental reality. The distinction of functions, attested by a traditional difference in ordination, can be expressed like this: the *episcopos* exercises the pastoral ministry of presidency and unity, with the whole range of his responsibilities towards the particular church and the universal church; the presbyters exercise the same ministry within the framework of the particular churches in communion with their *episcopos* and acknowledging his authority.

34. The ministry of the *episcopos* in union with his community is to ensure and signify "the church's dependence on Christ, a source of its mission and foundation of its unity" (Dombes 1972, no. 20). It is in this relationship with Christ the chief Shepherd, which is experienced within the church, that the presence of the *episcopos* is a reminder to all of the priority of the divine initiative.

35. The *episcopos* expresses the church's obedience to Christ first of all by his own submission to Scripture, which is the declaration of God's Word and the heritage of the apostolic ministry. This is how, in the church, he guards the deposit of faith as recorded in the Scriptures and presides over the teaching of it. In submission to Scripture the *episcopos* exercises an authority for regulating the way in which the gospel message is interpreted, in order to guide the church, in freedom and obedience, to Christ, who has given us the supreme example of freedom and obedience to the Father.

36. The ministerial succession of the original symbolic college of the Twelve is expressed in the whole episcopal college as one universal reality, while the whole church succeeds to this college of the Twelve insofar as it symbolizes and already brings into existence the Israel of the new covenant.

37. The ministry of *episcopē* thus expresses the permanence of the pastoral charge which the risen Christ guarantees for his church, in the fullness of the Holy Spirit, so that she may be "one, holy, catholic[9] and apostolic." The continuity of mission cannot be separated from the bond of communion between the different communities.

9. Here we are deliberately using the traditional term "catholic," which expresses both the universality of the whole church and the catholicity of each particular church.

38. The *episcopoi*, in the midst of the communities entrusted to their ministry, are thus preeminent signs of the bond linking the past (the salvation event accomplished in Christ) and the future (the definitive victory of the risen Christ and the consummation of creation by the Holy Spirit); they are both witnesses to and servants of the catholicity of the whole church. As regards the past, the *episcopoi* inherit whatever can be handed on of the apostles' ministry. In the present and for the future, they guarantee the continuity of the church's advance in her pilgrimage to the kingdom. In the light of this understanding of episcopal ministry, which is already indicated in the primitive church, we can state that the succession of the apostolic ministry becomes a reality in the first place through the episcopal succession.

39. The ministerial authority of the *episcopos* is based on that of Christ, the servant of his church; the church receives this authority as "a service of Christ in the power of the Spirit" (Dombes 1959, no. 3); as such "it constitutes a part of the very being of the church" (Dombes 1959, no. 4a).[10]

The exercise of this authority has its norm and foundation in Christ's words: "Whatever you bind on earth shall be considered bound in heaven; whatever you loose on earth shall be considered loosed in heaven" (Matt. 18:18). It is "entirely oriented to the growth of the Body of Christ in holiness and truth, for the glory of God" (Dombes 1959, no. 4b).[11]

This authority of service and of communion is exercised not simply over an assembly of the faithful, but also over the other ministries.[12]

40. The authority of the *episcopos* is of the charismatic order, that is, it is a gift of the Spirit for the growth of the church; it recognizes the other

10. Groupe des Dombes, "1959 L'autorité pastorale dans l'Église [Thèses]," in *Pour la communion des Églises: L'apport du Groupe des Dombes 1937-1997* (Paris: Centurion, 1988), p. 17.

11. Groupe des Dombes, "L'autorité pastorale," p. 17.

12. "If I am overwhelmed by what I am for you," says Augustine, "I am reassured by what I am with you. For you, I am the *episcopos*. With you, I am a Christian. *Episcopos* is the title of a charge. Christian is the name of a grace. How much more attractive to me is the fact that I have been redeemed with you than the fact that I am your leader" (Sermon 340, 1; PL, 38, 1483). Also John Chrysostom: "It is certainly myself who stretch out my hand to the banquet first, like a senior surrounded by children. But everything is portioned out equally among us: the life that saves . . . the victim in which we all share. We each possess the same baptism, we have been judged worthy of the same Spirit; everything is held in common among us. So what carries the most weight with me? My cares on your behalf. But there is nothing more pleasing than such a pain" (Fourth Sermon on 2 Thessalonians 4; PG 62, 492).

charisms, discerns and authenticates them, and directs them towards the unity of the Body of Christ in space and time.

It must be always alert not to stifle the other charisms; equally, the Christian community for its own part has the obligation of recognizing the gift of episcopal authority and of helping it to function.

41. This is why the *episcopos* does not undertake his duty as the result of a purely juridical arrangement. He holds his ministry from Christ the chief Shepherd, and it is by Christ that he is consecrated in his new charge.

The invocation of the Holy Spirit with the laying on of hands expresses the origin of his ministry and gives him the spiritual gifts he needs to fulfill this service. This epiclesis also sets the *episcopos* within the ministerial succession and aggregates him to the college of those who, like himself, exercise *episcopē* in the church.

(II) The Relation of the episcopos to the Particular Church

42. The episcopal ministry is exercised "in the dependence of the community and the minister on one another" (Dombes 1972, no. 22). This means that *there is no episcopos without community*: because he is essentially at the service of the community. His ministry consists in summoning it to the eucharistic celebration and to the fulfillment of its mission in the world. Neither is there any *community without episcopos*: for the community cannot continue as such without taking its *episcopos* to itself in a freely given obedience, as an envoy of the Lord and the symbol of its unity.

43. This structure involves a twofold demand:

(a) The *episcopos* must live out his submission to Jesus Christ not simply in his relation with his church, but also in his collegial relation with the other ministers. His ministry of presidency does not constitute a domination over or a monopoly of every charge in the church.

(b) Likewise, a church or an assembly of communities having genuine and living bonds cannot be without a presidency as a sign and instrument of their unity, which is given by Christ.

44. The expression of the Lord Christ's relation to his church at the institutional level cannot purely and simply reproduce a system, of whatever sort

it may be, democratic, monarchical, or oligarchic. For these forms of government are only the translation of human methods of lordship.

Every model of social organization expresses the network of relations within that society's life. It is therefore the receiving of the gifts of the Spirit, openness to the Lordship of Christ, and filial obedience to the Father that ought to be visible through the sum of ministerial relations in the church.

45. The church professes that authority is in Christ's hands, not her own. As a result, she is obliged to reject the abuses of "parliamentarianism" and bureaucratic anonymity, the temptation of every college, and also of the lone exercise of power, the temptation of all presidency.

The purpose of the church's ministerial structure is to express that all her authority is a gift she has received, an embassy and stewardship in the name of Christ. It makes actual in the life of the church the fact that man is saved by the grace of Christ, according to the gospel of justification by faith.

(III) The Relation of the episcopos to the Universal Church

46. The episcopal ministry that each church has received as a gift from Christ functions not just within the college of ministers of the particular church, but also in the episcopal college, which ensures and signifies the communion of all the particular churches.

47. The communion of the *episcopoi* among themselves has as its foundation the communion of the churches within which and on whose behalf they receive their ministry.

This communion makes visible and effective the unity and catholicity the Lord willed for his church. The communion of the *episcopoi*, which is enriched by their differences, expresses the catholicity that is created by the diversity of particular churches.

48. The synods and councils are privileged moments in the exercise of episcopal vigilance over the faithfulness of the life of the churches to the apostolic witness. Their faithfulness can be guaranteed only through the mutual verification of unanimity in confessing the true faith. In return, each *episcopos* is responsible for making the faith of the whole church known to his particular church.

49. In the responsibility he bears to the universal church as much as to his particular church, the *episcopos* is thus a man of communion and of communication.

(IV) The Relation of the episcopos to Society

50. The church of Jesus Christ has been sent into the world to serve the human community. At the call of God, she bears a responsibility for the whole people, of whom she constitutes only a part. She is constantly being invited to go out beyond her walls to further the deliverance of mankind.

51. At the heart of his ministry and in communion with the people entrusted to him, the *episcopos* is charged with an equal concern for the society in which he lives. It is his task, along with his community, to be a "watchman" and "sentinel" in that society (cf. Ezek. 33). He proclaims the Good News in the midst of the efforts and conflicts of society. He keeps before it the demands of justice. He undertakes the defense of the poor and those whom society rejects.

52. Because of his position in the Christian community, the *episcopos* often personifies his church in the eyes of public opinion and public authorities. Whether he likes it or not, he is a representative person. It is his task in this delicate situation to be the spokesman of his community and also to challenge it. In the name of the gospel he will be capable of taking his stand with humility and courage.

(V) Conclusion: Outline of the episcopos

53. The *episcopos* is, then, a man who animates the life of the people of God, who watches over the birth and harmonious development of the different communities, and who makes possible the full expansion of the spiritual gifts that are given to every baptized Christian.

54. The *episcopos* is a man who ensures that all the ministries grow together towards Christ, and apart from whom these ministries run the risk of scattering the church instead of gathering her together and building her up in unity and peace.

55. The *episcopos* is a man with the task of helping to preserve the church's identity between Pentecost and the parousia, and this makes of him a constitutive element of the church's tradition.

Part Two: Proposals for a Way to Transcend the Existing Situations

56. The joint study of the New Testament and of the tradition that interpreted it constitutes for us, Catholics and Protestants, a serious challenge. The Word of God calls us to set out from our different ecclesiologies and to come together in the search for a common objective: the recovery of the wholeness of the one church of Jesus Christ, after centuries of division, in a common obedience to the one Lord. This does not imply a quest for uniformity, but fidelity to a single essential structure (cf. no. 31) that makes visible and operative the *episcopē* of Jesus Christ himself.

57. We indeed think that advance towards reconciliation presupposes on both sides a transformation of ecclesial life simultaneous with progress at the doctrinal level. Both are necessary if each confession is to be able to recognize the image of Christ's church more distinctly in its partner, and also to make this image more recognizable in itself.

58. It may be that our suggestions will appear timid or inopportune to some, and too daring to others. But we believe that any reform in the church will be pointless unless it aims at making its conformity to God's plan for the salvation of the world more transparent. This implies a change of mentality in the whole assembly of believers as much as on the part of those who have the responsibility of being "spiritual guides." This can be the work only of the Holy Spirit.

Today, the handing on of the gospel demands of all confessions a revision of the witness their institutions actually give.

59. As our confessional points of departure are different, ecclesial conversion *(metanoia)* will take different paths for each, but our whole group takes note of the various suggestions that follow, some of which are addressed to the Catholic Church, and others to the Reformation churches.

(A) *Proposals for the Catholic Church*

(I) *Towards a More Evangelical Exercise of the Bishop's Ministry*

60. The actual way in which the episcopal ministry is exercised arises from the permanent work of conversion, which always needs to be done afresh in submission to the Holy Spirit.[13]

This is why we think that new modalities in the exercise of the episcopate should witness to a type of authority of an evangelical nature that would not identify itself with any model to be found in the world (Luke 22:25-27).

61. In fact, the adaptation of the church to the life of the world is undergoing a radical change, and the application of the directives of Vatican II involves a profound renewal in the way in which the episcopal function is exercised. This renewal should be pursued with an eye to the following needs:

(a) the necessity of preaching the Good News in language that is accessible to people today;

(b) the necessity on the bishop's part for an increasingly genuine pastoral closeness to the Christian people;

(c) the development on the diocesan level of a collegial and synodical life in the exercise of authority;

(d) attention to the emergence of new church forms raised up by the Holy Spirit.

---

13. In the course of the centuries, the episcopal charge seemed at certain moments to lack concrete expression. This was particularly the case in the sixteenth century at the outbreak of the Reformation. In her official documents the church acknowledged this, but perhaps saw it too much as a matter of a series of personal failings on the part of particular bishops. We think that much more needs to be admitted. The real situation was that as a result of the social models it had adopted, the episcopal institution itself appeared to be contrary to the gospel rather than in its service, and in so doing it concealed the apostolic origin of the episcopate.

(II) Co-Responsibility with the People of God in the Diocesan Church

62. The way in which bishops have been chosen has undergone considerable evolution in the history of the Catholic Church, and consequently the current mode of their designation is not beyond alteration or the only one possible. To make it clear that episcopal authority is rooted in ecclesial communion it is important that the designation of the bishop should be the fruit of a living relationship and shared reflection between the Bishop of Rome, the neighboring bishops, the priests of the diocese, and all the people concerned. We would in fact find it desirable for the people of God to have a part in choosing their bishop.[14]

63. We think it desirable that when a new bishop is installed in his office the neighboring particular churches and also the other Christian communities of the region should have some role in the liturgical celebration of the installation.

64. Since the affairs of the diocesan church concern the whole people of God, it is important that the baptized make an effective contribution to preparing and guiding decisions that have to be made.[15] It is the task of pastoral councils, diocesan commissions, liturgical teams, theological and catechetical groups, and various movements to share in the work of animating the church and its service in the world with all the imagination this calls for.

(III) Contacts between the Bishop, His Colleagues, and Other Ministers

65. In conformity with the teaching of Vatican II, which declares that a bishop cannot govern alone, we think it right that he should be surrounded by genuinely collegial institutions, which would allow the episcopal function to be carried by a greater number of people and the bishop to be more effectively informed about the life of his church.

14. The norms concerning the designation of new bishops in the Latin church already open the way for this.

15. "Since the beginning of my episcopate," says Cyprian of Carthage, "I have made it a rule to decide nothing by my own opinion without the advice of yourselves (the priests and deacons) and the approval of my people" (Letter 14, 4); and again, "I must know these particular cases and carefully study their solution, not just with my colleagues but with the whole people" (Letter 34, 4, 1).

66. (a) For example, we would like the experience of diocesan synods to be tried out more often, despite the difficulties involved. Such a procedure could make it possible for concrete problems to be raised, and even for solutions to be traced out, and such synods would encourage ecumenical encounters.

67. (b) Another example: since the episcopal council should deal with the basic preoccupations of the diocese, it would be good for it to be made up of representatives (clerical or lay) of those who are responsible for the essential "pastoral fields."

68. We wonder whether apostolic regions could not foster fruitful exchanges between neighboring particular churches.

(B) Proposals for the Reformation Churches

(I) Protestantism's Original Orientations

69. Apostolic succession is based, in the Lutheran-Reformed tradition, on conformity of preaching with the apostles' witness, as the rule of all discourse and all sacramental life in the church. The authority of ministry arises exclusively from this conformity to the Word which the Lord entrusted to his church. The Holy Spirit who was promised to the apostles makes this word effective in the present, whatever the diversity of forms in which ministerial succession is expressed.

70. The legitimacy of the apostolic succession of the bishop has been hidden by the unilateral affirmation of this principle. Yet the episcopal function is exercised in some Reformation churches in a more personal way by bishops and "ecclesiastical inspectors."

71. The pastor's ministry has often accumulated the traditional charges of the episcopate and presbyterate. However, the episcopal ministry is now exercised at different levels of the church's life in three forms, through which the traditional charges are expressed:

(a) by synodical assemblies that are responsible for giving doctrinal and disciplinary directives;

(b) by councils that are responsible for church government and for applying the decisions taken;

(c) by individuals who undertake the pastoral ministry of unity in a specific place or region.

(II) Proposed Orientations

72. The importance claimed today in the Reformation churches by the functions of presidency (the ministries of the presidents of regional councils, of "ecclesiastical inspectors," and also of the presidents of consistories or synodical commissions) demands that the reflection on ministries that has already been started[16] should be deepened at the doctrinal level.

73. The restoration of the value of the ministry of *episcopē,* including its expression in particular persons, should lead the Reformation churches to rediscover the meaning and specific nature of a ministry of unity with the basic purpose of promoting reconciliation, maintaining communion, and directing the overall mission of the church.

74. If the presently existing plurality of theological and doctrinal options is to be lived out in a positive way, it demands this rediscovery of the value of the ministry of *episcopē.*

In the face of the increasingly numerous risks of division or rupture, this ministry would have the urgent task of making possible a common confession of faith and of directing the life of the communities into the path of more stringent fidelity to the Word of God.

75. Consequently, the following proposals are intended to indicate the direction that the theological and practical reflection of the Reformation churches should take:

(a) this reflection would give the work its proper ecumenical dimension by being undertaken in relation with the other churches that have preserved or rediscovered the episcopate;

---

16. Cf., for example, for the Federation of Reformed Churches, "La Dévolution de l'autorité et l'autorité régionale" at the national Synod of Saint-Jean du Gard, in 1964.

(b) the churches would benefit from reflecting on and extending the work of the World Council of Churches, in particular the work of Faith and Order;

(c) the historical equality of pastors in ordination to the ministry should not exclude the recognition of various levels of responsibility, and in particular a ministry of *episcopē* given expression in specific individuals;

(d) the specific role of a ministry of "pastor-*episcopos*" would be illustrated more clearly by various new forms of ordaining elders or lay preachers with theological training to the Word and the sacraments, as the ordained ministries undergo diversification.

76. We are aware that this attempt at doctrinal and practical reflection can be effective only if it is accompanied by an ecumenical pedagogy addressed to the whole Christian people and the local communities, and translated into catechesis and ongoing Christian formation. In this way the faithful will more readily understand and accept the perspective of living and confessing their faith in a new form of church.

Conclusion

77. At the end of this new study, we should not forget that our aim is the reconciliation of ministries, something indispensable to the reforming of visible unity that we know in fact to be broken. We cannot rest content with any developments towards institutional parallelism. These ought to lead to the emergence of a single *episcopē* in the one church.[17] On this depends our full communion.

78. Many people today lose their confidence when they look at institutional realities. They find the episcopal ministry, which we have been discussing, patently suffering from the rigidity of the letter, to the detriment of the freedom of the Spirit. This ministry can indeed grow stiff and become paralyzed, like other institutions.

But we have the hope that this charismatic institution will serve the vi-

---

17. Unity in *episcopē* does not mean uniformity in the ways it is exercised.

tality of the church, Christian freedom, and the defense of the weak and ne-
glected. The living stability and continuity of the episcopal ministry stand
as an irreducible pole of unity that makes it possible for the Christian body
to live through tension and change without tearing itself to pieces.

79. When episcopal ministry is carried out in submission to the Spirit, it is
an opportunity for openness and suppleness towards the ever-changing
situations of life. As a practical example, the emergence of spontaneous
communities that desire to live freely in communion with the church calls
for an episcopal function capable of watching over the unity of faith while
respecting those who are seeking new paths.

80. The reflections and proposals above carry on from those we made in
1972 and we still think valid. We shall approach the authorities of the
churches to tell us to what extent they find these reflections and proposals
acceptable and workable: Can they help in ecclesial conversion *(metanoia)*
and in progress towards the reconciliation of ministries?

PARTICIPANTS AT THE MEETING OF THE GROUPE DES DOMBES, 6-10 SEPTEMBER 1976:

Fr Jean-Noël Aletti
Pastor Jean Ansaldi
Pastor Jacky Argaud
Pastor Daniel Atger
Fr Paul Aymard
Fr Joseph de Baciocchi
Fr René Beaupère
Pastor André Benoit
Pastor Alain Blancy
Fr Edmond Chavaz
Fr Henri Denis
Fr Jacques Desseaux
Fr Claude Gerest
Fr René Girault
Fr Étienne Goutagny
Fr Pierre Gressot
Fr Joseph Hoffmann

Pastor Jean-Claude Ill
Fr Maurice Jourjon
Pastor Jean Kaltenmark
Fr Marie Leblanc
Pastor Louis Lévrier
Fr Robert Liotard
Pastor Marc Lods
Pastor Alain Martin
Fr Pierre Michalon
Pastor André Morel
Fr Jean Roche
Pastor Hébert Roux
Fr Bernard Sesboüé
Brother Max Thurian of Taizé
Pastor André Vermeil
Fr Maurice Villain
Pastor Gaston Westphal

The Holy Spirit, the Church,
and the Sacraments (1979)

───❦───

Introduction

1. In its document "Towards a Reconciliation of Ministries" the Groupe des Dombes recognized that "a study of sacramentality needs to be done in the future because of the importance of this concept in ecumenical dialogue." But despite the considerable progress made in recent years along the lines of reconciliation in faith regarding baptism, eucharist, and ministries, the churches still in fact remain divided in the way they understand the sacraments and do not even give them the same importance in their lives. This situation makes a joint clarification of the nature and significance of the sacraments in the life of the church and of Christians needed and urgent.

2. What do we mean by "sacrament"? We obviously agree in general terms in seeing it as a sign given by Christ the Savior at work today in the power of the Spirit. But difficulties crop up at once: What efficacy does a sacrament have? What link ought we to establish between the ordained ministry and sacramental validity? What sort of mutual suspicions linger on about "spiritualism" or about imprecision or ambiguity in our sacramental practices and doctrines?

We would therefore like to help elucidate this concept of "sacrament" by clarifying the relation between *the Holy Spirit and the church's sacramental action.*[1]

1. We studied the doctrine of the Holy Spirit in 1965 and of the church and the Holy

3. Our approach will have three stages:

First the preliminaries: the *words* we use provoke emotional reactions that are sometimes very sharp; *old disputes* reappear in a different cultural context; *sacramental practices* are themselves drawn into these confusions. We therefore need to provide a clarification of terminology, a proper appreciation of the difficulties inherent in the number of sacraments and in their significance, and an attempt to elucidate our contemporary mentality.

4. In the second stage we shall take up *the witness of the Scriptures* of the Old and New Testaments to God's covenant with his people. This is because the covenant constitutes the basic point of reference that enables us to understand the link between the Spirit and the celebrations that Christian tradition has called "sacraments."

5. In the third stage we shall set out a *doctrinal outline* describing in more detail the link between the Spirit, the Word, and the sacraments in the church's life.

PART ONE
Preliminaries

(1) A Short History of the Words We Habitually Use

6. Our desire to clarify the often contradictory perceptions, the results of differences in sensitivity and formation, that transmit the idea of "sacrament," and to propose the most suitable modern equivalents possible should not make us forget that here we touch on the mystery[2] of God's action and gift in our world. It is therefore not possible to define and explain

---

Spirit in 1969. When we speak of the Holy Spirit, we intend to be faithful to scriptural perspectives: before being revealed as a person distinct from the Father and the Son, the Spirit enters the human heart as a divine power. And "it is the economy taken as a whole, according to Scripture, which reveals to us the person of the Holy Spirit as he is related to the Father and the Son by making us understand his essential role in our own participation in the mystery" (Dombes, "La doctrine du Saint-Esprit, 1965," in *Pour la communion des Églises: L'apport du Groupe des Dombes 1937-1997* [Paris: Centurion, 1988], pp. 23-24).

2. The term *mystery,* used here in its ordinary sense, should be taken in its Pauline meaning in paragraph 8 and according to the particular usage of the Eastern tradition in paragraph 10, in the plural.

everything. The true and perfect light is not accessible to the gaze of reason alone; it issues from the Holy Spirit who enlightens the heart and opens it to knowledge of the faith. We undertake to present this little vocabulary of realities that always transcend anything we can understand about them in full awareness of this basic datum.

7. An important difficulty results from the fact that Christian concepts often take up concepts evidenced in the history of religions (the "holy," for example), but transform them radically as they do so. This transformation of meaning is not always realized by believers, nor adequately set out in catechesis and preaching.

(a) From the beginning to modern times

8. Scripture does not use the term "sacrament." It speaks of "mystery." The nature of mystery is to be revealed. Thus there is "the mystery of God" (Col. 2:2); "the mystery of Christ" (Eph. 3:4; Col. 4:3); "the mystery of faith" (1 Tim. 3:9); "the mystery of the kingdom" (Mark 4:11); "the mystery of the gospel" (Eph. 6:19); the mystery of the union of a man and woman, which "has many implications" because "it applies to Christ and the church" (Eph. 5:32). Only the Holy Spirit gives access to all these aspects of the one mystery of our salvation.

9. The New Testament did not, however, apply the term "mystery" to baptism or the eucharist since it had no single term for the two celebrations. The same is true of the second century, when, however, all the evidence agrees in attesting that the two celebrations determine how each person becomes a Christian.

10. The tradition of the churches of the East speaks later of *mysteries* with regard to the liturgy of baptism and of the eucharist. By using the word this tradition quite consciously borrowed a religious term from paganism (the mystery cults), but also understood that "mystery" in the Pauline sense was used of the person and activity of Christ as the source of the mysteries of the church's faith and sacraments.

The eschatological reality becomes effectively present and active for us through the medium of actions and words perceived by the senses. Such is the nature of the Christian mysteries. Hence the importance of the *epiclesis,* that is, of the invocation of the Holy Spirit as the agent and guarantor of the coming kingdom of God.

11. To look elsewhere, at the beginning of the third century Tertullian made the term *sacramentum* current in the Latin Church, and this later became the equivalent of *mysterion.* A study of the etymology of this word helps us understand how it came to be transposed into Christian language. On one hand, the *sacramentum* was the solemn oath (the supremely "sacred" act and "holy thing") by which every soldier pledged his loyalty to his commanders and to the state he purposed to serve. On the other hand, *sacramentum* was used of the bond or security that a litigant deposited with the courts as evidence of the veracity of the case he meant to defend. This is how the concept of *sacred commitment* emerges from the word's double sense.

12. The event which the East called "mystery" came to be called "sacrament" in the West. This translation involved a hardening of meaning in the ritual, visible sense of the word. Seen from this viewpoint, the words pronounced and the actions performed by the church spring from a twofold commitment: on the part of God who is faithful to his covenant, and on the part of man who is called to respond in faith. Thus the sacrament is the presence of the invisible gift within the visible. This is expressed in two definitions of sacrament found in St. Augustine's writings: "One thing is seen in them, but something else is understood";[3] the sacrament is "a visible form of invisible grace."[4] Calvin would later make use of the second definition.[5]

13. The high Middle Ages extended the use of the term *sacramentum* to a great many Christian realities and rites celebrated by the church.[6] This resulted in some confusion. The list of seven sacraments drawn up in the twelfth century represents an act of discrimination intended to limit the term to the essential acts constitutive of the church.

---

3. Augustine, *Sermon* 272 (PL 38, col. 1247).

4. Cf. Augustine, *Letter* 105, chap. 111, 12 (PL 33, col. 401).

5. Calvin, *Institutes of the Christian Religion,* IV, XIV, 1.

6. The events of salvation history and the mysteries of the faith were thus called sacraments in that they are "given" to us; so also were a number of liturgical rites (for example, the consecration of virgins).

14. The great Latin theology of the thirteenth century developed sacramental doctrine within the general category of sign. It taught that the sacraments are efficacious signs inasmuch as they are acts of Christ performed by the power of grace and celebrated by the church in obedience to the Word of the Lord. The efficacy of the sacraments belongs to God alone who creates, controls, reveals, and communicates his gifts and his presence, which requires faith and a sincere disposition to be perceived.

15. However, during the Middle Ages the theology and practice of the West, which had inherited the sacramental problematic worked out at the time of the Donatist crisis,[7] laid emphasis on the sacred rite, to the extent of leading people to think of the reality of the mystery as being entirely contained by and coterminous with the rite. This kind of weakening of sacramental doctrine and practice made the Reformers in the sixteenth century suspect that the sacraments were thought of in a quasi-magical way.

16. In their reaction against a sacramental practice they saw as a religion of quasi-magical words and gestures, the churches stemming from the Reformation laid a contrary emphasis on the spiritual reality, that is, on the indispensable intervention of the Holy Spirit. This basically sound reaction has often, especially in the nineteenth century, led to an underestimation of the close connection between sign and reality and to an impoverishment of the role of signs in the life of the church.

17. According to classical Reformed theology, the sacraments are given by God to confirm his Word, received in faith, and to certify the promises contained in his Word in a personal way for each believer as well as for the whole community.[8] "The Word is addressed to the unbeliever as well as to the believer; to the unbeliever to lead him to believe, to the believer to increase and deepen his faith. The sacrament speaks only to faith, which its function is to strengthen, enlighten, and renew in vitality, by setting on it the seal of the promise. It is always a Word of God, but a *Verbum Dei*

---

7. The Donatist controversy (named after Donatus, an African bishop who died about 355) divided the African church of the fourth and fifth centuries. It resulted in the church's declaration that the power of the sacraments did not depend on the holiness of the minister, but on the holiness of God active in the sacramental celebration.

8. "The sacraments are God's seals, the stamp on his coins and his household livery," wrote Jean Daillé (1594-1670), *Sermons sur le catéchisme des Églises Réformées* (Geneva, 1701), p. 646.

visibile. A Word of God, because while its substance is Christ who is now invisible, its matter consists of elements borrowed from the visible world: water in baptism; bread and wine in the eucharist."[9]

18. For its part, the Council of Trent intended to stress that the sacraments of the new Law confer the grace they signify on those who put no obstacle in the way,[10] that is, those who receive them with dispositions of faith ("the foundation and source of all justification"),[11] hope, and love. It therefore made use of the then controversial expression "by virtue of the action performed" *(ex opere operato)*, because the efficacy of the sacraments arises from the fact that they are acts of Christ celebrated by the church, not because they might be thought of as conferring grace independently of the necessary dispositions.

(b) Today

19. For many people today the term "sacrament" still carries an equivocal charge of "sacredness," which produces ambivalent reactions. A person may think he or she ought to keep at a reverent distance from the "holy thing," or may condemn it as conveying the idea of a materialistic efficacity.

20. When contemporary theological reflection analyzes the concept of sacrament it generally draws on the terms "rite" and "sign." It may well add "symbol" and stress the communitarian character of the sacrament.

21. The sacrament is celebrated in a liturgical action. This means it can be considered as a *rite,* as long as the word is taken in the specifically Christian sense.[12] The characteristic mark of a Christian rite is that it is the cultic expression of the salvation event accomplished in Jesus Christ. By the words spoken and the actions performed in it, it proclaims and realizes

9. A. Lecerf, *Études Calvinistes* (Neuchâtel and Paris: Delachaux et Niestlé, 1949), p. 34.
10. Council of Trent, Session VII, canon 6 on the sacraments in general (Denzinger-Schönmetzer 849/1606).
11. Council of Trent, Session VI, *Decree on justification*, chap. 8 (Denzinger-Schönmetzer 801/1532).
12. In the following section we shall deal with the interconfessional dispute and contemporary arguments about rite.

the words and actions that Jesus commanded us to carry out as a memorial of him.

But the liturgical action is also the expression of the faith of God's people in a particular historical setting with its own culture and mentality. The liturgy in which the sacramental rites as such belong, often in a very schematized form, therefore arises from a dynamic encounter of a given culture at a given moment with the church of always and everywhere as it celebrates its Lord in the Holy Spirit.

22. The sacramental *sign* expresses both a distance and an effective link between the visible form and the invisible, hoped-for reality. Beginning with what is visible, the sacrament gives access to a mystery that transcends everything available to the senses, a mystery that gives it its entire significance. Conversely, it is the privileged manifestation of this invisible reality and allows the resurrection-world to break through into our world.

23. The sacrament is also related to the category of *symbol*. We are not using this word in the attenuated sense given it by liberal theology or by the current Catholic thinking that merely sets it over against "reality."[13] On the contrary, we are taking note of the rediscovery of the symbolic order in our contemporary culture, for which "symbol" is pregnant with a rich and complex meaning and enables people to touch reality in an order deeper than rational thought, science, and technology.

"Symbol" is more expressive than "sign" and belongs to the meaning-spectrum of the primitive term "mystery." The characteristic mark of God's interventions in the covenant he initiates with his people is to bring them to experience his transcendent presence and saving activity in the visible events of our world. The existence of symbol is a consequence of the bridge that has been laid between the visible face of creation and God's plan worked out in the covenant.

A symbol is actually more self-concealing than self-explanatory. It belongs to a specialized vocabulary and can be interpreted in many different ways. This is why we shall generally speak of *sign*, though we always keep the symbolic dimension in mind.

24. The sacrament is an interpersonal and *communitarian* reality. It relates people one to another and brings them to communicate with one another

---

13. "Symbolic" in this sense means something with no solidity.

as they communicate in what God does for them and enter into the covenant he offers them. A sacrament cannot be experienced alone: it creates solidarity; it restores and unites. The Christ-event it celebrates becomes an event for the community.

25. To conclude this survey of ancient and modern terminology we shall sum up the best insights of standard teaching in the following definition:

The sacraments are the actions by which the God of Jesus Christ commits and pledges his Word and promises within the new covenant he has contracted on his people's behalf by the Easter event of his Son. Through the sacraments his people once again touch this mysterious reality in which the same God who once intervened in human history now comes to them, veiled by signs yet accessible through their transparency, to assure them of his presence and to live with and in them as their ally. The sacraments are celebrated in the ecclesial community, the partner who obeys the Savior's Word in faith, as effective encounters with God who gives himself to us by the presence of his Son and in the power of his Spirit.[14]

14. Because of the long way it has traveled in Christian faith, the term "sacrament" is equally susceptible of an analogical sense, broader than the framework of celebration. Since the sacrament is the presence and gift of the invisible in the visible, it is possible to call the very person of Jesus Christ, Word of God made visible in the flesh, "sacrament of God." There is an ancient line of tradition based on this thinking which is taken up in Luther's formula: "Holy Scripture knows only one sacrament — Christ the Lord himself" (*Disputatio de fide infusa et acquisita,* of 1520, 18; Weimar edition 6, p. 86).

To speak of Christ in these terms is a means not so much of shedding light on his own mystery as of increasing our understanding of the sacramental economy: it points up an incarnational logic at work in the Christian reality and an analogy of structures between the different aspects of salvation history. By definition, all sacramentality in the church must stem from Jesus Christ himself. Christ's action in giving the sacraments to his church is related to the Father's action in giving and sending his Son, since Christ is the sacrament of the Father.

The same discerning of incarnational logic has led contemporary theological reflection to speak about the church-as-sacrament. The church is a sacrament in an analogical sense insofar as it is the body of Christ extended through human history and the sign raised up amid the nations (Isa. 5:26); insofar as it is penetrated by the divine energies of the Risen Lord and called to let his face become visible through the lives of its members; insofar as it is the place where the sacraments are celebrated, and so a liturgical, baptismal, and eucharistic community.

However, since this terminology is not shared by all our churches and belongs to the domain of theological reflection, we shall not use it here, using by preference the expression: "the church, a living sign."

(2) An Ecumenical Difficulty: How Many Sacraments?

26. This brief historical survey of sacramental terminology enables us to put the remaining dispute about the number of sacraments in its proper context.

27. History teaches us that the number of sacraments has been reckoned differently over the centuries: the church of the Fathers did not count seven sacraments because it had not yet gathered under a single heading all the actions belonging to its praxis, which it derived fundamentally from Christ; the church of the high Middle Ages counted more than seven because it was ready to call sacraments realities or rites that were based purely on the church. Correlatively, history shows that the reckoning of the number of sacraments is tied up with the precise meaning given to this term.

28. Since the twelfth century, Orthodox and Catholic traditions have kept to seven sacraments, each of which, in its own way, brings us into contact with the mystery of Christ's death and resurrection: baptism, confirmation (or chrismation), eucharist, penance (or reconciliation, according to contemporary Catholic usage), the anointing of the sick, order or ordination, and marriage. Since the sixteenth century the churches stemming from the Reformation have generally kept only two sacraments in the strict sense, baptism and eucharist, because these are more clearly attested in the New Testament and because they are meant for all the faithful.[15]

29. On the Catholic side, contemporary theological reflection brings out increasingly clearly the differences between the rites that make up the seven sacraments. There seems to be an analogical use of the term "sacrament" in the case of several of these rites. Moreover, faithful to a conviction that has always seen the eucharist as the peak of the sacramental structure, this reflection underlines the fact that baptism and eucharist are the major and primordial sacraments around which the others seem to be organized. So it is legitimate to speak of a "hierarchy of sacraments" just as Vatican II spoke of a "hierarchy of truths."[16]

---

15. For its part, Anglican tradition affirms the preeminence of baptism and eucharist, but recognizes the sacramental nature of the other five rites.

16. Second Vatican Council, Decree on Ecumenism *(Unitatis Redintegratio),* no. 11.

30. On the Protestant side, churches born of the Reformation consider the following as liturgical acts which they practice without hesitation: confirmation, marriage, and ordination, and for some of them also penance and the anointing of the sick.[17] The general renewal of liturgical and sacramental life in these churches invites us to reflect again about several nuances in the Reformers' thinking and to continue ecumenical dialogue on these celebrations.

This is how Calvin spoke about ordination: "As for the laying on of hands which is done to introduce the true priests and ministers of the church into their state, I am not in the least opposed to anyone holding this to be a sacrament. In the first place, it is a ceremony taken from Scripture; and then it is not empty, as St Paul says, but a sign of God's spiritual grace (1 Tim 4:14). The reason why I have not included it with the other two is because it is neither ordinary nor common among the faithful, but relates to a specific office."[18]

The primitive Lutheran tradition recognized the sacramental character of absolution. Private absolution was transformed in the worship of Reformed churches into the communitarian "declaration of pardon."[19]

The basic problem raised by confirmation is the question of its link with baptism.

Marriage is at present the subject of thriving ecumenical dialogue.[20] The use of the term "sacrament" continues to cause difficulty but there is agreement in affirming a "relationship of grace between the mystery of

---

17. The liturgy of pastoral ordination currently in force in the French Reformed churches requires the pastor to keep secret confessions made to him. The ministry of absolution (declaration of pardon) forms an integral part of his pastoral charge.

A liturgy of the anointing of the sick was published in 1967 for the Reformed Christians of French-speaking Switzerland. The prayer union of Charmes in France has been involved in this celebration.

18. Calvin, *Institutes*, IV, XIX, 28. See also Melanchthon, *Apology for the Confession of Augsburg*, art. XIII, 11-13.

19. Cf. Calvin: "We see that ministers are ordained of God as witnesses and, as it were, as pledges to assure consciences that their sins have been remitted, so aptly it is said that they remit sins and unbind souls" (Matt. 16:19; 18:18; John 20:23), *Institutes*, III, IV, 12.

20. Cf. the "Doctrinal Agreement on Marriage" of the Roman Catholic/Protestant Joint Commission in France (*Doc. Cath.* no. 1623 [1973]: 24); *Theology of Marriage and the Problems of Mixed Marriage*, a dialogue between the Lutheran World Federation, the World Alliance of Reformed Churches, and the Secretariat for Promoting Christian Unity of the Roman Catholic Church, 1971-77 (LWF and WARC: 150, Route de Ferney, 1211, Geneva 20, Switzerland; SPCU, Vatican City; *Doc. Cath.* no. 1736 [1978]: 157-72; *One in Christ* [1978]: 162-96).

Christ and the conjugal state."[21] Further, it is recognized that "speaking in this way of the initiative of the promise in regard to the spouses and the recreative experience which the spouses are called to have of its power over them, is to speak of the sacramental character of marriage considered in light of the covenant. It also means that marriage is a sign of the covenant."[22]

31. These attempts to reach a basic agreement ought to stimulate the churches to stop fighting about words and to infuse new spiritual and theological life into practices that are already largely common to them all. Two requirements will have to be met in the ecumenical quest: the deepening out of the specific way in which each of these ecclesial acts is linked with Christ's paschal mystery; the proper appreciation of the invocation of the Spirit *(epiclesis)* as a common and necessary element of all these rites.[23]

32. To the extent that it may be possible, though difficult, to eliminate the term "sacrament," we propose a terminology that would associate unity and difference, for example, *sacraments* for baptism and eucharist, and *sacramental acts* for the other celebrations. This suggestion does not rule out the opportune use of a common term that would cover the traditional seven sacraments.[24]

---

21. *Theology of Marriage and the Problems of Mixed Marriage,* p. 18.

22. *Theology of Marriage and the Problems of Mixed Marriage,* p. 21.

23. The state of the baptized person is definitive and cannot be effaced, because God who is faithful never goes back on what he has done: the configuration of a new Christian to Christ and his incorporation into the church. The constant practice of the church, therefore, is to refuse any repetition of baptism, even when the baptized in one way or another puts an obstacle in the way of receiving grace and salvation. This extreme case — which forces us to distinguish an element other than the gift of grace in the sacrament — has led to the progressive clarification of the doctrine of *character,* considered as a mark of Christ, spiritual and indelible.

The doctrine of character has been extended by analogy to confirmation and ordination, neither of which can ever be repeated. It goes without saying that character must never be understood as a guarantee of salvation or as a human possession. It is achieved through the inalienable transcendence of God's gift.

24. In a rather similar way the Anglican/Roman Catholic International Commission (ARCIC) distinguishes between the primordial sacraments of baptism and eucharist "necessary to salvation" and the other "sacramental rites" (*Eucharistic Doctrine, Ministry and Ordination, Elucidations,* Salisbury 1979, no. 13; *Doc. Cath.* no. 1769 [1979]: 737f.; *One in Christ* [1979]: 238-48).

(3) Christian Existence and Human Existence, Rites and Sacraments

33. Our work needs more than a clarification of sacramental vocabulary and disputes. We also have to take note of the particular difficulties that our secularized culture has with regard to rites — new difficulties that are having an effect on confessional reservations about the sacraments.

34. Two data make an immediate impact: the extremely radical criticism of the way in which the sacraments are carried out by the churches is happening at a time when our contemporaries are rediscovering the value of signs and the part symbolic action plays in their personal and social lives. Both these two apparently contradictory aspects produce ambiguous attitudes towards an authentic understanding of sacraments in the Christian sense.

35. The sacramental rite is still nowadays the object of confessional dispute, at least at the level of personal opinion: taken as a whole, Catholicism is thought by many people to be characterized by the obligatory performance of rites necessary for salvation. For its part, Protestantism still seems to relegate these rites to a secondary position. These oversimplified interpretations produce mutual suspicion.

36. But the ritual side of the sacrament is often also perceived negatively: the rite is seen as programmed, repetitive, "religious," wielded by authority as an instrument of domination. As programmed, the sacraments seem to be shut away from personal spiritual freedom; as repetitive, they are out of harmony with our human rhythms; as "religious," they operate in a sacred world that must be appeased and preserved; the way in which they convey meaning is not always that of our own culture and sensitivity. Finally, they are worked out in advance by an apparently remote authority.

37. Other people see the sacraments as the local, concrete form taken by popular religion. They are no longer accepted as the celebration of the historical event in which God encountered his people through the action of his Son and the gift of his Spirit.

38. On the other hand, many of our contemporaries are rediscovering the meaning of celebration and festivity and the typical value of certain actions that come to express a "transcendence" mysteriously present in the great moments of human existence. Few of them would actually work out any theory about it, but this is what they do in their lives.

So, in considerable areas of society, we are involved in a rediscovery of symbolical actions springing from an anthropological, pedagogical, psycho-sociological, etc., approach. We are becoming aware again that human nature needs rites, in which the most important thing is the "experience" of actions that "mean something." This can arouse the desire to sacralize certain moments of life ("rites of passage," etc.).

This review of the present situation leads into a new sensitivity to sacramental celebration whose subjective value (the experience) is in practice understood better than their objective value (Christ's action and the gift of the Spirit).

39. From another angle, the phenomenon of secularization that conditions so much of contemporary life springs in fact from a belief in the objectivity of science and the efficacity of technology. The sense of the holy may take a new hold here. Now, every culture and civilized society lives by a twofold network that links it to a world both material and spiritual. While the first arises out of necessity and guarantees security, the second appeals to freedom and calls for personal commitment.

40. Even where Christian faith no longer determines how society thinks and behaves, the modern world may still not claim to have been delivered from magico-religious attachments to the holy. So true it is that man does not live by bread alone, but also needs the word that conveys meaning and the symbolic action that gives consistency to human existence.

41. This is the perspective from which we must speak about what is specific to the Christian sacrament.

Christian faith transforms the sense of the holy. It takes it into the order of the covenant, of the creation and incarnation, of the revelation and redemption, God's work realized in our history in the unity of the Father, Son, and Holy Spirit. When a sacrament is celebrated God is perceived in his active holiness, and men and women open up to his intervention.

42. A sacrament holds together two extremes: fullness and apparent emptiness, glory and deprivation. In this paradoxical coming together of opposites it is mutual gift, exchange and sharing, the human recognition of God, and the realization of the love of God as "all in all" (1 Cor. 15:28).

43. A sacrament is therefore something dynamic and liberating. If it looks programmed, that is only because God's plan calls us to make a memorial

of his Son's mysteries; its continual re-celebration is not so much a repetition as a renewal; it turns people not to the past but to Christ's future. It makes the churches responsible for not reducing it to a "religious" ceremony, but for allowing the Spirit to make of it an act of freedom.

PART TWO

The Witness of Scripture: Covenant, Spirit, and Sacraments

44. The Christian sacraments bring into play God's covenant with mankind through the mediation of Jesus Christ in the power of the Holy Spirit. They do so through the network of human relationships that make up the church.

45. In both the Old and the New Testaments God's covenant with his people has three poles that correspond to three temporal, historical points: a foundational event in the past; an actualization of this event in an ever-moving present; and an active orientation towards the future conceived of as the fullness and definitive consummation of the foundational event.

46. This is the datum that enables us to understand the meaning and nature of the actions that Christian tradition calls sacraments (cf. 25). For revelation proclaims the intervention of God's Spirit precisely in the history of the covenant.

(1) The Old Testament

(a) Covenant and Law

47. The originality of the first of God's covenants with his people stems from the following points:

> (a) its foundational event: God the Savior freed his people from the land of Egypt and made a covenant with them at Sinai, thus constituting them as a chosen people;

> (b) the ways in which it was actualized: initiating newly personal relations between God and this people by the mediation of a holy, just, and good Law in the midst of a world awaiting its transformation;

72

(c) seen in its relation to the future, where the fulfillment of the original promise is to culminate in the communion between the author and the beneficiaries of the covenant in a kingdom where this promise will be fully realized: "You shall be my people and I will be your God" (cf. Exod. 6:7; Lev. 26:1; Jer. 11:4; 31:33; quoted in Heb. 8:10; Ezek. 36:28; 37:27).

48. God chose the people of Israel and made a covenant with them. This free choice on God's part marks a series of foundational actions, from the promise made to Abraham until the event of the Passover and Exodus, when God revealed himself as creator and redeemer by accomplishing in our history the deliverance of a people in order to save all humankind (cf. Isa. 2:1-5; 56:1-8).

49. In order that they might live out the freedom acquired at such cost by the grace of the saving event, the people received a Law from God. The covenant drew on the Law to lay down the basic lines of its historical development by prescribing the conditions of the people's filial relations with God and fraternal relations among themselves. The Decalogue links the recalling of the deliverance from Egypt to the commandments, which were intended to combat the temptation to go back under the yoke of slavery (Exod. 20:1-17). The Law is therefore part of grace and promise.

50. The Law instituted a way of life and of celebrations that were meant to maintain the people in their loyalty and to enable them to repent and be converted every time they broke the covenant. We can therefore translate the demands of the promise and the means of grace into terms of word and sacrament. They are the way by which God reaches his people's hearts.

51. In a similar way circumcision, originating with Abraham, is for the priestly tradition a sign of the covenant, a physical sign that every son of Israel was obliged to bear in his flesh from the eighth day onwards "as a covenant in perpetuity" (cf. Gen. 17:10-13). No uncircumcised person was allowed to share in the Passover celebration in which Israel was renewed as a people chosen and saved by its God. But physical circumcision is also an appeal for circumcision of the heart, that is, for love of God preferred even to fraternal charity (cf. Deut. 10:12-22). Israel could receive this spiritual circumcision only by a gift of God (cf. Deut. 30:6).

52. So the Law included the institution of the Passover meal as a true memorial of the foundational event of the deliverance from Egypt. As she fulfilled the command given her to eat in all haste a yearling lamb, Israel celebrated a Passover in honor of her God (cf. Exod. 12:11-12); in the concreteness of her history, she experienced a saving encounter with the ever-faithful God who protected her and kept her on the path of his covenant. She likewise experienced the anticipation of a future in which deliverance would reach a plenitude never more to be reversed and would reach every person and all mankind.

53. This is the condition of the people of the covenant: to live under the Law of freedom in the obedience of faith. But such a demand exceeds the capacity and the courage of people who are too weak to dare to take up the challenge of freedom in their lives. Breaches of the covenant provoked by the people's sin, faithlessness and unbelief with regard to the promise, even their return to the deceptive securities of idolatry, did not mean the defeat of this covenant, but urged its renewal and deepening, thanks to the faithfulness of God who is always at work in his people's history.

(b) The Covenant and the gift of the Spirit

54. However, it was not enough to have been given a Law. It was also necessary that those who owed their new life of freedom to the Law should be disposed to obey it with indefectible faith, according to the spirit and not just according to the letter. But sin and the drag of the flesh showed how impossible it was for human beings to accept the Law's demands in their lives — the essence of the Law being self-oblation to the God of the covenant. It was therefore necessary that this attitude of trust and irrevocable faithfulness should itself be a gracious gift of God, making freedom possible for its recipient.

55. Israel grew in her understanding that God's Spirit had been at work from the beginning, for God always pours out his Spirit without measure. But the hearts of unreconciled men and women could not yet receive him fully. This is why the Spirit manifested himself in an extraordinary, sporadic fashion to confirm the people's faith in God's control of history; he came upon people who spoke and acted in God's name. Through the many

diverse modes of his intervention, the Spirit appeared as the seal of the covenant.[25]

56. Gradually, these startling manifestations came to yield more space to the fruits of the Spirit than to ecstatic phenomena, to the requirements of spiritual and moral rectitude than to spectacular psychic and physical disturbances. Interiority took precedence over the rapture of the senses, not because of any evolution on the side of the divine, but because of the educational process that was helping the people to develop. The presence of the Spirit was increasingly understood as a continual providence of God among men, and the very condition of the covenant's endurance.[26]

25. Thus throughout the history of the people of Israel, the Spirit "seizes" on men and women, old men and children, great and minor officials, political leaders and prophets of the Lord, in order to call or recall the people to faithfulness to the call of their God. He intervenes directly to "come on" a man (Judg. 6:34); to "penetrate" him (Judg. 14:6); to "be upon" him (Judg. 3:10; 2 Chron. 15:1); to "come upon" him (Num. 24:23); to "come down" on him (1 Sam. 10:6, 10; 11:6); and to "seize on" him (1 Sam. 19:20, 23; 2 Chron. 24:20); or again, as in the case of the prophet Ezekiel, to "fall" on him (Ezek. 11:5). [*Translator's note:* The English version of the Jerusalem Bible does not preserve the distinctions of the French original.] He bestows on the recipient a prophetic, or rather, an ecstatic power. The one seized by the Spirit leaves the normal order of things: he is changed into another person qualified for an extraordinary role: king, prophet, seer.

The Spirit intervenes also by conferring on a man a power corresponding to a particular function, as in the case of Moses and the elders of Israel (Num. 11:25). He legitimates those who hold office.

In some cases the Spirit intervenes in the handing on of a charge: Moses, for example, lays his hands on Joshua who is then presented as "a man in whom the Spirit dwells" (Num. 27:18; Deut. 34:9). There is likewise a clear charismatic kind of transmission of Elijah's spirit to Elisha. After Elijah's assumption, Elisha picks up his cloak and those who see it say: "The spirit of Elijah has come to Elisha" (2 Kings 2:15). The scene suggests both a permanence and a succession in the role of prophet. In David's case the gift of the Spirit is linked with the anointing with oil which he received from Samuel's hand and which made him a king (1 Sam. 16:13).

26. This is how the messianic oracles of Isaiah present the awaited king, as one upon whom "the spirit of the Lord rests" (11:2). Again, "the spirit of the Lord has been given to me, for the Lord has anointed me" (61:1). The act of anointing appeared to be so closely linked to the gift of the Spirit that the term "anointing" came to designate the gift independently of any application of oil.

Isaiah also proclaims the gift of the Spirit to the whole people (32:15). Ezekiel (36:26, 27; 37:14) and Joel (3:1-5) proclaim in an eschatological context the sending of the Spirit on all flesh. Using similar language Jeremiah had already proclaimed the concluding of a new covenant whose law would be inscribed in the person's inmost being and written on everyone's heart (Jer. 31:33).

Wisdom ends by assuming the features of the Spirit, the divine universal principle ani-

57. God's Spirit is always linked to the Word. His inspiration is in harmony with the divine plan of revelation and redemption. Leaders and prophets received the Spirit in order to serve this Word for the benefit of the people and of all the nations. Even if this is not explicitly said, the effects of the creative and liberating Word of God in history and among his chosen people can be understood as gifts and fruits of the Spirit. Thus from the time of the first covenant the whole Law is a law of the Spirit, a title never to be removed from it despite the inability of sinful mortals to live by it.

(2) The New Testament

(a) Jesus Christ, Mediator of the New Covenant

58. With regard to the old covenant, the new covenant is in a situation of both continuity and discontinuity. On the one hand, the new deliberately prolongs and fulfills the old by taking on its significance; on the other hand, it brings with it a total newness in the person of Jesus Christ, the one mediator between God and man, on whom rests the full measure of God's Spirit and who at the conclusion of his reconciling Passover sent the promised Spirit definitively and irreversibly.

So there are a number of evident analogies between these covenants that provide the basic lines for the historical existence of both and for the growth of a people in its relations with God.

59. The foundational event of the new covenant is the Passover of Jesus, accomplished once and for all by the one who was true man and true God. In Jesus Christ, the new Adam who responded perfectly as a son and loved his brothers to the very end, God succeeded in giving himself to us, delivered us from slavery to sin, and made of us a redeemed people.

60. Nonetheless the Law was not henceforward rendered void, since it had at last been wholly received as the Law of freedom and love; thanks to the gift of the Holy Spirit, it became the new Law of the new covenant. The Spirit is at work at the heart of our personal freedom as a source of faith, hope, and love; he ensures the cohesion of the believing community.

---

mating and penetrating the whole universe, unifying and containing it (cf. Wis. 1:6-7 and 7:22-23). The people thus discover that Wisdom has always been close to them, ever near at hand.

61. To enable his people to draw life from the definitive gift of the new covenant and from the Law of the Spirit until the end of the ages, the Lord Jesus gave his disciples the twofold command to baptize (Matt. 28:19) and to celebrate the Supper of the new Passover (Luke 22:19). The community of the new covenant has always understood itself to be founded on these two acts in which it discerns, in two different and complementary modalities, the memorial of its founding event.

62. These are the Christian sacraments by which the Spirit introduces us into, and renews us in, the covenant with God. They lead us into an encounter — beyond his absence — with the Crucified and Risen Lord who is always with us. They enable us to live the filial and fraternal relationships that are brought into being by the Holy Spirit in the living memory of Christ Jesus.

63. By virtue of God's call and promise, the new covenant is directed towards a definite future: the kingdom of God whose fullness will come about in the world when the Lord returns. Along with the gift of the Spirit the disciples of Jesus received the mission to proclaim the kingdom and to open the world to its coming by fighting against every form of evil for the sake of just, fraternal, and liberating relations among all peoples.

64. The different traditions of the New Testament each express in their own way the basic conviction that the new covenant, sealed in the event of Jesus Christ, constitutes the definitive gift of the Spirit to mankind. It is the same Spirit who passes from the person of Jesus to the community gathered in his name and to which the pagans are summoned. It is the gift of the same Spirit which the itinerant community is invited to receive, celebrate, and live in the sacraments of baptism and eucharist.

(b) The Spirit in the life of Jesus[27]

65. The baptism of Jesus is a baptism of water and Spirit, constituting the type of Christian baptism. The opening of the heavens at the time of his

---

27. Our text follows the Lucan tradition for which the Spirit is already at work before the coming of Jesus (cf. the many references to the Spirit in the infancy narratives: Luke 1:15, 35, 41, 67; 2:25, 27). This gift prepares for the definitive, universal gift of Pentecost.

Note the difference from the Johannine tradition for which the Spirit is given only after

baptism means that the Spirit is to become a gift offered to every person to empower them to love. It was the moment when Jesus was invested as prophet by the voice of the Father (Luke 3:21-2).

66. And so Jesus carries out his entire mission "filled with the Spirit" (Luke 4:1). He is led into the desert by the Spirit; he returns to Galilee "with the power of the Spirit in him" (Luke 4:14); in the synagogue at Nazareth he proclaims that Isaiah's prophecy is fulfilled: "The Spirit of the Lord has been given to me, for he has anointed me" (Luke 4:18); later he exults under the action of the Holy Spirit (Luke 10:21). The permanent presence of the Spirit in Jesus already has an eschatological character.

67. Jesus was baptized in the Spirit, too, in view of his coming Passion. He thought of this as a baptism he was eager to receive (Luke 12:50).

68. For all who have faith in him and receive his signs and miracles as anticipated blessings of the coming kingdom, Jesus is in his own person the manifestation of the kingdom; it is through him that the kingdom arrives, with him and through him that the blessings of the kingdom are given; everything he does is rooted in the kingdom.

This is what theological language is saying when it states that Jesus is the sacrament of the encounter with God for all who have faith in him.

(c) The Spirit in the life of the church[28]

69. Three modes in which the Spirit intervenes can be discerned in the Acts of the Apostles: a direct intervention that happens for the good of the entire

---

the death and glorification of Jesus (cf. the promise of living water, John 7:37-39; the promise of the sending of the Spirit in the discourse after the Supper, 14:26; 15:26; 16:7, 13; the symbols of the "giving up" of the Spirit ("Breath") by Jesus on the Cross and of the spear-thrust that let blood and water flow out for the life of the church, 19:30, 34; the gift of the Spirit to the disciples on the eve of the resurrection, 20:22-23).

However, the miracles of Jesus have a sacramental coloring. Jesus indicates through them the gift he is to offer when he is glorified: the multiplication of the loaves (John 6) prefigures the eucharist; the healing of the man born blind (John 9) baptism, which was already described in the dialogue with Nicodemus in terms of being born of water and Spirit (John 3:5).

28. As in Luke's Gospel, the Spirit intervenes in the Acts of the Apostles in a decisive fashion on the occasion of great beginnings: at Pentecost (1:5; 2:4); at the new Pentecost of

community or for the good of the apostles' mission and authority; sometimes also for the good of particular charismatic persons (e.g., Agabus, 11:28 and 21:11); a direct intervention linked with the apostolic preaching (10:44-46 and 11:15); and an intervention working through the mediation of the act of baptism (2:38; 9:17-19) and of the laying on of hands (8:17; 19:6).

70. The different manifestations of the Spirit in Acts are the sign that the new world of the last days has arrived and is offered even to the pagans. The Holy Spirit is given to all who believe in Jesus Christ. The same Spirit who lived in Jesus continues to animate the church, and the apostolic authority is itself based on the action of this same Spirit.

71. The letters of Paul give the Spirit a central place. The divine adoption that defines the Christian is simultaneously a gift of the Spirit (Gal. 4:6; Rom. 8:15-16). To be a Christian means to have received the Spirit who makes us sons and daughters.

Having become sons through the Spirit they have received, Christians are henceforth free in regard to any law by which they were enslaved and to the flesh and its passions (cf. Gal. 5:13-25).

Receiving the Spirit means receiving his gifts which are bestowed for the good of all the believers, in particular love *(agape),* the basis of Christian freedom (1 Cor. 12-14; Rom. 5:5; Col. 1:8). And it is the Spirit who reveals to us the mysteries of God (1 Cor. 2:11-13; Eph. 3:5).

72. Paul compares baptism to passing through the Red Sea, and the eucharist to the spiritual food and drink given in the desert (1 Cor. 10:1-13 and 16-

---

the evangelization of the pagans (10:44-46; 11:15); in Paul's apostolate (13:24). This gift of the Spirit creates a new people. It institutes a community in the midst of whom the reality of this gift is experienced and verified. From now on remarkable signs will show forth the community's dynamic life and it will renew its link with the Spirit as it draws its life from baptism and the breaking of bread. This is how the Spirit arouses, accompanies, and directs apostolic activity (4:31; 8:26-29, 39; 9:31; 11:12; 13:19; 20:22-23).

The Acts of the Apostles does not on the whole conceive of the Holy Spirit being received without charismatic manifestations of power (speaking in tongues, prophecies, cf. 6:10; 10:44-47). Linked with the laying on of hands or with the hearing of the Word, the gift of the Spirit nonetheless does not make baptism of no avail: it presupposes it (8:16) or requires it (10:47). These powerful gifts of the Spirit underline the force of the gospel and its efficacy among those who accept it.

Luke also connects the gift of the Spirit with the celebration of baptism (2:38) or with the laying on of hands, which accompanies it (9:17-19) in a more interior sense.

17). Just as the passage through the sea, the food, and the drink were the first-fruits of the promised land, so baptism and eucharist are the first-fruits of the eschatological gifts.

These two sacraments are related to the Easter event of Jesus (both of them are a "passing over") and to the final coming of the kingdom (revealed by the gift of the Spirit who is identified with communion with Christ). They are entirely determined by these two poles.

These two sacraments are the conditions of access to the blessings of the kingdom; they are the means by which the movement of the death and resurrection of Christians with Christ begins with baptism (Rom. 6:3-11) and unfolds towards the Lord's Supper. Nonetheless, they are not magical acts whose results would be guaranteed no matter how people behaved (cf. 1 Cor. 10:7-11; 11:27-29). They are without meaning where there is no living communion with Christ. They call people to step out in faith.

73. In the pastoral letters the laying on of hands is linked with the charismatic gift of the pastoral charge (cf. 1 Tim. 4:14 and 2 Tim. 1:67).

74. The historical and eschatological event of Jesus Christ, dead and risen, is thus in its totality the central, fundamental "sacrament" of salvation, the sacrament in which God gives himself to the whole world in the eternal covenant from which all previous covenants and all authentic human steps towards God draw their definitive significance and whatever saving power they contain.

75. Thanks to the event of Jesus Christ the Spirit is given to all who believe without exception and without discrimination between races. In and through Jesus Christ the end time penetrates our human "today" and the Spirit of Jesus Christ penetrates the church and communicates to it all the gifts of salvation.

76. The Spirit is sovereignly free in his ways of manifesting himself, in his interventions and his gifts. However, he gives life to the church by means of institutional signs: the Spirit is received at baptism, and the life of the baptized believer is a life in the Spirit. The Spirit is also linked to the ministry, for he governs Christ's church: he is therefore given to those who are responsible for the apostolate. The final evidence of the New Testament connects the gift of the Spirit for this ministry with the act of the laying on of hands.

77. The gift of the Spirit to the church is the fruit of a trinitarian initiative: everything begins with the Father's creative power and plan of salvation; everything comes through the incarnation of the Son, the visible manifestation of God; everything is completed in the eschatological gift of the Spirit to believers. To put it the other way, the Spirit who renews their hearts gathers the believers together in Jesus Christ, as sons in the Son, and brings them to confess God as Father.

PART THREE
Doctrinal Outline

(1) The Church: People of the Covenant, Temple of the Spirit, Body of Christ

78. The people of God who at Pentecost became the temple of the Spirit and body of Christ are the sign and reality of God's gift to mankind, the sign and anticipated reality of the kingdom, the memorial and expectation of the Lord in thanksgiving, the baptismal and eucharistic community. This election and vocation are at the service of the world in which and for which the witnesses are being made holy.

79. It is in this sense that the church gathered by the Word and built up by the sacraments can be called the *living sign* of salvation for the world. For the church is not primarily a social organization but an institutional event, a real communion established between God and mankind. It is the place of the covenant where the sacraments are both given and received.

80. As the people rooted in the covenant, the original covenant of God who is faithful to his promises and the ever-new covenant of God who fulfills his promises through Christ and in the Spirit, the church is the one, holy, catholic,[29] and apostolic community that follows the Christ of the gospels in faith, hope, and love.

81. The church as a community is open and offered, turned towards the memory of the Lord's coming and towards the future when he will come

---

29. "Here we are deliberately using the traditional term 'catholic' which expresses both the universality of the whole church and the catholicity of each particular church" ("The Episcopal Ministry," no. 30).

again. It is universal through the freedom of the Spirit who governs it and leads it to the ends of the earth and the end of the ages in order to gather all things into Christ and to reconcile them with God the Father.

82. The church is the temple of the Spirit who fills and guides it. The Spirit of Pentecost is within it as the memorial of the creation, incarnation, passion, and resurrection. He is within it also as the expectation of salvation and of the glory of the kingdom. Where the Lord's Spirit is at work, there the church of Christ declares its presence. "Where the Spirit of the Lord is, there is freedom" (2 Cor. 3:17). And so he makes the church a *living sign* of the Lord for the world.

83. The church, the body of Christ, is constantly called to reproduce Christ's image (cf. Rom. 8:29) in order to become, thanks to the newness of the Spirit, the messianic community and living sign of God the Creator and Redeemer of the universe.

84. The church as sign of the covenant is the place where Christ the Head is joined to the believers who are the members. By receiving the divine life in the church, believers become children of God. This is what tradition means when it speaks of the church as mother.

85. To speak of the church as a living sign is to describe it as the place of both *presence* and *distance*. This tension will be resolved in the face-to-face communion of the kingdom that will come about when there is neither temple nor sign (cf. Rev. 21:22). In the church, on the other hand, there is a distance between the body and the head, that is, Christ, who is the judge of the body; there is a distance between the church and the gospel as its abiding norm, between the church and the kingdom as its consummation. Despite the real gift of the Spirit to the church, this distance remains.

86. The church is a living sign within a concrete reality that gives rise to its institutional and social character. Its sign-value will therefore be inevitably affected by all the burdens caused by sin. Instead of being dynamic the church has, at certain historical times and places, looked anemic, exhausted, and divided. This is why the Spirit who is himself "the forgiveness of sins" invites the church — through a process of death and resurrection — to a perpetual reform, a constant purification, and a future of reconciliation as it awaits its eschatological transfiguration.

87. The church is the living sign of Christ not simply because it celebrates the sacraments but also because it receives within it the fruits of the Spirit flowing from the sacraments. Christ "made her clean by washing her in water with a form of words . . . so that she would be holy and faultless" (Eph. 5:26-27). Scripture also speaks of "the new self that has been created in God's way, in the goodness and holiness of the truth" (Eph. 4:24), and of the "saints" and "the sanctified" (cf. 1 Cor. 1:2). For Jesus our High Priest "has achieved the eternal perfection of all whom he is sanctifying" (Heb. 10:14). The church's holiness is thus necessary for her witness to be recognizable as the sign of God.

88. The church does not live this in secret. It is a sign for the world. The sacraments, which are the heart of its life, prevent it from closing in on itself and urge it to go beyond its own limits.

89. Always and everywhere, the Spirit puts himself at the service of Christ's Lordship among people who do not profess the Christian faith. He did this before the incarnation and he does so in civilizations where Christ is practically unknown. Thanks to him, human longing can always stretch out, even unconsciously, for the kingdom of God. Under the action of the Holy Spirit the symbols that convey this longing can direct towards Christ and his coming reign people who have not yet been able to make an assent of faith in him.

This is why the church is called to recognize this one Spirit wherever he goes ahead of it in the world, as Peter did in the episode of the centurion Cornelius (Acts 10).

(2) The Gift of the Spirit in the Word and in the Sacraments[30]

90. The church is the charismatic community that receives God's gift through the ministry of Word and sacraments. This is the way in which Christ gathers and sanctifies the children of God, and in which the church builds itself up at the initiative of the One whose body it is, in the power of the Spirit. Word and sacraments conform it to the will of God so that it can exercise its basic ministry of proclaiming the gospel and of making it present in the world.

---

30. Cf. the theses of 1957, "La médiation du Christ et le ministère de l'Église," dealing with Word and sacraments. In *Pour la communion des Églises*, pp. 13-15.

(a) The necessary link between the Word and the sacraments

91. The link between the Word of God as it is heard and the Word of God as it is seen must never be broken in the life of the church, for sacrament is implicit in Word, and Word in sacrament. This is why, "from the table of both the Word of God and of the body of Christ, the church unceasingly receives and offers to the faithful the bread of life, especially in the sacred liturgy."[31]

92. The fact that Word and sacraments imply each other forbids us either to set one against the other or to assert the primacy of either over the other.

93. The indissoluble link between Word and sacrament is based on the mystery of the Word made flesh, for Christ is himself both Word and sacrament. The specific character of each stems from the complementarity of speaking and acting in human living. They correspond concretely to two different states of the church's constitution and mission. In the New Testament the ministry of Jesus Christ and the apostles attests that the proclaimed Word is the source of the calling and gathering of the people of God; the preaching of the Word engenders faith (cf. Rom. 10:17); the gospel preached to all the nations results in the entry of the pagans into the covenant of grace. The sacrament accompanies and fulfills the Word by carrying out in action the gift of God proclaimed by the Word (cf. Acts 8:34-38; 10).

94. The Spirit is present and given in the proclaiming, hearing, and sharing of the Word of God. The proclaiming belongs to the public reading of Scripture and to preaching based on Scripture. The ministry of the Word must be exercised and received in invoking the Spirit. This is why a prayer of *epiclesis* has its liturgical place before reading and preaching.

95. The Word of God arouses the response of faith. This faith testifies, by the activity and fraternal relations of Christians, to the Good News of reconciliation, freedom, justice, and love according to God, the first-fruits of the kingdom.

---

31. Second Vatican Council, Dogmatic Constitution on Divine Revelation *(Dei Verbum)*, no. 21.

96. Under the impulsion of the Spirit of Pentecost, the ministry of the Word communicates and interprets the gospel message of salvation to the ends of the earth and the end of time, and assimilates it to historically diverse cultural conditions.

(b) The gift of the Spirit in the sacraments

97. The Spirit is present and given in the ministry of the sacraments, which carry out what the Word proclaims. A sacrament is not solely a figurative rite; it is primarily the celebration of the Christ-event among a number of people who come together to open up their lives to his paschal presence. This common celebration always consists of symbolical words and actions, in harmony with the basic structure of speaking and acting in human life, and is in profound accord with the church's faith in the Word made flesh.

98. As acts of Christ whom the Father has sent into the world with the power of the Spirit, the sacraments bring people into the fellowship of the Father, Son, and Spirit from whom they receive their efficacity.

By expressing and actualizing the *Father's plan* to reconcile everything in the Son "to make us praise the glory of his grace" (Eph. 1:6), they are vehicles of the creative power of the Word of God.

By commemorating the *mystery of Christ,* his incarnation, his passion and death, his resurrection and glorification, and his coming at the end of time, they are invested with the regenerative power of the Word made flesh.

By signifying the *grace of the Spirit,* they bear within them the fruitfulness of the Spirit himself.

This is why sacramental acts are performed in the name of the Father and of the Son and of the Holy Spirit. In addition, the structure of every developed sacramental celebration usually consists of thanksgiving to the Father, the memorial of the Son's actions, and the invocation of the Spirit.

99. The sacrament draws its reality from the fact that the saving work of Jesus Christ is active in it as well as being expressed by it. Thanks to the Spirit, the church's sacramental action makes real what it signifies. The words of which it consists do not just report past events or promises; in the prayer and faith of the church, they create a new situation. For, while the sacraments are administered by human beings, their principle is the Holy Spirit.

100. Thus the reality of a sacrament does not come from the faith of the person who receives it or administers it, but it is received in faith for the sanctification of believers. This is why a response of faith is necessary for the power of the sacrament to be discerned and for it to be fully understood and its fruitfulness received. It is the particular responsibility of catechesis and sacramental liturgy to express and develop this "faith that makes its power felt through love" (Gal. 5:6).

101. The Word which is active in the sacrament is the commandment given by Christ and carried out by the church's ministry. Its power transcends our lack of faith. This is why, as St. Augustine says,[32] it is capable of purifying even the child who cannot yet believe in its heart and confess with its mouth. However, the church may not confer the sacrament in this limit-situation if the people presenting a child for baptism lack faith.

102. The Holy Spirit keeps the sacrament from falling into the error and bondage of becoming a relation of possession and power, domination and dependence, which is alien to its nature. Conversely, the sacrament prevents our understanding of the Holy Spirit from yielding to the illusion of spiritualism or to the vanity of a moralism incapable of achieving what God alone can give.

(3) The Role of the Community and Ministerial Authority in Celebrating the Sacraments

103. The church is a living sign of the Holy Spirit for the world; its community is ministerial and its ministry is communitarian. Thus the celebration of the sacraments by the church relates these three realities to one another: the community of the people of God, the ordained ministers, and the world. This relation implies both a distinction and a mutual solidarity. For while the ministers stand over against the people, they remain members of it; and while the people of God are distinct from the world, they remain in the world.

---

32. Augustine, *Treatises on Saint John* 80, 3 (PL 35, col. 1840).

(a) The role of the community

104. Christ does not gather or save people against their will. Christians receive the Word and the sacraments with faith and let themselves be reconciled with God (cf. 2 Cor. 5:20) as they faithfully live out the terms of their ecclesial communion. The church is a sacramental community because it receives God's gifts in its prayer and celebrations, with the mission of communicating them and witnessing to them before the world.

105. While the community is the beneficiary of Christ's acts when it celebrates the sacraments, it also plays an active part. The whole membership of the community is the first agent of the celebration. It is the community that celebrates baptism and the eucharist. The gathered community thus exercises an overall ministry in celebrating the sacraments, as the Spirit works through the prayers and obedience to the faith of all the baptized.

(b) The authority of the ordained ministers

106. The church receives Christ's acts performed in the power of the Spirit and declares its recognition of its Lord in the reciprocal dependence of the community and its ordained ministers (cf. "Towards a Reconciliation of Ministries," no. 22).

107. Ordained ministries act in the sacraments as ministers both of Christ and of the church. This cannot be dissociated.

> (a) The act they carry out in the faith of the church and in accordance with its intention is not their own personal act but an act of Christ, who alone possesses the authority and power that are at work in the sacramental celebration. They show that the new life into which the sacrament engenders men and women has its source in the free initiative of God and that it is not we who have first loved God, but God who has first loved us (cf. 1 John 4:10 and 19).[33]

33. "When we say it is Christ who baptizes," wrote St. Augustine, "we are by no means trying to say that he does so in a visible way . . . but by a secret grace, by the hidden power of the Holy Spirit. . . . He has never stopped baptizing, no, he still baptizes, not by a physical act but by the invisible operation of his majesty. When we say: it is he who baptizes, we are not saying: it is he who takes the believers bodily in his hands and plunges them in the water of

(b) The thanksgiving and invocation *(epiclesis)* which the ministers pronounce are the prayer of the whole church, and this prayer is answered because of Christ's promise.

108. The ordained ministers of the church are thus the visible "artisans" of the sacraments in faith and obedience to Christ's commandment. They are instituted and given to the church for this service, that is, they receive the faculty, capacity (cf. 2 Cor. 3:5), mission, and charge and thus also the authority that corresponds to their ministerial responsibility to carry out the sign of Christ's acts in the faith of the church.[34]

109. The church has always held that the sacraments do not depend on the personal holiness of the ministers. If the sign is truly carried out according to the church's intention by an unworthy minister, the transcendence of Christ's action remains.[35]

110. Nonetheless, the practice of the church has to take account of the consequences of human sin. Sacraments are acts of the supremely Holy One; and they are ordered to the sanctification of Christians. Thus it is necessary that the ministers who celebrate them should do all they can to give an example of holiness in their lives.

---

baptism, but that he invisibly purifies not only the baptized but the entire church. . . . It is Christ who sanctifies, Christ himself who washes and purifies by the bath of water in the word, since his ministers are seen acting bodily" (*Against the Letters of Petilian*, 3, 49, 59 [PL 43, col. 379]).

34. "It is one thing to baptize by the ministry, another thing to baptize by power." Augustine, *Fifth Sermon on Saint John*, 6 (BA 71, p. 302); "Even given by Judas, baptism was Christ's baptism. . . . Christ's baptism is through power; the disciple's baptism through ministry" (18 [BA 71, p. 334]).

"And so only his true and legitimate officers have the right of administering them and if anyone takes it on himself without having received this ministry and commission from the Lord, he plainly incurs the guilt of sacrilege and what he does is worthless, something nonexistent, as it were, performed without any right or authority." Jean Daillé, *Sermons sur le catéchisme des Églises Réformées* (Geneva, 1707), p. 646.

35. "Grace always comes from God. Sacraments always come from God. The only human factor is the minister. If he is a good man he cleaves to God and cooperates with him. If he is unworthy, God uses him to create the visible form of the sacrament, and himself gives the invisible grace." Augustine, *Letter* 105, 3, 12 (PL 33, col. 401).

"Truth and the catholic church say that it is improper to place one's hope in men instead of in the One who justifies the unrighteous, not simply when the minister of baptism is a bad man, but even when he is saintly and good." Augustine, *Against the Letters of Petilian*, 3, 49, 59 (PL 43, col. 379).

(c) *The sacraments and the world*

111. The sacramental and liturgical celebration unfolds in the midst of the world. While it invites the world to break with sin by joining itself to the church, it nevertheless borrows from the world certain cultural elements that it transfigures. The intercessions of the Lord's memorial mention the names of members of the human society. The liturgical assembly of the community is turned to the world from whose midst the Lord calls them and to which he sends them out again.

112. The Holy Spirit poured out into the hearts of the faithful transforms the people who are called into people who are sent. He converts men and women to the Lord so that they may serve his plan of creation and salvation. Carried out corporally in the mystery of Christ, the sacrament will achieve its end in the reconciled, pacified, and glorified universe.

(4) The Spirit and the Church in the Liturgy of the Sacraments

(a) *The Spirit and the sacraments: the epiclesis*

113. Ancient and modern liturgies practice in different ways the invocation of the Spirit *(epiclesis)* which every sacramental celebration includes.

114. In the case of baptism, the Spirit is invoked on the candidate, and often on the water as well, in order to show that there is a single baptism in water and the Spirit. Here by way of an example is how the ancient Syrian liturgy (fifth-sixth century) invokes the gift of the Spirit on the catechumen who is to be baptized: "You who sent the Holy Spirit in the form of a dove upon your only Son, God and Word, who has instituted upon earth the economy of baptism; you who sanctified the waters of the Jordan: be pleased, Lord, to send down now your Holy Spirit upon your servant here present who is to be baptized. Perfect him and make him a fellow of your Son by purifying him in this divine and redeeming bath."[36]

115. The *epiclesis* in the eucharistic prayer was a common property of the undivided church, and it is today being rediscovered by the churches of the

36. Cf. E. Pataq-Siman, *L'Expérience de l'Esprit par l'Église* (Paris: Beauchesne, 1971), pp. 84-85.

West. It is found in the great majority of liturgies, ancient and modern —
Orthodox, Catholic, Anglican, Lutheran, and Reformed.

116. St. John Chrysostom clearly points out the significance of this *epiclesis:*
"The priest extends his hand to the gifts only after he has invoked the grace
of God . . . ; it is not the priest who performs whatever it is that is happening . . . it is the grace of the Spirit who carries out this mystical sacrifice, by
coming upon it and covering it with his wings."[37]

117. According to the traditions, the eucharistic *epiclesis* is found either before Christ's words of institution, to show that the Spirit's action actualizes
and carries out the Son's words to the glory of the Father; or after the
anamnesis (memorial) of the mysteries of salvation, to show the gift of the
Spirit who perfects the work of the Father and the Son; or sometimes before the institution and after the anamnesis, to show the role of the Spirit
who constitutes Christ's eucharistic and ecclesial body.

118. This invocation of the Holy Spirit also occurs in the celebration of the
"sacramental acts," which the churches of the Catholic and Orthodox tradition also hold to be sacraments. Western Catholic tradition practices an
epiclesis in the second sacrament of initiation, confirmation. Eastern tradition practices the *epiclesis* in the blessing of marriage. Both practice it in
the liturgies of ordination to the ministry. Some other churches that do
not recognize these ecclesial acts as sacraments practice the *epiclesis* when
they celebrate them.

119. When the ecclesial community, presided over by its ministers, celebrates baptism and the eucharist, it publicly attests by its double reference
to Christ and to the Spirit the significance of what it is carrying out to the
glory of the Father. Its obedience to Christ's command and its invocation
of the Spirit show that the efficacy of the liturgy has nothing magical
about it. It celebrates in faith the sacraments of faith. These constitute its
official prayer: the church never acts in its own name, but is confident of
being heard every time it does what Christ gave it to do and asks the Spirit
to grant its words the same efficacy he granted the words of Jesus.

---

37. John Chrysostom, *On Pentecost,* Homily 1, 4 (PG 50, cols. 458-59).

(b) The Spirit and the ordained ministry

120. The ministry of Word and sacraments, which has the purpose of communicating the Spirit, is itself given by the Spirit. Its purpose — and the function of the ministers — is to make the church capable of exercising its mission in the world. To do this, it has the task of discerning the gifts the Spirit gives to each person for the sake of the common service.

This is why in certain churches, in the course of the ordination of ministers, the liturgy gives an active role to laypeople, thus indicating that the ministry does not simply share in a collegiality that unites all ministers, but also shares in the community of service that unites all Christians within the church to which the mission of God has been entrusted.

121. The ministry of Word and sacraments continues in time and space the service of those acts that constitute the church. As an ordained succession it is the sign and guardian of the church's communitarian and ministerial continuance.

122. Since the service of Word and sacraments in which God gives himself is thus a gift of the Spirit, it is itself attested by a sacramental sign. For the ministers of the acts on which the church is founded are themselves part of this foundation.

123. The sacramental sign of this gift is ordination. According to the tradition of the church rooted in the New Testament "the ordination of ministers comprises the prayer asking for the gifts of the Holy Spirit and the laying on of hands which signifies them. It proclaims that the church is joined to the acts of Jesus Christ and his apostles" ("Towards a Reconciliation of Ministries," 34; see also 35).

124. Here by way of example is the ancient witness of an *epiclesis* of presbyteral ordination (Serapion of Thmuis, in Egypt, from the fourth century): "We raise our hands, sovereign God of heaven, Father of your only Son, over this man and we pray you that the Spirit of truth may fill him; grant him understanding, knowledge and a pure heart; may the divine Spirit be in him, so that he may minister to your people, dispense your divine words and reconcile your people with you, uncreated God. You poured out the Holy Spirit upon the elect through the spirit of Moses: grant the Holy Spirit to this man through the Spirit of your only Son; so

that he may serve you with a pure conscience through your only Son Jesus
Christ; may glory and honor be given to you through him in the Holy
Spirit, now and for unending ages. Amen."[38]

125. The doctrinal outline we are here presenting together makes us feel
more sharply the anomaly of a situation of division where the same baptism does not lead to a shared eucharist.

126. And so Christians — constituted and acknowledged as members of
the body of Christ through the church's sacraments — are appointed, in
accord with the very dynamism of the sacraments, to show forth the unity
of the body of Christ. In this sense ecumenical advance is an essential aspect of the mission that flows from the church's sacramental life.

Conclusion in the Form of Theses

(I)

127. *The salvation of the world,* the merciful plan of God who wills to reca-
pitulate everything in his Son, is in progress today. It is visible *in the church*
which has the task of proclaiming the coming kingdom and so of offering
everyone the baptism of the Spirit.

(II)

128. The proclamation of the kingdom originates with Christ, *the Word of
God made flesh,* in order to reveal the Father to us. The proclamation of the
gospel gathers the church: this is the Word on which it is founded. The actualization of the saving acts performed by Jesus is the living memorial of
them: these are the sacraments. Word and sacraments imply one another
and are inseparable in the action of the one Spirit.

---

38. Serapion of Thmuis, *Eucologia,* XXVII; ed. Funk, *Didascalia et Constitutiones
Apostolorum,* vol. 2 (Paderborn: Schöningh, 1905), pp. 188-90. The text refers to the account
in Numbers (11:24-30) in which a part of Moses' spirit is given by God to the seventy elders
(who were elected, chosen to help him).

(III)

129. To anyone who asks "Why sacrament?" we reply that it is a visible Word and act celebrated in faith. It conforms us to the economy of the incarnation as our way of learning of Christ, who speaks through symbolical acts. The sacrament is an appropriate way of making the speaking of the Word become real and concrete in us. Its specific function is to *set the seal of the Covenant* concluded between God and his people upon a community or an individual.

(IV)

130. Gift of God without repentance, saving act of Christ, sanctification by the Spirit — under this threefold title a *new situation* comes into being in the church. This situation will be *fruitful* only if it is received in faith.

(V)

131. By the power of the Spirit, Christ is present and gives himself in person in the sacrament. By the very manner in which the sign works, this *presence* both discloses and respects the *distance* between man and God who gives himself to man. As an anticipation of the coming kingdom the sacrament renews longing for it without giving full possession of it.

(VI)

132. By beseeching the Father to send the Spirit *(epiclesis)* to fulfill the words of the Son on which the sacrament is founded, the church celebrates the sacrament under the form of *prayer,* not as a magical act. This is wholly a prayer of hope, since its certainty that it *will be heard* rests on Christ's promise.

(VII)

133. The *ministry* of Word and sacrament cannot be reduced to human or ecclesial organization; it is a *gift of the Spirit* signified and realized by a sac-

ramental act of ordination: the service and communication of the Spirit is itself received from the Spirit by the church.

(VIII)

134. When the church speaks of the presence, in different cultures and civilizations, of elements recognized and adopted by its mission as "preparation for the gospel," it is declaring that the Spirit goes ahead of it to prepare for its sacramental action, which can find in these new territories *characteristic symbolism* for translating the newness of the gospel.

THE FOLLOWING HELPED TO PRODUCE THIS TEXT DURING MEETINGS OF THE GROUPE DES DOMBES (1977-79):

Fr Jean-Noël Aletti
Pastor Daniel von Allmen
Pastor Daniel Atger
Fr Paul Aymard
Fr Joseph de Baciocchi
Fr René Beaupère
Pastor Andre Benoit
Pastor Alain Blancy
Fr Bruno Chenu
Fr Marc Clément
Fr Henri Denis
Pastor Edouard Diserens
Pastor Daniel Fricker
Fr Paul Gay
Fr René Girault
Fr Etienne Goutagny

Fr Pierre Gressot
Fr Joseph Hoffmann
Fr Maurice Jourjon
Pastor Jean Jundt
Pastor Jean Kaltenmark
Fr Marie Leblanc
Pastor Louis Lévrier
Fr Robert Liotard
Pastor Marc Lods
Pastor Alain Martin
Fr Pierre Michalon
Pastor André Morel
Fr Jean Roche
Fr Bernard Sesboüé
Br Max Thurian of Taizé
Pastor Gaston Westphal

The Ministry of Communion
in the Universal Church (1985)

—⁌∞⁍—

Introduction: Towards the Third Millennium

1. Our 1976 document, *Episcopal Ministry,* recognized the need for a future study of "the thorny question of the ministry of *episcopē* and unity for the universal church."[1] Today the time has come for us to undertake this task, in spite of the obstacles involved.

2. Since that time we have decided that it would be preferable to use the expression "ministry of communion in the universal church" in order to show clearly that the concept of unity we are using does not imply a centralizing and reductive uniformity. Indeed, the term "communion" refers to living and diverse expressions of the church.

3. At the close of the second millennium, all churches and Christian confessions are marked by deep and persistent movements that come together in a concern to express their "catholicity."

- *The World Council of Churches,* on the basis of a trinitarian confession of faith, strives to promote "a conciliar fellowship of local churches

---

1. Groupe des Dombes, *Le ministère épiscopal* (Taizé: Presses de Taizé, 1976), "Commentaire," p. 81; this commentary is not included with the English translation, "The Episcopal Ministry."

which are themselves truly united."[2] It has encouraged the establishment of councils of churches or Christian councils in diverse regions and countries. The Roman Catholic Church participates fully in its doctrinal studies through the Council's Commission on Faith and Order.

- The *Roman Catholic Church* has made efforts since the Second Vatican Council to restore a balance between the functions of the episcopal college and those of the Bishop of Rome. It has expressed its commitment to unity, notably by participating in numerous doctrinal dialogues.

- The *Orthodox churches* manifest a desire to witness to a supranational unity through pan-orthodox conferences and the preparation of a "Holy and Great Synod."

- The *Anglican Communion*, through its worldwide extension and its original notion of "comprehensiveness," witnesses to the necessity of visible signs of communion within the contemporary ecumenical movement.

- The *churches issuing from the Reformation* manifest a desire to establish and develop bonds of communion among national and regional churches through diverse confessional alliances and federations. They take part in numerous dialogues, both bilateral and multilateral. Here and there, they have sought to establish united churches. Other evangelical churches and communities have heard the call to manifest the universal communion of all witnesses of Jesus Christ.

4. All churches, in spite of their present divisions, are committed to the task of serving the plan of God for all people by seeking a visible expression of their communion in unity. In this way, they will remain faithful to the apostolic faith and to their vocation of common witness.

5. The Groupe des Dombes desires for its part to contribute to the search for a "catholicity" that is visibly served by a ministry of communion. In light of this, we consider that two pitfalls must be avoided:

- That which consists in thinking of the ministry of communion in an *atemporal* manner. In contrast, we propose a historical reflection that combines fraternal good will and critical freedom.

---

2. Report of the Central Committee, *Uppsala to Nairobi*, 1975, p. 79. Cited in *Breaking Barriers: Nairobi 1975: The Official Report of the Fifth Assembly of the World Council of Churches, Nairobi, 23 November–10 December 1975*, ed. David M. Paton (London: SPCK / Grand Rapids: Eerdmans, 1976), p. 60.

- The other danger consists in privileging one particular situation in the Scriptures and in transferring partial data onto a single and obligatory model.

We believe that our study of the Scriptures enables us to discover some "hidden treasures" capable of regenerating and reforming the ministry of communion from within the diverse and separate heritages that have shaped us to this day.

6. Since its birth the church has seen, under the impulse of the Spirit, the development of ministries and charisms destined to assure its continuity and its growth in the world. By studying the history of the church, marked by human sin yet sustained by God's fidelity, we are invited to discern and recognize that which comes from the Holy Spirit.

7. In this way, we are led to *interpret* the relationship between sacred Scripture and ecclesial tradition. There is no Scripture, in fact, except that which is read and interpreted by the Christian community, just as all tradition is subject to the norm of Scripture. The work underway on this difficult question, like that already completed in the texts of Faith and Order at Montreal and Venice, and of Vatican II, offer a hope that we will soon see an ecumenical agreement on this subject.

8. Our reflection on the ministry of communion rests on the double requirement of confessing the faith and missionary witness.

9. Our previous studies recalled that there are three dimensions to the exercise of the ministry of communion: the personal, the collegial, and the communal.[3] In their understanding of the New Testament and in their own history, the churches have often privileged one of these dimensions to the detriment of the others. We believe, and we will verify throughout our study, that this three-dimensional structure must undergird every model of ecclesial organization and become an authentic element of our respective confessional conversions.

---

3. See Dombes, "The Episcopal Ministry," nos. 42-44. This triple dimension of ministry is first noted at the World Conference of Faith and Order in Lausanne, 1927. See the Commentary in *Baptism, Eucharist and Ministry* (Geneva: WCC, 1982), Ministry, no. 26.

10. In approaching a question that has so deeply characterized our divisions, we find it necessary to begin with the facts of the history of the church from the post-apostolic era to our day. Without confusing the times and the events, this journey through some of the most decisive centuries of history will permit us to distinguish the part played by historical or cultural contingencies and by human weakness. It will help us discern that which belongs to the mystery of the church and constitutes a gift of Christ to the church in the fidelity of the Spirit. For communion through space cannot be dissociated from communion across time. This approach will enable us to take stock of the complementary forms for the exercise of the ministry of communion. It will liberate us from confessional prejudices that can lead to exclusivity. The great book of history will teach us to recognize that which ought to be relativized so we can better grasp the essential. In this spirit we will traverse the first and second millennia of church history respectively (Part I).

11. Recourse to the authority of Scripture without this obligatory passage through history would risk hiding our respective presuppositions in a selective reading and a skewed interpretation. Our task is rather to reread the Scriptures as keenly informed as possible of the suppositions that we bear. We can thus receive the biblical teaching in its fullness, with respect for the richness and complementarity of its content. We do so in the knowledge that Scripture is not outside of history. We read it as a testament to all that concerns the founding event of our faith. Our reading of it is an act of submission to its qualified authority. We shall establish criteria for discerning its multi-secular trajectory, just as an obedient reading commits us to translating the Scriptures faithfully in the church of today and of tomorrow (Part II).

12. This is why, in light of this mutual enlightenment between history and Scripture, we conclude by proposing some elements of confessional conversion to our respective churches in the hope of a rapprochement between them, and of bringing us closer to the day when our communion can be visibly signified and fully lived out (Part III). We acknowledge that we have not resolved all remaining points of contention. In particular, we have not touched upon problems concerning the doctrinal role of the magisterium.[4] We hope, however, to prepare a way that will permit us to

---

4. Every ministry of Christian communion is a service of the unity of faith in Christ. (See Groupe des Dombes, "Towards a Reconciliation of Ministries," no. 6, and "The Episco-

advance boldly towards the day when we will enjoy the unity that the Lord desires.

I
Historical Overview

A. The First Millennium

13. The first differentiated and complex evidence concerning the ministry of communion in the universal church that we find in the witness of the first millennium is of interest to us all, for in this period the divisions relating to this ministry had not yet occurred.[5] The first millennium dates from the patristic period to the high Middle Ages. In our consideration of the patristic age, it is essential to take into account the first ecumenical council of Nicea (325) as an event of paramount importance. While the ante-Nicene church witnesses the establishment of precise marks of communion and forms of ministry, the post-Nicene church presents more marked institutionalization. The gathering of the Second Council of Nicea in 787 marks a transition towards the developments of the early Middle Ages that led to the schism of 1054 between East and West.

---

pal Ministry," no. 35.) The magisterium does not invent doctrine, but exists to be an institutional guarantor of the fidelity of the Church to the teaching of the apostles.

Infallibility, which Catholicism recognizes in certain limited cases as belonging to the Bishop of Rome, is not an exclusive prerogative. That same infallibility is recognized as belonging to the episcopal college (united with the Bishop of Rome) acting with these qualities on points that engage the fidelity of the Church to the apostolic faith (particularly in ecumenical councils). Infallibility is also recognized in the whole Christian community when it is unanimous in its faith.

When Vatican I defined certain acts of the papal magisterium as infallible, it characterized these as applications of "that infallibility which the divine Redeemer willed his Church to enjoy in defining doctrine concerning faith or morals" (DS 3074).

This is a question of major importance but one that goes beyond the limited case of the *universal* ministry of communion and poses multiple specific problems. The universal ministry of the Bishop of Rome was recognized by the Church long before the definition of infallibility (1870).

5. Nonetheless the first millennium saw more than transitory schisms, but enduring divisions arising from the Councils of Ephesus and Chalcedon, e.g., with the Assyrian Church of the East (sometimes called "Nestorian"), the Coptic, Ethiopian, Armenian, and Syrian Orthodox churches (sometimes called "Monophysites").

Ante-Nicene Church

14. During the first three centuries, the *tradition of the apostles* is the fundamental criterion and common reference that enables one to recognize the unity of the churches of God that spread quickly through the known world. The appeal to apostolic tradition is concretized in two ways: first, diverse signs that belong to the content of the profession of faith (canon of Scripture, confession of faith, the celebration of one baptism, and one eucharist); and second, structures of the ministry of faith and of communion (the episcopal structure, synods and regional councils, the role of the church of Rome). These signs and structures are all interdependent.

a) The Marks of Unity of Faith in the Church

15. Towards the end of the second century considerable agreement developed among the churches regarding the acceptance of an almost identical canon of biblical writings. Despite the dispute with Marcion, the Jewish Scriptures were received by all. For all churches, the canon of the New Testament included the four gospels, the Acts of the Apostles, and the Pauline epistles. If some churches expressed hesitation regarding other apostolic letters and the Book of Revelation, the dominant conviction was that this canon ought to be the same for all the churches. For Irenaeus, one of the criteria for true "knowledge" is: "An immutable conservation of the Scriptures has come down to us, implying three things: an integral account, without addition or subtraction; a reading exempt from fraud and in accord with the Scriptures; a legitimate and appropriate interpretation, exempt from the danger of blasphemy."[6] In contrast, the characteristic of heresy is the making of exclusive choices in the use of Scripture. The establishment of the canon of Scripture thus provides a fundamental point of reference for the unity and communion of the churches.

16. The first confessions of faith sought to express the common faith received from the apostles. They are diverse in their expression, yet one in their christological and trinitarian structure. "In fact, the church," says Irenaeus, "though dispersed throughout the world even to the ends of the

---

6. Irenaeus of Lyons, *The Treatise of Irenaeus of Lugdunum: Against the Heresies*, trans. F. R. Montgomery Hitchcock (London: Society for Promoting Christian Knowledge, 1916), vol. II: IV, 33, pp. 67-68.

earth, having received from the apostles and their disciples the faith in one God, Almighty Father . . . , and in one Jesus Christ, the Son of God . . . , and in the Holy Spirit . . . , guards it with care, as if inhabiting a single house. She believes in an identical manner, as if having but one soul and the same heart. She preaches, teaches and transmits it with a unanimous voice, as if she had only one mouth. For, if languages differ throughout the world, the content of the tradition is one and the same."[7] The apostolicity of faith thus leads to catholicity. In turn, catholicity becomes the expression of apostolicity. The formation of the confessions of faith maintains the churches in the unity of faith and allows them to mutually recognize one another. This process would lead to the later formation of the great Symbols of faith promulgated with the same intention by the ecumenical councils.

17. The celebrations of baptism and eucharist belong to the tradition of the apostles. One baptism is recognized in all the churches. The preparation for and celebration of baptism are privileged places for the flowering and expression of the confessions of faith. Sharing in the eucharist was the sign *par excellence* of communion between the churches. By the celebration of the eucharist the Lord gathers them from the four winds.[8] Every Christian who travels is welcomed at the eucharist of the church they visit.

b) Ministerial Structures

18. The appearance and the general diffusion of the episcopal structure have their foundation in the relationship of each church to the apostles. Where do we find the tradition of the apostles, namely the truth of the gospel, says Irenaeus, if not with those "to whom they entrusted the churches themselves, those they left as successors and to whom they transmitted their own mission of teaching"?[9] This episcopal structure, which is similar in all the churches, is the foundation of the unity of the particular church. It is equally at the service of the communion and the unity of all the churches. It is in solidarity with the canon of Scripture, since it was the churches presided over by the *episcopoi* that, little by little, received the canon of Scripture.[10]

7. *Against Heresies,* I: I, 10, p. 28.
8. "The Didache (Teaching of the Twelve Apostles)," in *The Apostolic Fathers,* rev. and ed. Michael W. Holmes (Grand Rapids: Baker Books, 1999), 10, 5, p. 263.
9. *Against the Heresies,* I: III, 3, 1, pp. 84-85.
10. See Dombes, "The Episcopal Ministry," no. 23.

19. Each time that the church becomes conscious of itself and of its necessary unity — even in the midst of challenges posed by distance and the inevitable difficulties that affect relationships among communities — it gathers in a synod or council. From the end of the second century until the fourth, we see the spontaneous appearance of local and regional gatherings of the faithful and the ministers (bishops, presbyters, and deacons) that quickly become a regular occurrence. They reflect a concern to maintain communion among the churches in question and to communicate to other communities the decisions taken so as to maintain diverse practices in the unity of faith and the harmony of the whole body. The authority of these synods binds each particular bishop. The sending of synodal letters to other churches expresses the ecumenical concern that marks these gatherings.

20. At the end of the first century, the church of Rome intervened in the affairs of the Council of Corinth where a "revolt" had arisen. The Letter of Clement to the Corinthians appeals, in its exhortation, to the example of Peter and Paul.[11] At the beginning of the second century, the church of Rome is recognized by Ignatius of Antioch as the church "that presides over charity" and "teaches the others."[12] But Ignatius does not claim to give orders to the Romans as the apostles Peter and Paul had done.[13] For Irenaeus, the church of Rome stands as a model of faith. Its preeminence is derived above all from its foundation on the apostles Peter and Paul who are buried there.[14] This double reference is the basis for the authority of the "very great, very ancient church known to all that the two glorious apostles Peter and Paul founded and established in Rome;[15] . . . for with this church, because of her most excellent origin, the whole church must necessarily be in accord, the faithful from everywhere — she in whom, for the benefit of people everywhere, the tradition that comes from the apostles has always been preserved."[16]

11. "The Letter of the Romans to the Corinthians (1 Clement)," in *The Apostolic Fathers*, 5, 3-7, pp. 34-35.

12. Ignatius of Antioch, "To the Romans," in *The Apostolic Fathers*, greeting and 3, 1, pp. 176-79.

13. 1 Clement, 4, 3, pp. 170-73.

14. The socio-political and cultural power of Rome, capital of the Empire, also played a role in the acknowledged preeminence of the church of this city.

15. Irenaeus's affirmation must be nuanced: a Christian community existed at Rome before the arrival of Peter and Paul. Nonetheless, for the ancient tradition, their common presence and their martyrdom at Rome belong to the founding acts of this church.

16. *Against the Heresies*, 3, 2, pp. 85-86.

21. As the church of Rome possesses a greater founding authority, the Bishop of Rome becomes first among the bishops. Through the Bishop of Rome, Peter remains present in some way in the church. This bishop is called "the Successor of Peter," and also "the Vicar of Peter," for he exercises his ministry in the same locale and in the place of Peter.[17] Unfortunately the exclusive invocation of the "chair of Peter" at Rome allows the relationship of this church to the apostle Paul to be almost forgotten.[18] From the end of the second century the Bishop of Rome was a partner in the synodal life of the church. He himself initiated the convocation of several regional synods.[19]

22. In the early church, reference to the texts of Scripture concerning the role of Peter appears to play a secondary role in relation to an earlier practice.[20] Tertullian is the first to appeal to Matthew 16:18-19 to speak of Peter

17. Cyprian calls Pope Stephen "vicar and successor" of his predecessors (Letter 68, in St. Cyprian, *Letters [1-81]. The Fathers of the Church,* vol. 51, trans. Rose B. Donna [Washington, DC: Catholic University of America Press, 1964], p. 243). For Cyprian, the place occupied by the Bishop of Rome is "the place of Peter" (Letter 55, in *Letters,* vol. 8, p. 139). With some irony he speaks of Pope Stephen, "who so glories in the place of his episcopate and contends that he has the succession from Peter, on whom the foundations of the church were established" (Letter 75, in *Letters,* vol. 17, pp. 306-7). In 431 the papal legate to the Council of Ephesus declares that he was sent by Celestine, "the successor and vicar of Peter"; "Peter, until now and always lives and judges in his successors." (Cf. *Éphèse et Chalcédoine,* trans. A. J. Fustigière [Paris: Beauchesne, 1982], p. 404.) The title "Vicar of Christ" is much more recent. It is claimed by Innocent III (1198-1216), supplanting the expression "vicar of Peter" (*PL,* 214/92 A; see J.-M. R. Tillard, *The Bishop of Rome* [London: SPCK, 1983], p. 218, n. 124).

18. Despite the link between Peter and the successive bishops of Rome the church of the capital remained that of Peter and Paul. The feast of Peter and Paul on June 29 shows that the witness of Clement, Irenaeus, Caius, and even the graffiti of the catacombs of St. Sebastian could not be forgotten. We can cite at least one papal text referring to the two apostles: the letter of Pope Hadrian to Irene (772-95) calls the popes successors of the two apostles (*Mansi,* XII, cols. 1078-84; see also "Nicée" [IIe Concile de]," in *Dictionnaire de Théologie Catholique,* XI, col. 421). The mention of the two apostles does not appear in the Greek translation of the letter: a discreet Oriental reminder regarding the Bishop of Rome?

19. For example, Pope Victor, during the Easter controversy of 190, according to his correspondent Polycrates of Ephesus, seems to have demanded the convocation of synods concerning Palestine, Rome, the Pontus, Gaul, Osrhoene, and Corinth. Eusebius, *Ecclesiastical History: The Fathers of the Church,* vol. 19, trans. Roy J. Deferrari (New York: Fathers of the Church, 1953), 5, 23-24, pp. 333-39.

20. Things seem to have occurred in this manner: first the church acted in the name of a deep and spontaneous conviction; afterward it felt the need to verify and justify its practice in regard to the founding event through precise scriptural texts.

as the source of the episcopate and of universal unity.[21] On the basis of Matthew 16:18-19 and John 21:17, Cyprian develops a theology of church unity that rests on both the chair of Peter and on the collegiality of bishops gathered in council: "It is on one only that the Lord builds the church. He entrusts his sheep to him to be fed. And though he dispenses an equal share of power to all the apostles, he has nonetheless established but one chair and organized by his word the origin, the mode of unity. In any case, the other (apostles) were also what Peter was, but the primacy is given to Peter, and one unique church, one unique chair is revealed (to us) . . . He who is not joined to this unity (recommended by) Paul, does he believe himself bound to the faith? He who abandons the chair of Peter on which the church is founded, can he flatter himself at being in the church?"[22] Thus, Peter is in some sense present in each church, but the unicity of the chair of Peter alone assures unity among all the successors of the apostles.

23. What constitutes the primacy of the see of Rome in this early period? It entails deference and respect for the chair of Peter. It is the recognition of a "primacy of honor,"[23] inseparable from a real responsibility: to maintain unanimity in faith and a communion of charity among the churches. Thus, primacy entails an authority in the church, but not the government of the church. For this reason it is exercised either in the form of an exceptional initiative in regard to one or several churches in difficulty, or in response to an appeal by other churches for an arbitration. But one must not confuse this unity of faith with a unity of customs. That is why Irenaeus reminded Pope Victor, in regard to the quarrel over the determination of the date of Easter, that "the different practices of fasting confirm the agreement in faith."[24]

21. Cf. Tertullian, "The Prescription Against Heretics," in *The Ante-Nicene Fathers. Vol. III* (Buffalo: Christian Literature, 1885), XXII, p. 253.

22. St. Cyprian, "The Unity of the Church," in *Treatises: The Fathers of the Church*, vol. 19, trans. and ed. Roy J. Deferrari (New York: Fathers of the Church, 1958), 4, pp. 98-99. Two versions of this text have come down to us. Contemporary criticism recognizes the authenticity of text A, in spite of the absence of important expressions of text A, notably "primus Petro datur," in text B.

23. The expression "primacy of honor" comes from canon 3 of the First Council of Constantinople (381), expressing a reality that was already established for the church of Rome.

24. According to Eusebius, *Ecclesiastical History*, 5, 24, p. 334.

From Nicea I (325) to Nicea II (787)

24. With the Council of Nicea another mode of conciliarity appears: an ecumenical council; that is to say, the gathering in one place of the "directing personnel" (Louis Duchesne) of all the churches, the bishops. This way of acting together, thanks to the decisive role played by Constantine, constitutes a new step in conciliar tradition. Such councils maintain the church's conviction that when the churches recognize and confess one faith in unanimity, they do not invent the faith, but proclaim its apostolic origin.

25. This fundamental truth, clarified for us by Athanasius, gave rise to the seven[25] ecumenical councils of the undivided church. The councils were not lived out according to canons that had been established in advance. Certain customs evolved slowly: convocation of the council by the emperor; the absence of the Bishop of Rome, represented by delegates; the acceptance of the acts of the council by the Bishop of Rome; the discipline of the debates and the implementation of conciliar decisions undertaken by the emperor.

26. It is especially with Leo the Great (440-61) that we see the pope claim for himself a universal authority, accorded by Christ, which ought by right to supersede that of the council. Thus, the Bishop of Rome "with the whole Council of the West, condemns all that was done"[26] at the so-called "Robber Council" of Ephesus in 449. The "Petrine-Roman" ecclesiology of Leo would play a decisive role in the later direction of Catholic doctrine.

27. In spite of Leo's precise affirmation of primacy, the Council of Chalcedon refuses to simply ratify papal decisions. In so doing, it demonstrates for its part the role of the council in assuring unity of faith in the universal church. In short, the reciprocal relationship of the council and the Bishop of Rome is not understood in the same way in East and West, as we see in the sad days that follow Chalcedon.[27]

25. Admittedly, problems exist concerning the number seven and the progressive recognition of the ecumenicity of certain councils.

26. Cf. Letter of Hilary of Arles to Pulcheria in the corpus of Letters of Saint Leo, 46; PL, 54/837-39. Leo writes elsewhere to the emperor and asks him to disregard the Council of Ephesus of 449.

27. See W. de Vries, *Orient et Occident. Les structures ecclésiales vues dans l'histoire des sept premiers conciles oecuméniques* (Paris: Cerf, 1974).

28. Structures of regional unity are institutionalized in the churches of the East with the first ecumenical councils (canon 6 of Nicea, canon 3 of Constantinople, canon 28 of Chalcedon). In addition to the metropolitans, the apostolic sees of Jerusalem, Antioch, and Alexandria — to which that of Constantinople was added by reason of its political importance — exercise a jurisdiction over the churches of the region. These are the four "patriarchates" of the East. The apostolic see of Rome constitutes the only patriarchate in the West. By reason of its primacy of honor, the see of Rome is considered the first of these five sees. The churches of the East would give the name "pentarchy" to this governing structure of the churches.[28]

29. As the only apostolic see in the West was that of Rome, a pope such as Gregory the Great (590-604)[29] exercised the authority proper to a metropolitan in Italy. He exercised a patriarchal authority over the ecclesiastical provinces of the West in the aid of unity in discipline. In relation to the patriarchs of the East he enjoyed a primacy of honor that conferred upon him solicitude for the unity of the faith and for communion in charity.[30]

From Nicea II (787) to the Gregorian Reform

30. This brief patristic overview has set before us a variety of structures of communion among the churches, each intended to serve the unity of the catholic faith of the church wherever it is found. From this time forward a

28. Canon 6 of Nicea mentions Alexandria, Rome, and Antioch. This is why the church of Rome, which refused to ratify canon 3 of Constantinople I and canon 28 of Chalcedon, preferred to speak of a "triarchy" to which it had in fact consented (see no. 32).

29. Who never accepted the title "universal pope" for himself (cf. Letter to the Patriarch of Alexandria cited by Tillard, *The Bishop of Rome*, pp. 53-54).

30. It is most necessary to recall this portrait of the different functions of the see of Rome today, not all of which have the same value, because since the separation of East and West the [geographical] extent of the Western Patriarchate has come to coincide entirely with the Roman Catholic Church. Because of this we have lost sight of the fact that the pope *administers* this church, not in the name of a primacy of all the churches, but by virtue of his role as the Patriarch of the West.

The period of Gregory the Great represents a time of equilibrium and merits consideration. When there is a question of "faulty" attitude, the Bishop of Rome intervenes by virtue of the authority of the apostolic see of Peter. When no "fault" requires his intervention, the bishops are his equals because of Gregory's humility (PL 77/996; PL 77/36). Gregory does not hesitate to speak of more than one chair of Peter, recognizing the link between Peter and the Patriarchates of Rome, Alexandria, and Antioch (PL 77/899).

new world evolves under the persistent influence of the Byzantine Empire in the East and the effects of the assimilation of the barbarians on the West. Are the unity in the faith of the apostles — of which the Symbols are but a pluralistic expression — and the communion of the churches in charity specially guaranteed by the Bishop of Rome, to whom the title of "pope" is accorded in the West beginning in the fifth century?[31]

31. The imperial coronation of Charlemagne (800) accentuates the tension between Byzantium and the see of Rome. An undeniable restoration of the church in the West is carried out in the name of the idea of the Roman Empire and to the benefit of Rome. Relations between East and West are strongly marked by these events that lead the Western church towards a new level of Roman centralization.

32. Rome's reception of the Council of Constantinople (869-70) is also an acceptance of the fact of the "pentarchy" (canon 21). The authority of the Bishop of Rome, which is a sort of monopoly in the West, is, in the eyes of the East, only that primacy recognized by the four Eastern patriarchs as belonging to the Patriarch of the West.

33. The missionary witness of Sts. Cyril (d. 869) and Methodius (d. 885) is a reminder to the churches of the ancient and the new Rome. They are not only servants but also models by the nobility of their souls, that the proclamation of the gospel is in itself a sign and a requirement of the communion between the churches.

34. In the West, the spiritual and moral decadence of the clergy, the constraints of feudalism, the repeated temptations to seize imperial power by a papacy that had fallen prey to the ambitions of the great Roman families, provoked a movement of reform in the first half of the eleventh century. The three main expressions of this movement were the project of the German emperors, the Cluniac reform, and the Gregorian reform.

35. The project of the German emperors (962-1050) was to reestablish order in Rome, to intervene in the choice of the popes, and to patronize the

---

31. The title "pope" *(papa)* was given to every bishop, from the second to the sixth centuries, as a sign of respect. The practice continued for a longer time to designate the four patriarchs of the East. Following the sixth century in the West it begins to be reserved for the Bishop of Rome. After the reign of Pope Gregory VII, it was used exclusively for the holder of the papal office in the West.

promotion of as many Germanic prelates as possible, albeit worthy men of valor.

36. The Cluniac reform (910-1048) was a factor of religious unity and proved a civilizing force. The important role played by the Abbot of Cluny risked making him into a sort of parallel pope. Nonetheless, the abbot's desire to admit no other jurisdiction with respect to his role but that of the pope contributed effectively to an accentuation of the authority of the papacy. The Cluniac ideal only served to enhance attempts at papal reform.

37. Nicolas II sought to seize the election of the pope out of the hands of princes and rulers, that is to say, from the emperor and the Roman nobility. Yet this positive initiative, which in 1059 entrusted the election to the cardinals alone, also contributed to the clericalization of the church.

38. The character of the Gregorian reform was not only to purify the church of its imperfections, but to set the church free from the institutional system that hindered the realization of its mission. The spirit of this reform is reflected in the *Dictatus papae* of 1075.[32] In this document the pope appears as the absolute monarch of the universal church: "Only the Roman pontiff merits the name universal; only he can depose or absolve the bishops; the pope is the only man whose feet all the princes kiss; he may depose the emperors."

39. These affirmations come twenty-some years after the schism of 1054. They are incontestably a charter of freedom from temporal power for the Western church. But they accentuate its centralization and contribute to the belief that such centralization is necessary for unity. Finally, do they not give a new face to the papacy? None regrets that it is Gregory I and not Gregory VII who is still known as Gregory the Great.

Summary and Conclusion

40. The memory of the Gregorian reform leads us beyond the threshold of the second millennium to the separation of East and West (1054). Having

---

32. The *Dictatus papae* are 27 propositions that figure in the registry of the Roman Chancellery for the year 1075 (cf. Fliche et Martin, *Histoire de l'Eglise*, t. 8 [Paris: Bloud et Gay, 1944], pp. 79-80; or Caspar Edition [Berlin, 1930], pp. 202-7).

sketched the centralizing turn taken by the church of Rome which perhaps contributed to this split, we now propose an assessment of the principal teachings of the first millennium. Until Nicea II their authority belongs to the "founding" period of the Fathers; from Nicea II to the Gregorian reform a new state of affairs was progressively established in the church where East and West were yet still united. To what extent can we recognize in this period the "data of tradition," that is to say, facts rooted in the tradition of the apostles?

41. Throughout the whole patristic period, all churches lived in communion according to the same signposts of faith and had the same ministerial structures, namely, the episcopate, local and regional synods, then ecumenical councils. These are facts of tradition. The churches also consider that the church of Rome, the church of Peter and Paul, is first among the churches, not according to chronological order (from this perspective Jerusalem is the Mother of all churches), nor according to the political order (from this point of view Constantinople progressively becomes the new Rome), but according to the apostolic order (it is the church of the chief of the apostles and the apostle to the nations). This fact of tradition, which puts Rome at the head of the list of all the churches, constitutes a primacy: a primacy of honor that implies, of course, a precedence, but also a duty to exercise a presiding role over *agape,* that is to say, the communion of the churches.

42. The presiding over charity that belongs to the particular church of Rome is exercised by none other than the bishop of this church.[33] There is one bishop who, because he is the Bishop of Rome, is responsible for what this church is. This church is *apostolic.* Its bishop cannot consent to a break in the communion of the apostolic churches. This church is the *first* of the churches. Its bishop ought to have a solicitude worthy of the apostle Paul toward all the churches. This church is the *chair of Peter.* Its bishop responds consciously with the faith of Peter to Christ's promise to build his church upon the rock. The Bishop of Rome exercises all of these responsibilities because he presides over this church.

---

33. It is because he presides in the church of Rome that this bishop presides over the charity between all the churches. In this sense there is not a "president of the churches" in the same sense that there is an emperor of the Roman Empire.

43. All of this belongs to the conviction of the church of Christ: the will of the Lord is to build his church on the mission of the apostles and by the collegial ministry of the bishops, all of them "figures" of the apostle Peter. It receives the Bishop of Rome as "successor of Peter," as a sign of unity in the midst of the college, even if East and West perceive the content of this succession differently.

44. Beginning in the ninth century there is concern to maintain these structures, and the principles of communion remain. But serious signs of decadence appear in the Iron Age church, affecting even the face of the papal institution. These abuses necessitate serious reforms that contribute in fact, by successive waves, to a first movement of Roman centralization. However legitimate a certain centralization might have been in these times of crisis, this evolution is the portent of new developments that cannot be confused with the ministry of communion in the universal church as such.

45. The Bishop of Rome is conscious of receiving a specific ministry from Christ. This ministry, however, is none other than the episcopal ministry. Yet popes sometimes confused solicitude for the churches with abusive intervention, the Western patriarchate with universal supremacy, and the Roman episcopate with pontifical monarchy.

46. This presentation of the "facts of tradition" may reflect a tendency towards idealization. It is true that they leave many weaknesses and problems in the background. These undeniable faults have indeed contributed to preventing the Christian people from placing their confidence in the human officeholder. The enduring portrait of the pope is that of Gregory the Great: Bishop of Rome, servant of the servants of God, who defined his ministry and lived it according to the gospel.

B. The Second Millennium

47. The second millennium is that of a divided church, following the separation of East and West in 1054. At the close of the twentieth century, the unity of the churches is no longer a utopian dream. As yet, however, it remains but a hope on the way towards fulfillment.

48. To facilitate an examination of these ten centuries we distinguish three great periods: the medieval period (eleventh to fifteenth centuries), the

Reformation period (sixteenth to eighteenth centuries), and the ecumenical awakening (nineteenth to twentieth centuries).

The Medieval Period

49. The second millennium of Christian history opens with the separation of the Eastern and Western churches (1054). More than a tragic consequence of this or that passing event, this division results from a process of estrangement between two worlds, both so sensitive to differences of the ritual, cultural, and political orders that they forgot their common tradition.

a) Western Christianity

50. This separation reverberates in the internal life of the Western church. Henceforth the Catholic Church, reduced to the sole patriarchate of Rome, is centered exclusively on the personal principle of unity represented by the pope. Consequently, it tends to confuse communion *with* Rome and centralization *in* Rome.

51. Effective decision-making, missionary expansion, and protection from heresy are fruits of this Roman centralization. But these consequences also serve the papacy in the struggle between church and Empire, as it does in the establishment of what has been called, perhaps with some exaggeration, the pontifical theocracy from Innocent III (1198-1216) to Boniface VIII (1294-1303).

52. Councils, far from disappearing in this period (there are six general councils in the twelfth and thirteenth centuries), bring together more Western bishops than ever before. But these "general synods of the West"[34] held at the initiative of the pope make the Bishop of Rome appear as the keystone of the apostolic collegiality. Thus, they are distinguished from the ecumenical councils of the early church, marked more by imperial convocation than by the influence of papal legates. The ecumenical

---

34. In a letter to Cardinal Willebrands on the occasion of the seventh centenary of the Second Council of Lyon in 1974, Pope Paul VI affirmed that this was "the sixth of the general synods held in the West." See *Doc. Cath.* 1688 (1975): 63. By distinguishing the purely Western councils from the ecumenical councils that included both East and West, this language indirectly reconsiders the list of ecumenical councils received since the end of the sixteenth century.

councils held in the East, for that matter, had only limited participation by Western bishops.

53. Considered in itself, medieval Christianity displays a rich diversity. First, it is often in protecting the rights of every man that the popes become omnipresent and all-powerful. As well, the thirteenth-century mendicant orders spread the concrete and popular image of the Roman pontiff as head of all Christians.[35] Finally, respect for the rights of communities in all their diversity is fundamental to Christianity (chapters, universities, monasteries, confraternities, etc.).

54. The period of the Crusades contributes to reawakening the West's memory of Eastern Christians in their struggle against the conquests of Islam. But this armed intervention gives rise to hostile reactions. The West is accused of imposing its ecclesiology and predominance on the East. The sack of Constantinople, the creation of a Latin empire (1204), and of several Latin patriarchates in the East, accentuate the gulf between Catholic and Orthodox Christians. The general synod of Lyon's failed attempt at reunion (1274) contributes further to the deepening separation.

55. Our historical study would not be complete without recalling certain evangelical messages addressed to the popes of Christianity. Thus, Bernard of Clairvaux wrote to Eugene III (1145-53): "People call upon you from throughout the world. This is certainly an homage to the unique character of primacy. Now then, if you are wise, you will not rejoice in the primacy, but in the good that it allows you to do. . . . The ostentation that makes of you a successor of Constantine and not of Peter — tolerate it as a concession to our times, but be careful not to take it as your due. . . . Do not go taking offense at the pastoral task and solicitude, you, the heir of a pastor. Never be embarrassed at the gospel! . . . Evangelizing is feeding the sheep. Fulfill therefore your role as evangelist. At the same time you will fulfill that of a pastor."[36]

---

35. The title "Sovereign Pontiff" (summus pontifex) "should not be confused with that of pontifex maximus, a pagan title mistakenly said to have been assumed by the popes. Sovereign Pontiff . . . was used to designate all the popes from the fifth to the eleventh centuries. Non-Catholics have great difficulty understanding its use. It cannot be translated into Greek, as we see in the Acts of the Council of Florence." Initiation à la pratique de la théologie, III, 2 (Paris: Cerf, 1983), p. 316.

36. St. Bernard, La consideration, trans. P. Dalloz (Grenoble: Didier & Richard, 1945), pp. 121 and 170.

b) The End of "Medieval Christianity"

56. Some have been tempted to sum up the history of the relationship between the pope and the early councils as a shift from recourse to an ecumenical council to definitively resolve a question in the church, to the appeal to papal power, the supreme recourse to settle similar debate. Can one present this evolution as a sort of irreversible progress? Such an attempt to translate history into theology, and to consider the papal ministry as the object of a coherent and continuous development, belies the facts of two important centuries of history.

57. The fourteenth and fifteenth centuries were marked by the residency of the popes in Avignon (1309-76), by the Great Schism of the West (1378-1417), and by the phenomenon of nations imposing themselves on the churches of Christianity. This period is filled with debate that was more than theoretical. At issue was knowing what constituted the supreme ecclesial authority in the Western patriarchate: the pope or the council? The question was posed all the more sharply when three rival popes confronted each other.

58. The decree *Haec sancta* affirms, concerning the Council of Constance from which it emerged, "The synod, legitimately gathered in the Holy Spirit and forming a general council, representing the catholic church militant, receives its power directly from Christ; every man, regardless of his state or dignity, even papal dignity, is bound to obey it in all matters concerning the faith and the eradication of schism" (4th session, 30 March 1415; 5th session, 6 April 1415).[37]

59. In a more radical manner the Council of Basel, whose authority, it is true, has since been rejected, decreed on 27 April 1433 that a pope who would not be faithful to the decisions of Constance would be "*ipso facto* suspended from the administration of his papal dignity . . . and this administration would *ipso jure* devolve to the council."[38]

60. The struggle ended in the condemnation of the principle of conciliar superiority (Council of Florence, 21 April 1441). Yet conciliarism continued

---

37. Cf. J. Gill, *Constance, Bâle et Florence* (Paris: Orante, 1965), pp. 307-8.
38. Gill, *Constance, Bâle et Florence*, p. 338.

to be taught in the universities of Germany and France. The Council of Lateran V (1512-17) returned to the pattern of the medieval councils, being a "council of the pope." It seems, in any case, that by the end of this conflict both conciliarists and partisans of the pope were in agreement on two very important points:

- the council does not draw its authority from the pope but from Christ;
- the government of the church is dominated by realities that transcend pope and council: the good of the faith and the good of the body of Christ.

61. Throughout the Middle Ages in the West, many Christian movements reflected a deep need for a return to the sources and to the simplicity of the gospel. Francis of Assisi (1181-1226) is a living symbol of this. The success of his efforts should not let us forget Peter Waldo (Vaudès) of Lyon, a forerunner of Francis with an analogous objective, who met with rejection. Later, John Wycliffe (c. 1329-84) and Jan Hus (c. 1369-1415) were precursors of the sixteenth-century Reformers. Like them, they were denouncers of abuse and passionate seekers of truth.

c) The Christian East

62. The development of the concept of a "papal monarchy" in the West, beginning in the eleventh century, and the subsequent claims by the pope of Rome to rule with sovereign power over the patriarchal sees[39] of the East, would have an effect upon the East. Byzantine Orthodox theologians developed an ecclesiology of their own, establishing a theory of the "pentarchy," organized around the five patriarchal sees recognized by the Council of Chalcedon and juridically structured according to the laws of Justinian.[40]

63. This theory is founded upon the idea that a council cannot be considered ecumenical or that a decision does not engage the ecumenicity of the church without being approved by the five patriarchs. St. Maximus the

39. This theory dominates from the time of Innocent III in 1204 to the papacy of Boniface VIII.

40. Cf. L. Bréhier, *Les institutions de l'Empire byzantin* (Paris: Albin Michel, 1949), p. 449, which cites Justinian's *Novellae* 109 (541), 131 (545), 123 (546). In the latter text, Antioch is referred to as Theopolis.

Confessor, in the disputes with the Monothelites, and later Theodore Studite in the time of the iconoclast controversy, often referred to this criterion. This theory was elaborated and explained most extensively in the twelfth century by the great Byzantine canonist, Theodore Balsamon.[41]

64. The politico-religious context, the claim of the Slavs to create new Bulgarian and Serbian patriarchates, and the tutelage of the "Melkite" patriarchates of Alexandria, Antioch, and Jerusalem tend to promote the preeminence of the ecumenical see of Constantinople. In the eyes of the Greeks this "New Rome" inherited the privileges of the ancient one from the moment that the old Rome entered into schism. The creation of the Ottoman Empire contributes to the increased role of the Patriarch of Constantinople in regard to the Orthodox of the Empire and reinforces the influence of his Holy Synod.

65. The idea of an ecumenical patriarch is at the origin of the creation of the Patriarchate of Moscow. Its titular bishop, supported by the tsar, the legitimate heir of Basileus, later considers himself as the holder of the privileges of Rome (hence, the theory of the "third Rome"). In the end, this development put an end to any theory of pentarchy. Several Orthodox theologians had preferred that of the "tetrarchy" for some time, allowing them to account for the failure of Rome.

66. The suppression of the Patriarchate of Moscow by Peter the Great (1721) and the founding of a so-called "synodal" organization would lead numerous Russian theologians to prefer the concept of an ecclesial structure founded on the equality of all the bishops and the solidarity of the whole Christian people *(sobornost)*. The reestablishment of the patriarchate (1917) did not put an end to the diversity of ecclesiologies.

The Reformation Period

67. Rome's rejection of the sixteenth-century reform project led to a split in the Western church. Thus, the Reformation movement continued to develop outside of communion with the pope. These factors meant that

---

41. Cf. particularly *PG* 119/1161f. for numerous references and citations in "Patriarcat," in *Dictionnaire de Théologie Catholique*, XI, 2267-75 and 2289-91, and in M. Jugie, *Theol. Dogm. Christ. Or.* (Paris: Letouzey & Ané, 1931), t. IV, p. 450.

churches issuing from the Reformation could no longer consider the ministry of the pope a ministry of unity. In their desire to remain in the true tradition of the church, they organized themselves according to three poles of unity, namely:

- The sovereign authority of Holy Scripture and its interpretation by the councils, ecumenical creeds, and confessions of faith of the Reformation.[42]
- The ordained ministry of the Word and sacrament, which constitutes one of the signs of the universality of the church.
- A synodal life that strives to maintain, while taking into account local political conditions, a bond of communion between the churches.

68. The ministry of Word and sacrament becomes very important alongside other ministries that are less well defined (that of teachers, deacons, and elders). It includes the New Testament charisms of *episcopos* and presbyter. This ordained ministry is constitutive of the church. Preaching, the administration of the sacraments, and care for unity are the essential tasks of the pastor-*episcopoi*. The ministry assures the growth and the communion of the ecclesial body through these functions.

69. It is worth recalling that the major preoccupation of the Reformation churches was to develop and affirm the ecclesial implications of the doctrine of justification by faith and of the authority of Scripture. In the realm of ecclesiology, different emphases and tensions sometimes appear between the diverse confessional families of the Reformation:

70. *For Lutherans,* the establishment of a particular type of ministerial organization was never considered an essential or normative element for the authenticity and unity of the church. The Lutheran tradition willingly accepted the ministerial structures such as they existed before the sixteenth century, notably the episcopal ministry, and even the papal ministry, rec-

---

42. "We willingly embrace and reverence as holy the early councils, such as those of Nicea, Constantinople, Ephesus I, Chalcedon, and the like, which are concerned with refuting errors — insofar as they relate to the teachings of faith. For they contain nothing but the pure and genuine exposition of Scripture, which the holy fathers applied with spiritual prudence to crush the enemies of religion who had arisen." John Calvin, *Institutes of the Christian Religion,* ed. John T. McNeill (Philadelphia: Westminster Press, 1960), IV, IX, 8, pp. 1171-72. Subsequent citations of the *Institutes* are taken from this edition.

ognized as having accomplished a beneficial historic task.[43] Some Lutheran theologians declare that they accept a ministry of unity that belongs to the Bishop of Rome in relation to the evangelical ministry of Peter.[44]

71. *For Reformed churches,* an element of radicalism often seemed to disregard the tradition. Calvin and Bucer notably sought to reestablish a structure of ministry founded directly on the New Testament, where a universal ministry does not appear to be clearly instituted. Roman centralism is considered a major obstacle to the spiritual growth of the churches. Nonetheless, Calvin accepts a conciliar structure and a patriarchal system that do not present the same difficulties.[45] Less dependent than Lutheranism upon

43. In teaching the Smalcald Articles, Melanchthon recognized the benefit of the Roman primacy and wrote: "As for the pope, I am of the opinion that, if he would give free rein to the gospel we should leave him the supremacy that he possesses *by human law* over the bishops, and this in the interest of the peace of the universal union of Christians who are and who will in future be under his authority." *Oeuvres de Martin Luther,* t. II: *Les livres symboliques* (Paris: Je sers, 1946), p. 10.

44. See the American Lutheran–Roman Catholic declaration mentioned above, which affirms: "We have found it appropriate to speak of a 'Petrine function,' using this term to describe *a particular form of Ministry exercised by a person, officeholder, or local church, with reference to the church as a whole.* This Petrine function of the ministry serves to promote or preserve the oneness of the church by symbolizing unity, and by facilitating communication, mutual assistance or correction, and collaboration in the church's mission. . . . The single most notable representative of this Ministry toward the church universal, both in duration and in geographical scope, has been the Bishop of Rome." Lutheran-Roman Catholic Dialogue (USA), "Differing Attitudes Toward Papal Primacy," in *Papal Primacy and the Universal Church,* Lutherans and Catholics in Dialogue 5, ed. Paul Empie and Austin Murphy (Minneapolis: Augsburg, 1974), pp. 11-12, nos. 4-5.

45. "That each province had one archbishop among bishops, and that at the Council of Nicea patriarchs were ordained to be higher in rank and dignity than archbishops, were facts connected with the maintenance of discipline. However, in this discussion it cannot be overlooked that this was an extremely rare practice. These ranks, therefore, were established so that any incident in any church whatever that could not be settled by a few might be referred to a provincial synod. If the magnitude or difficulty of the case demanded larger discussion, the patriarchs, together with the synod, were summoned, from whom there was no appeal except to a general council. Some called the government thus constituted 'hierarchy,' an improper term (it seems to me), certainly one unused in Scripture. For the Holy Spirit willed men to beware of dreaming of a principality or lordship as far as the government of the church is concerned. But if, laying aside the word, we look at the thing itself, we shall find that the ancient bishops did not intend to fashion any other form of church rule than that which God has laid down in his Word." Calvin, *Institutes,* IV, 4, 4, pp. 1071-72.

the protection of princes, the Reformed churches, national and regional, appear to favor a synodal organization for each church from the outset, the model of which is found in the college of the apostles. This preference gives rise to a "presbyterian-synodal" form of government, from which the Lutherans were later to benefit greatly. Originally this system implied the participation of all ministers (pastors, teachers, elders, deacons, and civil magistrates) in the government of the church in a given land. A hierarchy of assemblies sought to maintain a common discipline among the churches and to preserve them from a personal authoritarianism of the ministers responsible for the Word and sacraments. Hence, a constant reminder of "the equality among pastors."[46] This system seeks to avoid the excesses of congregationalism (autonomy of the churches in relation to one another) and those of personal power.[47]

72. The first Reformers — both Lutheran and Calvinist — despite the sad memory left by the Council of Constance which condemned Jan Hus, deeply desired and called for the gathering of a general council convoked by the pope that would be truly open to reforming the church in its faith and morals. They set aside this idea, having little by little lost confidence in the reforming intentions of the popes and most of the bishops. Calvin, however, did not exclude the possibility of recourse to a general council, on the condition that it was made up of "true" bishops. Such a council, in his view, could not be valid or legitimate unless it submitted to the Word of God and only took decisions that were based upon it.[48]

46. "All those to whom the office of teaching was enjoined they called 'presbyters.' In each city these chose one of their number to whom they specially gave the title 'bishop' in order that dissensions might not arise (as commonly happens) from equality of rank. Still, the bishop was not so much higher in honor and dignity as to have lordship over his colleagues. But the same functions that the consul has in the senate — to report on business, to request opinions, to preside over others on counseling, admonishing, and exhorting, to govern the whole action by his authority, and to carry out what was decreed by common decision — the bishop carried out in the assembly of presbyters." Calvin, *Institutes,* IV, 4, 2, p. 1069; also: La Confession de foi de la Rochelle, art. XXX, cited in Roger Mehl, *Explication de la Confession de foi de la Rochelle* (Les Bergers et les Mages, 1952), p. 122.

47. This system was only able to function imperfectly due to the fact, notably in France, that historical circumstances long prohibited the synods from developing a permanent executive (or episcopal) ministry.

48. "We indeed willingly concede, if any discussion arises over doctrine, that the best and the surest remedy is for a synod of true bishops to be convened, where the doctrine at issue may be examined. Such a decision, upon which the pastors of the church in common,

73. In the seventeenth century, several Reformed theologians developed this conciliar perspective in a more systematic way. The goal of such a council is specified by the Synopsis of Leiden (1652): purity of faith, holiness of life, integrity of the sacraments, and correct modalities of discipline having as their objective the good government and edification of the church, and thus the glory of God.[49] Such a council should, according to these theologians, promote the unity of the church through a common submission to the Word of God. This rough plan for a council never came into being, and came up against the nationalism of the "magistrates." But the theological and juridical principles that inspired it found many practical applications at the level of regional and provincial synods and remain very much alive today.

74. The question of a universal and permanent ministry of communion in the church was not at the center of concern for the Protestant Reformers and their successors. In the centuries that followed, different attitudes emerged:

- For some, the "ministry of communion" is assured directly by Jesus Christ, without a human intermediary.[50]
- For others, the Confession of Faith alone assures the visibility and unity of the church.
- For yet others, a ministry of communion should necessarily have a concrete manifestation to assure the fidelity of the churches to their Lord.

75. The upheaval provoked by the Reformation made clear, on the Catholic side, the urgent necessity of a general reform of the church and awakened

---

invoking Christ's Spirit, agree, will have much more weight than if each one, having conceived it separately at home, should teach it to the people, or if a few private individuals should compose it. Then, when the bishops are assembled, they can more conveniently deliberate in common what they ought to teach and in what form, lest diversity breed offense." Calvin, *Institutes,* IV, 9, 13, p. 1176.

49. *Synopsis purioris theologiae doctorum et professorum in academia Leidensi Joh. Polyandri, Andr. Riveti, Ant. Walei et Ant. Thyssi* (Lugduni Batavorum ed. Sexta, 1881).

50. Very early on, Reformed theology affirmed that the universal episcopate could only be exercised by Christ himself, to the exclusion of any vicarious ministry. See, for example, "The Second Helvetic Confession (1566)," in *Creeds of the Churches,* 3rd ed., ed. John H. Leith (Louisville: John Knox Press, 1982), chapter 27, pp. 143-44; and "The Westminster Confession of Faith (1646)," in the same volume, chapter 25, no. 6, p. 222.

the desire to respond doctrinally and pastorally to the disputes raised by the Reformers. Such was the task before the Council of Trent, which labored over three intervals (1545-63). Even though the power of the sovereign pontiff had been violently contested during the crisis, the council was silent on the question of the ministry of the pope in the universal church. However, this council, which could not have met and of which the decrees could not have been promulgated without the authority of the sovereign pontiff, reinforced his role in the church considerably.

76. Successive popes undertook the responsibility for implementing the decrees of the council in the half century that followed. Thus, the pope emerged as the guarantor of unity in faith in the face of "heresy" and as the condition of reform and the good functioning of the church. As well, Catholic controversial literature, represented by Robert Bellarmine (1542-1621), glorified the role of the pope as the supreme head of the church, conceived according to the model of the absolute monarchies of the time. A theology of authority supplanted an ecclesiology of communion.

77. However, within the Catholic world sovereigns jealously guarded their authority and contested the interventions of the papacy in their states. Thus the king of France and the Parliament of Paris refused the promulgation of the decrees of Trent in their kingdom until 1615.

78. National churches, such as the Gallican church, saw in the evolution of the Roman interventions a disregard for their rightful traditions and a restriction of the rights of diocesan bishops, successors of the apostles. For this reason a current of theology arose, represented in particular by Bossuet, to defend an ecclesiology of communion. According to this theory, bishops and councils maintain all their prerogatives. The pope, understood as a bishop among bishops, is presented as the successor of Peter, charged with conserving the deposit of faith and maintaining the unity of the body of the church. In France, a sometimes-exaggerated link between this theology and the teaching of the jurists or parliamentarians and certain currents of Jansenism, served to discredit this doctrine. By the time of the Revolution it was almost completely obscured.

79. To resolve the crisis caused by the religious politics of the Revolution, the Concordat of 1801 accorded an authority to the pope that he had never exercised previously: to require that 130 bishops resign in a single act. Soon

a papacy persecuted by the imperial power would emerge as the supreme and sure safeguard of a church under siege on all sides.[51]

80. During this period the Reformed churches of France were deprived of their synodal structure. Following the Revolution, the organic articles prevented them from developing a unifying structure. This contributed to the development of congregationalist tendencies among them.

The Ecumenical Awakening

a) Attempts at Communion among the Churches of the Reformation

81. From the middle of the nineteenth century we witness a flourishing of efforts that aim to ensure communion within the diverse confessional families born of the Reformation. Thus was born the Lambeth Conference in 1867, which gathers the bishops of the Anglican Communion every ten years. In this same period, the world confessional alliances were born. In 1868 a Lutheran organization on a worldwide scale was founded that would later become the Lutheran World Federation. The World Alliance of Reformed Churches gathered for the first time in 1877. This was followed by the Methodist ecumenical conference in 1881, the international conference of Congregationalist churches in 1891, and the World Baptist Alliance in 1905. These diverse alliances sought to help their members become more aware of the universal dimension of the church. While they do not all have an ecclesial status, these alliances, together with other interconfessional and missionary initiatives, nonetheless constitute important signposts in the development of the ecumenical movement.

b) The Two Vatican Councils

82. The First Vatican Council appears as the triumph of the personal ministry of unity in the church. Henceforth, the Bishop of Rome is the specially venerated head of all Catholics, who see in him the irrefutable sign of their Christian identity, the infallible sovereign pontiff. In spite of the terms that were carefully chosen to limit his "charism of truth," he can

---

51. In his *Promenades dans Rome,* dated 3 August 1827, Stendhal wrote: "The sovereign of this country enjoys the most absolute political power and, at the same time, he directs his subjects in the most important affair of their life, that of salvation."

seem to represent the whole church in himself alone. Moreover, the conciliar majority had surely sought to proclaim before the world the most extensive papal primacy possible by qualifying it as an "ordinary, immediate and truly episcopal power."[52]

83. However, the exact juridical meaning of the terms used ("ordinary" is not opposed to "extraordinary," but to "delegated"; "immediate," which permits the pope direct access to every member of the faithful, does not in any way suppress the jurisdiction of the bishop; "truly episcopal" means "really pastoral"), as well as the presence at the council of a minority that made all aware of the historical and doctrinal objections that prohibit the church from having an absolute monarch or a "super-bishop," permitted a significant moderation of generally held opinion.

84. The First Vatican Council's definition of papal primacy in no way weakens the ministry of each bishop. Neither does it challenge their apostolic authority ("by divine right" according to the usage of the Roman canonists). It seems, it is true, to ignore the collegiality of [the episcopate]. Nothing in the definition obliges us to make of the pope a "bishop of the bishops,"[53] and even less so the first bishop of every Christian. It is because he is the Bishop of Rome that the pope is the common pastor of the bishops and the faithful.

85. Devotion to the pope remains a concrete characteristic of the Roman Catholic Christian. In regard to the Catholic Church in France, we note that the blows born by the papacy from the left and the right failed to diminish this devotion. It burned brightly among the militants of the Sillon movement, shone during the first wave of the Jeunesse Ouvrière Chrétienne (Young Christian Workers), and was renewed with the beginning of each new pontificate. The multiplication of encyclical letters — of-

52. First Vatican Council, "First Dogmatic Constitution on the Church of Christ *(Pastor Aeternus),*" in *Decrees of the Ecumenical Councils.* vol. 2, ed. Norman Tanner (Washington, DC: Georgetown University Press / London: Sheed & Ward, 1990), p. 814, no. 3.

53. This expression comes from Tertullian. He uses it with irony to speak, not of the Bishop of Rome, but of the Bishop of Carthage. Cf. "On Purity," in *Treatises on Penitence,* Ancient Christian Writers, vol. 28, translated and annotated by William P. Le Saint (Westminster, MD: Newman Press, 1959), pp. 53-125, at 54, note 1. In any case, Vatican I does not use it. Nothing obliges us to understand the formula as establishing the same relationship between the pope and the bishops as exists between the bishops and the faithful.

ten considered mistakenly as infallible[54] — on diverse subjects where the authority of the church can at times appear to be added on to that of the Word of God, has troubled consciences and provoked a lack of zeal to obey. Nevertheless, the most common reception of Vatican I reinforced among many the image of the pope as God's God, Vicar of Christ,[55] and bearer of the sovereign priesthood.

86. Perhaps the most spectacular act accomplished by a pope armed with all the possibilities accorded by the First Vatican Council for acting of his own initiative, was the convocation of a council by John XXIII (25 January 1959). That is to say, he chose to appeal to another sign of unity and of communion.

87. Today the Vatican Council of 1870 is merely Vatican I. Vatican II (1962-65) renounced nothing of the preceding council and even recalls its bluntest assertions: the pope still possesses full and supreme power in the church, and without doubt can still exercise it freely, that is to say, without being obliged to associate the episcopal college in an explicit way.[56]

88. Yet Vatican II opened up immense possibilities. It defined the church as the people of God. It rediscovered episcopal collegiality. It renewed the theology of the particular churches and of the communion among the churches. Finally, it was a turning point for the Roman Catholic Church in regard to ecumenism. It thus permitted us to hope that the exercise of papal primacy would be first and foremost a universal ministry of communion. In this way the conciliar texts and their initial effects in the life of

---

54. Next to the great encyclicals promulgated by the popes of the nineteenth and twentieth centuries, one must recognize that there have been some whose teaching was later revealed as ineffective and out of date. To give but one example within the realm of our study, the extremely harsh judgment of the early ecumenical conferences born by Pius XI in *Mortalium Animos* (1928), together with the refusal of any participation by the Catholic Church in the ecumenical movement, was in fact reversed by the decisions of the Second Vatican Council.

55. Speaking recently to seminarians in Rome about the title "Vicar of Christ," Pope John Paul II said: "I must tell you that I prefer not to abuse this expression and use it rarely. I prefer to say 'Successor of Peter.' In fact, I prefer even more to say 'Bishop of Rome.'" *Osservatore Romano* (5-6 March 1984) [French Edition].

56. Cf. Second Vatican Council, "Dogmatic Constitution on the Church *(Lumen Gentium),*" in *Decrees,* II: no. 22, p. 866 and the "Preliminary Explanatory Note *(Nota praevia),*" in *Decrees,* II: no. 3, p. 899.

Christian communities have made possible the restoration of a balance between the personal, collegial, and communal dimensions in the ministry of communion exercised in the universal church.

c) The Evolution of Orthodoxy

89. In response to the invitation addressed by Pius IX (*In suprema Petri sede,* 6 January 1848) to reestablish communion with the see of Peter, the four Orthodox patriarchs composed a common encyclical letter (May 1848) in which they presented an exposition of the Orthodox conception of the unity of the church: a fraternal communion, assured by the presence of the Holy Spirit among the diverse particular churches, organized within the framework of the traditional patriarchates, and excluding all other primacy except a primacy of honor among the bishops responsible for each of these churches.

90. In Russia we witness the development of an ecclesiology under the influence of Khomiakov that considers the entire Christian people (the faithful and pastors) not only as guardian of the faith, but also as the unique authentic guarantor of its expression *(sobornost).*

91. In 1902 the Ecumenical Patriarch sent a letter to the Orthodox sister churches concerning relations with the non-Orthodox and the search for greater unity with Catholicism and Protestantism. At the close of World War I, the same patriarchate took a wider and stronger initiative. An encyclical letter was published in 1920, addressed to "all the churches of the world," proposing a permanent organism that would give form to the spiritual community that already existed among them, a "union of different denominations in a league *(koinonia)* of churches." It was this idea that took flesh in the World Council of Churches and of whom the principal redactor of the encyclical — the future Metropolitan Germanos of Thyateira — was one of the first presidents.

d) The World Council of Churches

92. The World Missionary Conference at Edinburgh launched the contemporary ecumenical movement officially in 1910. This meeting led to the establishment of the International Missionary Council and the Commission on Faith and Order. Thanks to the concerted efforts of many great church-

men such as Nathan Söderblom, J. H. Oldham, William Temple, Marc Boegner, and W. A. Visser t'Hooft, the two movements of Life and Work and Faith and Order gave birth to the World Council of Churches in 1948.

93. At the present time the World Council of Churches includes more than 300 Anglican, Protestant, and Orthodox member churches, with theologians of the Roman Catholic Church participating as official members of the Commission on Faith and Order. According to the text of the "Basis," the World Council is "a fellowship of churches that confess the Lord Jesus Christ as God and Savior according to the Scriptures and seek to respond together to their common vocation for the glory of God the Father, Son and Holy Spirit." Through all of its activities, the World Council calls the churches to "to grow towards visible unity in one faith, one eucharistic community of worship and a common life in Christ, and to advance towards that unity so that the world may believe" (Constitution of 1975).

94. From the beginning, the World Council of Churches has specified that it is not a super-church, nor the church of the future (Toronto Statement, 1950). A privileged instrument of the ecumenical movement, the council allows its member churches to speak together in the name of the gospel and to act together in the service of humanity. It is an incentive for the common journey of the churches, at once the expression of their commitment and a call for their faithfulness. As was said in 1973 by the General Secretary, Philip Potter, "The search for the unity of the church is for us inextricably linked to the struggle for the unity of humanity."[57] In this way the World Council of Churches encourages a greater catholicity of its member churches through an apprenticeship of communion, the encounter of faith, and growth in common witness. Without constituting a new model of unity, it nonetheless offers prophetic signs of "conciliar fellowship."[58]

---

57. Report of the Central Committee of the World Council of Churches, Geneva, 1973.

58. Cf. "Conciliarity and the Future of the Ecumenical Movement," in *Faith and Order, Louvain 1971: Study Reports and Documents* (Geneva: WCC, 1971). See also the report of section 2, par. 6 of the Nairobi Assembly (1975): "Our present inter-confessional assemblies are not councils in this full sense, because they are not yet united by a common understanding of the apostolic faith, by a common ministry, and a common eucharist. They nevertheless express the sincere desire of the participating churches to herald and move towards full conciliar fellowship, and are themselves a true foretaste of such fellowship." In *Breaking Barriers,* p. 61.

II
The Witness of Scripture

95. The reconciliation of our churches requires a reconciliation of our interpretations of Scripture. Yet, our readings of Scripture concerning the ministry of communion are conflicted in proportion to the divergence in our ecclesiological convictions. Before undertaking a common rereading of the New Testament texts — especially in regard to Matthew 16:17-19 — it is helpful to recall how this text was interpreted before and after the great historical divisions of our churches. Taking this into account will help us to better understand and identify the significance of that which separates us and to discern the path towards doctrinal reconciliation. We will therefore proceed in two stages:

A. *Examining the Interpretations of Matthew 16:17-19*

In the Early Church

96. From their first appearance in the patristic literature at the beginning of the third century, we find various interpretations of Matthew 16:17-19. They apply the words spoken by Jesus to Peter to every Christian because of their faith, or to all the apostles and the bishops that succeed them, or finally, to the person of the apostle Peter, either because he himself is constituted as the foundation of the church or because his confession of faith is the foundation of the church. But it is never forgotten that Christ himself is the first rock[59] upon which the church is built.

97. Every Christian who makes a confession of faith merits in a certain sense the name of Peter. "The rock," says Origen, "is every disciple of Christ, the spiritual rock whom they follow and from which they drank and were refreshed" (*In Matt.*, PG 13/997). In the same sense John Chrysostom speaks of Flavian, Bishop of Antioch: "Because he has come

---

59. *Translator's note:* In this sentence there is a play on words that cannot be rendered into English. The French name for Peter is "Pierre." This same word "pierre" means rock or stone, in keeping with the double meaning of the Greek term "petra" used in Matthew 16:19. Thus the use of "rock" in the paragraphs that follow should be read keeping this double signification in mind.

to the confession and the faith of Peter, he has become worthy of this name" (*In inscriptione Actorum,* II, PG 51/87).

98. As well, in a manner that is just as direct even though different, Peter, who confesses the faith and receives the promise of Christ, represents all the apostles who also receive the same promise to bind and unbind in Matthew 18:18 and are called the foundations of the church (Eph. 2:20). "Our Lord . . . speaks in the gospel and says to Peter, 'And I tell you, you are Peter, and on this rock I will build my church. . . .' From this flows, through the passing of time and successions, the election of the bishops and the organization *(ratio)* of the church. The church rests on the bishops and its whole conduct obeys the direction of these same heads." Thus wrote Cyprian of Carthage (Letter XXXIII, I, 1; éd. Bayard, Budé, t. I, p. 84).[60] The attribution of the words of Christ to the apostles expresses the conviction of the Fathers of the Church that Peter and the apostles still occupy their chairs through the succession of bishops as constant foundations of the whole church, which confesses its faith in Christ through Peter (cf. no. 22).

99. For Tertullian, "the rock upon which the church should be built" is the person of the apostle "who received the keys of the kingdom of heaven and the power to bind and unbind in heaven and on earth" (*The Prescription against Heretics,* XXII, 4). "It is upon Peter that this church is built" (*On Modesty,* XXI, 11[61]). On what basis did Simon merit being called Peter *(petra)*? It was not only due of the strength of his faith, but also because "Christ desired to share with his dearest disciple one of his 'symbolic' titles, that which would indicate to him the double vocation of his Master: a 'spiritual rock' (1 Cor. 10:4), but also 'a stone that makes them stumble and a rock that makes them fall' (1 Pet. 2:8)." (Cf. *Contra Marcion,* 4, 13, 5-6.[62])

60. Later Jerome would say the same: "The church is founded upon Peter, yet this same foundation is expressed in another place as being all the apostles; all receive the keys to the kingdom of heaven, and the strength of the church is equally assured by all of them. However only one is elected from among the twelve so that the establishment of a head removes all occasion of schism" (*Adv. Jov.* I, 26; PL, 23/247).

61. It is remarkable that Tertullian, in this polemical work from his Montanist period, denies the claim of the bishop to whom he writes that "the power of binding and loosing have devolved upon you also, that is, upon every church that is akin to Peter." This would "pervert and . . . change the manifest will of Christ, who grants this to Peter personally." *On Modesty,* XXI, 9-10.

62. See the summary of Tertullian's position in J. Doignon, *Revue de sciences philosophiques et religieuses* 66 (1982): 419.

100. According to Hilary of Poitiers, Peter became the foundation of the newly established church by reason of his confession of faith. "The confession of Peter obtained fully the reward that he merited for having seen in the man the Son of God. . . . Oh foundation that he had the fortune to give to the church, by way of his new name, and rock worthy for building it, such that it broke the laws of hell . . ." (*Sur Matthieu*, 16, 7; trad. J. Doignon, *SC* 258, pp. 54-55). We find a similar teaching in the writings of John Chrysostom. The apostle Simon receives the name of Peter due to his faith in the rock that is Christ. "It was not for raising the dead or healing the lame that he was thus named. He received it for having manifested his faith in an authentic confession: 'You are Peter and upon this rock I will build my church'" (*In inscriptione Actorum*, II; PG 51/86). And elsewhere: "Upon this rock, that is, on the faith of this confession" (*In Matt.*, PG 58/534).

101. Because of his confession of faith in the rock that is Christ, the first of the apostles becomes the image of the whole church that confesses faith in Christ. "Because Christ is the rock, the Christian people is Peter" (Augustine, *Sermon*, 76, I, 1; PL, 38/479). "Only Peter was worthy to play the role of the whole church" (*Sermon* 295, II, 2; PL 38/1349). While he often speaks in this way, Augustine never denied the truth of the other opinion, according to which the church is founded upon Peter as upon a rock (*Retract.*, I, 21; *BA*, 12, p. 401).

102. Finally, Christ himself is the rock upon which the church is built. If the first among the apostles receives the name of Peter, it is due to his confession of faith in Christ. He draws his name of Peter from the Christ whom he confesses. "Peter comes from rock *(petra)*," writes Augustine, "and not the rock *(petra)* from Peter; in the same way Christ does not come from the Christian, but beginning from Christ we speak of the Christian. . . . 'It is upon myself, the living Son of God, that I will build my church. I will build you upon me, and not me upon you'" (*Sermon* 76, I, 1; PL 38/479).

103. From the ecclesial reading of Matthew 16:17-19 there thus emerge three dimensions in the church's confession of faith:

- A communal dimension: the whole church confesses its faith in Christ;
- A collegial dimension, manifested in the college of the apostles who, receiving a power that is equal to that of Peter, are also established as foundations of the church;

- A personal dimension, manifested in the person of the apostle Peter, who expresses the faith of the whole church and is established as foundation and source of the unity ("*origo unitatis*," says Cyprian[63]) of the church in its confession of faith, and first among the Twelve.

Following the Separation of the Churches

104. We note that the separation of Christians led the churches to favor, sometimes in an exclusive way and often in a polemical context, one or other dimension of this interconnected and complementary set of meanings. The text of Matthew 16:17-19 was a focal point for the more or less unilateral choices around which divergent lines of interpreting the New Testament were established.

105. The Catholic Church, always concerned to justify the ministry of the Bishop of Rome, saw in the rock upon which Christ built his church the very person of Peter the apostle and the bishops who succeeded to the see of Rome in an almost exclusive way. The words of Jesus to Peter in Matthew 16 were thus linked to those of Luke 22:32: "I have prayed for you that your own faith may not fail; and you, when once you have turned back, strengthen your brothers"; and to those of John 21:16-17: "Feed my lambs." The figure of Peter in the New Testament stands out in a privileged manner in this group of texts.

106. The Orthodox churches read in the text of Matthew 16:17-19 either the confession of faith of the church, or the apostle Peter as representative of all the apostles and thus of all the apostolic sees, or again of every believer who is steadfast in faith. The institutional value of the text is recognized for the succession of bishops to the Twelve, but not for founding a special primacy of the Bishop of Rome.

107. The churches born of the Reformation saw in this rock the confession of faith in Christ, and the apostle Peter as the first among those who confess their faith in Christ. They denied any institutional significance of this text for the "successor" of Peter, reacting against the claims of the Bishop of Rome. In the same way, they held that what was said to the disciples in

---

63. Cyprian, Letter 73, in *Letters (1-81)*, 7, p. 272; "The Unity of the Church," *Treatises*, 4, pp. 98-99.

Matthew 18:18 was addressed to the Christian community in general. This reading is linked to an interpretation of Ephesians 4:5: "one Lord, one faith, one baptism," which sees unity in faith and baptism as a sufficient basis for the communion of the whole body. Likewise, these churches, in a sometimes polemical manner in relation to the Catholic insistence on Peter, underline the role of Paul as witness to the freedom of the gospel and as one who was capable, when necessary, of openly opposing Peter (Gal. 2:11).

B. The Dimensions of Unity in the New Testament

108. Confessional readings of a same text — in this case Matthew 16:17-19 — refer us back to the conflicts around which they have progressively solidified. This heritage, which we cannot ignore, reflects our respective presuppositions. However, for some time now this confessionalism has been surpassed on more than one controverted point. Scholars have reexamined the files on Peter, on ministry, and on the unity and diversity of these early theologies with fresh eyes. Need we also enter into the labyrinth of these analyses? Another possible approach would allow us to understand the data of the New Testament in a fresh way without rejecting secular traditions and recent research.

109. Indeed, a presentation of the data, however precise it may be, will not suffice. Everything will depend upon the interpretation one makes of it. As there are several models of unity or communion in the New Testament, one may conclude that this diversity is normative. One could say that for Paul the unity of the churches is expressed by the contribution for the poor; in Acts by the fact that the college of apostles and the elders can decide and legislate for the whole church; in the gospel of Matthew by the universal power of keys that reverts to Peter. The New Testament thus attests to diverse types of unity. Would not a presentation of the ministry of unity in the figure of Peter alone then disfigure and narrowly constrain the richness of these beginnings?

110. These questions are themselves subordinated to the manner in which the New Testament unfolds. Does the New Testament emphasize the diversity of models of unity such that, according to needs, place, and time we are authorized to choose that which best suits us? Or, on the contrary, does

it favor one type of ministry of unity (collegial, individual, or other)? Which New Testament traditions will we take into consideration: the most ancient, because they better reflect the purity of the message? Or those which, attested by the greatest number of witnesses (gospels, Acts, epistles) are more universal and because of this more normative?

111. Today we are all aware of the extreme difficulty posed by these questions that come into play when we attempt to evaluate the interpretation of the texts. Therefore, it will not suffice to present the levels or the means by which unity and communion are expressed according to the different New Testament traditions. It is above all important to consider how the various New Testament data relate to one another and whether we must think in terms of exclusivity or complementarity. That is what we propose to do here.

Each Church, Sign of the One Body of Christ

112. Paul describes the relationship among Christians by a comparison to the unity of a body made up of many members (1 Cor. 12:12f.). Clearly, in this passage the apostle is not only considering the churches in general. The comparison applies first to the church at Corinth to whom his letter is addressed, and which should form one body, the body of Christ. In other words, each church is already fully responsible to convey an image of the body of Christ. Unity is not in the first place or solely linked to the relationship between the churches. It is that which permits the Christians in a given place — Corinth, Philippi, Rome — to be called church, body of Christ. The union of members, sealed by *agape* (1 Cor. 13), the unity of the body, is nourished by the one Bread (1 Cor. 10:17).

Communion between the Churches

113. The diverse churches described by the New Testament are concerned to remain in contact with one another. News is relayed from one community to the next, and this stimulates the faith of other churches and gives them cause for rejoicing (1 Thess. 1:7-9; 2 Thess. 1:4; Rom. 1:8; 16:19; 2 Cor. 8:24; 9:2; Eph. 1:15). The sharing of material resources also strengthens the bonds between the church of Jerusalem and other churches (Rom. 15:26; 1 Cor. 16:1; 2 Cor. 9:13-14). These contributions show that the gentile churches are

animated by the same charity, and that the Spirit is at work wherever the gospel is announced (2 Cor. 8). The good news and the gifts that are sent are perceived as the signs and the normal fruit of a common faith. Whether the initiative for the contribution to the poor comes from the churches (Acts 11:29) or from the apostles (Gal. 2:10), the churches take up the challenge and more than respond to the need. Certain churches take part in this service without being asked (2 Cor. 8:3), while others set a limit on the duration of their participation (2 Cor. 8:10). These exchanges also offer an occasion to send delegates to the other churches (1 Cor. 16:3; 2 Cor. 8:23), confirming the practice of visiting from church to church (cf. Rom. 16:1, 5, 7; Col. 4:12; and, at the end of the epistles, personal salutations that presuppose prior relations among the members of diverse communities).

114. Such is the evidence of the Pauline epistles concerning the churches founded by the apostle to the Gentiles. Nothing is said there with regard to the eventual exchange of letters with other churches (Antioch, Alexandria, etc.) but one may reasonably conclude that these existed. As well, little is said concerning the relationship between the Jewish-Christian and gentile communities. All the same, Paul perceived the importance of the issue of communion between the churches because it concerned the credibility of the gospel.

115. Although Paul viewed the contribution towards the needs of poorer churches as a duty for the gentile communities (Rom. 15:27), he did not, however, say that the church of Jerusalem was more responsible for unity or had any precedence over the others. In the first chapters of Acts, the church of Jerusalem nevertheless appears as a mother church, from which missionaries, delegates of the apostles, and decrees go forth. It is to Jerusalem that envoys return after a mission and where one journeys to visit Peter and the apostles (cf. Acts 9:26f.; Gal. 1:18f.[64]). Finally, Jerusalem is the place where the apostles and elders gather to examine the question of Christians of gentile origin (Acts 15).

116. In the subsequent chapters of Acts concern is expressed for the brothers, elders, and saints at Jerusalem (21:17f.; 26:10[65]). Yet, compared with

---

64. Even if Paul insists that he is late in going up to Jerusalem to show that the gospel was revealed to him directly by God and not transmitted by the apostles, he cannot avoid going there.

65. Acts 18:22 could also be an allusion to the church at Jerusalem.

Acts 1–15, these rare references are somewhat surprising. The redactor no longer describes Jerusalem as the see of the leading church, but as the place where Paul suffers his passion in a manner similar to the passion of the Lord. Does this mean that Jerusalem is no longer charged with the unity of the churches and that this role would be undertaken by Rome, to which Paul, a prisoner, seems mysteriously sent? The second part of Acts does not provide a response to this question. It is more concerned with the paradox of the spread of the gospel thanks to the passion of the apostle. Elsewhere in the letters of Paul we find allusions to the control that certain Judaizing missionaries from Jerusalem wished to exercise (1 Cor. 9:1f.; 2 Cor. 11:5, 13; 12:11f.; Gal. 1:9; 5:2; 6:12; Phil. 3:3).

117. Did the church of Jerusalem's initial responsibility in regard to unity derive from the historic and symbolic role of the holy city or from the fact that the apostles resided there? Both factors are undoubtedly important. The destruction of the city before the end of the first century could also explain the loss of preeminence by the church that was established there. But nowhere does the New Testament suggest that another church took over the role once played by Jerusalem. The primacy of the church of Peter and Paul, that is to say, Rome, postdates the New Testament.

Communion and Collegiality

118. The interecclesial dimension of communion reveals the vitality of the churches, the truth of the *agape*, the harmony of the body, and the power of the gospel. There is another dimension of the church that we might call collegiality, and which the New Testament presents as one of discernment, supervision, and jurisdiction. It even seems that the redactor of Acts underlines this collegial aspect to show unanimity in decision-making, in other words, the unity that reigns among the disciples of the first generation. This emphasis on unanimity is very clear in some passages (Acts 6:5; 15:22). Yet, quite apart from the theology of the redactor, collegiality appears as an essential element of the communion of the churches.

119. The decision of Jerusalem (Acts 15) is indeed of paramount importance:

- Though convinced of the merit of their position, the different apostles nonetheless accepted that litigious questions be examined and resolved in a collegial manner.

- The object of their decision concerned all the churches: it pertained to the identity of the believing community, in other words, the relationship of the church's Jewish roots to diverse cultures. Was this identity symbolized or not by circumcision and obedience to the ritual regulations?
- The apostolic letter is addressed to all gentile believers everywhere the gospel had spread.

Yet similar gatherings of a universal legislative character did not take place, it seems, except for exceptional circumstances when the identity and unity of the communities were at risk.

120. Thus, in Acts, the collegial dimension pertains to crucial decisions and deliberations, in a turning towards the common witness of faith (second therefore, but not secondary). A text like that of Galatians 2:7-10, which may refer to the same assembly as Acts 15, confirms the importance of unity among the apostles when it comes to discernment and decisions concerning the communion of the churches.

121. One might ask whether the collegial dimension was exercised after the apostles were separated, when they no longer had the occasion to compare their respective experiences so as to ensure better coordination. In any case it remains true that *the* great historical decision of the New Testament was made collectively. It was even necessary that it happen thus, given what was at stake: harmony among the apostles could only enhance the communion of the churches and the obedience of faith.

122. These facts nonetheless give rise to some questions: According to the New Testament do important decisions relating to the communion of the churches have to be taken collectively? Is collegial authority superior to that of each of the apostles and elders? These are modern questions arising from history and conflict, questions that the New Testament does not address.

123. When at the house of Cornelius, Peter is guided by the Spirit without consulting the other apostles (Acts 10). The same Spirit led Paul and Barnabas to judge the circumcision of gentile converts useless, even before discussing it at Jerusalem (Acts 15:1f.). One could give other examples. The grace received by each apostle is essential: it is a dynamism, a strength that

gives rise to new initiatives. Similarly, in a second stage, discernment, reflection, and coordination exercised collegially are equally essential, and led by the same Spirit. Moreover, it is when they are gathered together that the apostles recognize the grace that is given to each one (Gal. 2:7-9). The New Testament therefore invites us to think in terms of complementarity.

The Personal Dimension

124. The collegial dimension of ministry does not suppress the initiative of the different apostles. The letters of James and Peter are addressed to all the churches. Paul sends a letter (Romans) to the Christians of a church that he did not found and speaks of visiting them "so that we may be mutually encouraged by each other's faith" (Rom. 1:12). In the same way, he employs every means to stimulate the fervor of the churches he has founded in support of the collection to meet the needs of the church at Jerusalem. Without oversimplifying, we could say that even though the apostles are spread out in different fields of mission, they nevertheless each and all feel responsible for the communion of the churches.

125. However, the question that has captured the attention of theologians for several centuries (cf. 96-107) is not that of the rapport between the responsibility of each apostle to collegial authority, but rather, that of a primacy within the group of apostles. They have thus looked to the New Testament to discover whether one of the apostles (Peter) had received a special responsibility and authority from the Lord in regard to what we have called the ministry of communion.

126. In recent decades we have seen a multiplication of exhaustive exegetical studies.[66] It would be difficult, even impossible, to summarize them here. Their conclusions remain bound by the argument and the criteria of their initial premises. It is generally admitted that Peter received a special mission from the Lord regarding the people of God, for there are numerous New Testament traditions relating to this apostle. Paul accords him an important place in his letters (1 Cor. 1:10f.; 9:5; 15:5; Gal. 1 and 2),

---

66. Cf. Two excellent studies were published recently: *Peter in the New Testament,* ed. Raymond Brown, Karl P. Donfried, and John Reumann (Minneapolis: Augsburg, 1973); J. J. von Allmen, *La primauté de l'Église de Pierre et de Paul,* Cahiers Oecuméniques, 10 (Fribourg: Éditions Universitaires de Fribourg / Paris: Cerf, 1977), especially pp. 62-79.

the gospels mention him several times, and a text from the early second century (2 Pet.) claims his authority to comfort and guide the churches.

127. Matthew 16:17-19 undoubtedly remains the most controverted passage because it has no equivalent in Mark and Luke, and its vocabulary does not seem to come from Jesus but from a later tradition arising from the Matthean community. We concede today that such an objection is not decisive, for even if the words reflect a later ecclesial context, a special mission could well have been entrusted to Peter by Jesus before or after the resurrection. Neither can we dismiss this tradition because there exists only one witness to it, for according to the same gospel (cf. Matt. 18:18), Jesus does not withhold from the apostles any of the authority that he grants here to Peter. Again the New Testament requires that we avoid thinking in exclusive terms. However, Matthew reveals nothing about the way in which these two authorities can and must relate to one another.

128. Do the words of Jesus in Matthew 16:17-19 apply only to the historical Simon, or do they have any bearing on the church? Do they call for a universal ministry of communion? An *exegetical* analysis of this text alone does not provide a definitive answer to the question. A *theological* reflection on the context of the passage and on the whole complex of New Testament traditions concerning Peter is necessary. It enables us to recognize, in the person and the role of the apostle in these diverse writings, the emergence of an essential component of the ministry of communion. For it appears that Matthew 16:17-19 simply makes official or sanctions an authority whose reality is revealed in other New Testament traditions concerning Peter.

129. Thus, to give an example, more light can be cast on Matthew 16:17-19 by the theological construction found in the sequence of gospel scenes where we find the words Jesus addressed to Peter. Contemporary exegesis commonly admits the symbolic and ecclesial connotation of this group of texts. Before this passage the multiplication of the loaves refers us to the exodus and to the eucharist (14:13-21 and 15:32-39); the episode with the Canaanite woman symbolizes the salvation of the Gentile (15:21-28); the sign of Jonah announces the passion of Jesus (16:1-4). In subsequent passages the question about Elijah refers us to John the Baptist (17:10-13); the episode of the temple tax (17:24-27) has a symbolic meaning, since Jesus indicates to Peter, representative of all pastors, the relationship that the church should have with the authorities of the world. It is within this complex group of texts

that one can come to some conclusions concerning the figurative significance and ecclesiological value of Matthew 16:17-19.

130. Still, even when one accepts the ecclesiological value of the passage, it
leaves untouched the problem of the form of the ministry of communion
that might be called for. Numbers 96–107 of this study identified three
lines of interpretation — collegial, communal, and personal — which are
not mutually exclusive. The texts, like their early interpretations, invite us
to reject simplistic oppositions.

131. Moreover, the Johannine tradition reveals that the special mission entrusted to Peter does not exclude other personal charisms. The fourth gospel provides an example in the bond established between Peter and "one of
his disciples — the one whom Jesus loved" (chapters 13, and especially 20
and 21). At the discovery of the empty tomb and Jesus' appearance on the
shore of the Sea of Tiberias the primacy or seniority of Peter is affirmed,
but it is completed by the charism and vision of faith of his companion
(20:6, 8; 21:7-8). Further on, are not the words of Jesus concerning the des-
tiny of he who is called to "remain" until the Master comes (21:22-23) an
indication that, together with the authority of Peter, the Risen One established another permanent charism in his church — the spiritual precedence of the vision? This is not to be confused with pastoral authority, nor
does it contradict such authority. Yet it stands in a relationship of necessary tension to the pastoral authority.

132. The New Testament does not claim to say everything about the organization of the early communities, nor about the forms through which communion is experienced. But it does express the essential components of that
communion. We have attempted to recall these and to underline them.
Without them the unity of the church would become but an empty word.

III
Proposals for Confessional Conversion *(Metanoia)*

A. Proposals for the Catholic Church

133. The ministry of communion and of unity has always had a prominent
place in the Catholic Church. The role inherited by the Bishop of Rome is

traditionally the keystone of this ministry. That which constitutes a charism belonging to the Catholic Church ought to become a gift for all Christians with the restoration of full communion. We consider a genuine conversion of its form and exercise an absolutely necessary prerequisite to such a ministry being accepted by our brothers and sisters as a necessary element of ecclesial structure. We are, indeed, heirs of a historical evolution in the course of which concern for unity became a factor in the promotion of uniformity, where the service of communion led to an exaggerated centralization of the church, and where the personal role of the pope has obscured other forms of the unique ministry of communion.

134. We are mindful that the required *metanoia* must involve the mentality of all the faithful of the Catholic Church. We have not forgotten this need even as we center our reflection on the complementary institutional forms of the ministry of communion. The conversion of the Catholic Church will involve maintaining a balance among the *communal, collegial,* and *personal* dimensions of the ministry. The latter dimension cannot be exercised in truth unless it is supported by the other two.

The Communal Dimension

135. Communion among Christians is first of all the work of the Holy Spirit who converts our hearts and fills them with love and charity. The Spirit of Christ gathers us in one body and makes us brothers and sisters. Visible signs of communion are the fruits of the action of that same Spirit and are at the service of the Spirit's activity. The best institutional guarantors prove ineffective if they are not born by the spirit of communion, fruit of the one Spirit. Our way of living in the Catholic Church ought to manifest a greater confidence in the action of the Holy Spirit.

136. The communion of the universal church rests upon the dynamic of communion that dwells in the particular churches. Human weakness often leads to the development of centrifugal tendencies among them, to which the see of Rome responds by centralizing activity. Quite to the contrary, concern for the communion of the particular churches among themselves and with Rome ought to permit a real decentralization of responsibilities in the universal church. We need to experience this double movement of conversion.

137. The communion of the people of God is also operative through the bonds that unite the local churches. This network of bonds of charity constitutes the living fabric of the seamless garment. As in the early church, we see today the development of numerous spiritual and material exchanges among churches near and far. Through these exchanges an ecclesiology of communion, the legitimacy of which is recognized fully by Vatican II, is already being experienced. However, this ecclesiology has yet to find its proper expression within the Catholic Church and to develop corresponding levels of responsibility rightly suited to it, while respecting legitimate diversities.

138. The communal dimension of communion in the universal church requires that the laity, because of the common priesthood of believers, participate more and more in initiatives and responsibilities in the whole body of the church. Such participation would be preferable to the "ultramontane" attitude that leads certain laypeople to appeal directly to Rome, going above their bishops and sometimes against them.

139. Recent devotion to the person of the pope, characteristic of the Roman Catholic Church, is not without an evangelical significance if understood as a call to apostolic obedience in view of submission to the Word and docility to the Spirit. Pastors have a duty to see that it is understood and lived in this sense. Does not the proud and humble language of a Laberthonnière on this subject find a hearing in every Christian heart? "If those charged with the guidance of the church are saints, God knows, and if they are geniuses, posterity will say so. In the meantime, they are for us through their very humanity, even though weak, like all humanity, much more than saints and geniuses, since they are the instruments through which the life and the truth of Christ are maintained and circulate in the world to bring unity and harmony. For this reason we spare them neither our deference, nor our respect, nor our submission. By envisaging them at the same time under their human aspect, our deference, respect, and submission cannot miss their mark, and we no longer risk erecting them as idols in the place of the true God, as some have claimed."[67]

---

67. L. Laberthonnière, *La notion chrétienne de l'autorité*, éd. L. Canet (Paris: Vrin, 1955), p. 36. (This text belongs to the manuscript "Dogme et théologie.")

The Collegial Dimension

140. The college of bishops plays a pivotal role in the exercise of the ministry of communion since it "assures and signifies the communion of the particular churches"[68] and all the bishops share in the "solicitude for the universal church" (*Lumen Gentium* 23). In the service of communion every level of episcopal assembly has a role to play.

141. The episcopal conferences are precious instruments of the ministry of communion within their nations and territories. It is our hope that in the future they might become real centers of initiative in the life of the church. To this end, the scope of their competence could be extended, and it would be normal that their decisions, apart from those that are of immediate interest for the common good of the universal church, would have no further need to be confirmed by the Holy See.

142. Historical study has shown that, owing to the separation of East and West, the Catholic Church coincided with the ancient patriarchate of the West or the Latin Church. Because of this the Bishop of Rome has exercised, in a practical confusion, a double responsibility within the church — that of the ministry of communion and that of the Patriarch of the West — in a way that has fostered a growing centralization. Moreover, the intense missionary effort of the Latin Church extended the territory of the Western Patriarchate virtually throughout the entire world, without weighing the consequences. This "abnormal development" compromised the image of the papacy "by confusing it with freakish turgidity."[69]

143. So long as the distinction between these two functions is not made visible in the living organization of the church, the necessity of a ministry of communion exercised by the Bishop of Rome will not be receivable by our Orthodox, Anglican, and Protestant brothers and sisters. Only an internal decentralization of the Catholic Church will give them a concrete perspective on the nature of the commitment that they would undertake in reestablishing the ties of full communion with the Catholic Church.

68. Dombes, "The Episcopal Ministry," no. 46.

69. Louis Bouyer, *The Church of God*, trans. Charles Quinn (Chicago: Franciscan Herald Press, 1982), p. 453.

144. For this reason we hope that the present continental assemblies of bishops might receive, with a canonical recognition, a wide range of competencies in regard to the organization of the churches, the nomination of bishops, the liturgy, catechesis, etc. In this way continental "great churches" would be established as renewed and adapted forms of the ancient patriarchates. Such decentralization, a veritable *metanoia* in relation to the centralizing tendency of the Catholic Church, would be particularly opportune at a time when numerous churches are confronted with the challenges of inculturation.

145. A decentralization of this nature would have to be undertaken in ecumenical dialogue with the Orthodox churches and with a total respect for their patriarchates. If the bonds of full communion were reestablished with the Anglican Communion, the latter might take the form of a new "patriarchate," maintaining its originality. This new face of the church would enable us to seek more favorable solutions were these bonds to be reestablished with the families of Reformation churches.[70]

146. In the same spirit, we hope for a revival of synodal activity at all levels of the life of the church. In particular, we believe that the new institution of the triennial Roman Synod ought to be accorded a wider deliberative competence.

147. In the tradition of the church the ecumenical council has always been a privileged form of the ministry of communion. We believe that it will play an important role, taking on forms and frequencies adapted to new needs in view of rediscovering full communion with our Christian brothers and sisters.

The Personal Dimension

148. The Catholic members of the Groupe des Dombes fully adhere to the church's doctrine of faith concerning the ministry of communion in the universal church that devolves to the Bishop of Rome. With the whole tradition we believe that it is as the Bishop of Rome that the pope exercises a

---

70. We are aware of the inevitable difficulties posed by crossing over territorial and personal jurisdictions. Yet history and the present mobility of men and women in the world have created a state of affairs that must be considered.

rightful ministry in regard to the universal church and that this ministry is necessary to the structure of the church.

149. In a spirit of *metanoia* we would hope that the dogmatic expression of this ministry given since the First Vatican Council, which deeply offends the Christian sensibility of our separated brothers of East and West, will be replaced by an official and updated commentary, even a change of vocabulary, more consistent with an ecclesiology of communion. The early tradition of the church gives evidence of a similar effort to unceasingly improve the language of faith and to "correct" it, if need be, by expressing it according to balanced perspectives.

150. In the same spirit we also hope for a renewal of the concrete face of the papal ministry of communion. The distinction invoked above [between the ministry of communion and that of the Patriarch of the West] would contribute powerfully to such a renewal, with the creation of great continental churches that enjoy considerable autonomy. We also recommend a recovery of the honor of the exercise of the ministry of the Bishop of Rome in his particular church. A pope assuming greater episcopal responsibility in the place where he is held to and qualified to exercise authority would undoubtedly contribute to an important change in the image of the papacy. He would stand as a true Pastor, the servant and guide in solidarity with his brothers in a common ministry of *episcopē*.

151. We do not wish in any way to see an impoverishment or a weakening of the personal ministry of communion in the universal church. Out of respect for those who have exercised it in the past, in the present, or in the future, we desire that it become a more transparent sign of the gospel. This ministry must remain a force of initiative, proposing and supporting all the churches as they face the challenges of the present world or the pressures of certain powers.

B. Proposals for the Churches of the Reformation

152. The churches born of the Reformation each and all confess their faith in "the holy, catholic church." Yet they are not yet in a position to say clearly and to manifest on a universal level this "catholicity" of the church in a visible way. This results from the fact that they are tributaries of a con-

tentious history that accentuated the confessional character of each group. It is also due to the historical fact that only the Roman Catholic Church has claimed the primacy of the Bishop of Rome as sign and expression of the universality of the whole church. At the outset, the Reformation did not envisage the establishment of separated churches. For this reason it did not consider the question of visible unity at the universal level. When communities were "set up" through the preaching of a rediscovered gospel, concern for visible unity was concentrated at the local and regional levels. The universal church, an object of faith, was understood as a purely spiritual reality that did not seem to require a particular structure. On the other hand, this concern was manifested when emigration overseas and missionary expansion brought separated Christians together. In the twentieth century, the ecumenical movement emphasized this new awareness of the universality of the church in the Reformation churches and of the need to provide it with visible structures.

153. The true catholicity of the church began when the repentance of some led to that of others in order that, under the impulse of the Holy Spirit, together we might give a concrete witness to our conversion to Christ, head of the church and source of any rediscovered communion. To the extent that the church of Rome today, renouncing the privileges of a primacy of power and of centralization, intends to commit itself in the path of a primacy of service and of unity in faith, its attitude of *metanoia* will put a crucial question to all churches — one that none can escape.

154. To give consistency to this common desire to inaugurate a new era of the whole church's "catholic" visibility, we recommend that three approaches should be developed:

- At the communal level;
- At the collegial level;
- At the personal level.

155. *At the communal level,* the World Council of Churches partially expresses the desire for a "conciliar fellowship" of the member churches. But the risk remains that this locus of dialogue does not sufficiently engage the various separated churches. The basis of the World Council of Churches is embryonic and still far from a veritable confession of faith. Its decisions are but proposals, and the member churches do not feel bound to one an-

other in an organic manner. In other respects, the gathering in confessional alliances at a worldwide level represents real progress so long as it avoids the double risk of remaining a simple fraternal association or, on the contrary, of provoking a hardening of positions along confessional lines. If such were the case, *rapprochement* with the Catholic Church and the Orthodox churches would suffer. Bilateral and multilateral dialogues are important signs of progress and invite churches born of the same tradition to persevere in cohesion and openness.

156. *At the collegial level,* the presbyterian-synodal system that characterizes most of our churches has developed an experience of collegiality to which they are particularly attached. This experience has been lived in a positive fashion with the participation of diverse ministers and responsible members of the faithful. But the emphasis upon this form of collegiality has sometimes caused the communal and personal exercise of the ministry of communion within our churches to atrophy. Congregational and charismatic tendencies have developed in reaction to this deficiency, often in an anarchical manner. These movements arose in response to a legitimate need. Our desire for *metanoia* must therefore take into account the spiritual necessity for a harmonious development of communal, collegial, and personal expressions in the very midst of the structures of communion that have developed at the local and regional levels of our churches.

157. *At the personal level,* the experience of the ministry of Word and sacraments in the local church and that of presiding at assemblies and councils offers a presentiment that every visible expression of the universal church calls for a ministry of communion. The churches of the Reformation should examine themselves concerning the reasons that prevent them, at present, from conceiving of and recognizing such a ministry exercised for the benefit of the communion of the whole church.

158. Certain dialogues among Lutherans, Anglicans, and Catholics have deepened our reflection on the personal form of a ministry of communion in the universal church. Do the Reformed churches not need to consider the question of this personal ministry in a manner that testifies to their particular heritage while at the same time being open to the perspective of this ministry? Assuming this were the case, such a ministry would meet the following ecclesiological requirements:

- This ministry can only be assumed in a vigilant obedience to the Word of God. The minister of communion ought to be freely reminded of that Word through the fraternal exhortation that is the responsibility of every minister and every member of the faithful in the church.
- This ministry of universal communion can only exist on the basis of the exercise of a ministry of personal *episcopē* in a particular church that gives it its communal dimension.
- This ministry must be exercised in a collegiality that is expressed in councils, synods, and mutual consultation where not only the *episcopoi* are represented, but also presbyters, deacons, and the laity.
- When freed of the pressures that might be unduly brought to bear, this ministry would ensure the role of arbiter in the episcopal collegiality and in conciliar assemblies, a responsibility of universal *episcopē* to stimulate unity among the particular churches, and a prophetic service to open new perspectives for the church.

159. The whole people of God is called to rediscover the path of communion that occurs first in the places where we ordinarily live and express our faith, worship, witness, and service. Concrete signs of this communion are already being expressed through a progressive symbiosis of ecclesial life at the local level. It is here that, despite the weight of heartbreaks and historical divisions, the ecclesial fabric is slowly being reestablished through frequent communal celebrations, through hospitality and a practical recognition of ministries, through sharing in a concerted service for justice and peace, and through genuine spiritual exchange. Here authentic communion is manifested and deepened. By persevering in this path we mean to give substance and a face to our *metanoia*. Then it will cease to be a pious intention that is belied by the facts. What good, indeed, would be the convergence of our common efforts in biblical, patristic, historical, and diaconal studies if they were not applied in the will and the capacity to live together among Christian communities who cannot be churches of Christ without one another?

160. In order to persevere on the path that we set before ourselves, we recommend that the proposal elaborated in 1976 by the Groupe des Dombes for a revalorization of the episcopal ministry be taken up again. What has become of it? Has not our search for a diversification of ministries, useful as it may be, obscured the necessary rediscovery of the episcopal ministry without which this diversification will inevitably lead to a scattering of the

community? The hour has come to recognize the necessity of this rediscovery that surpasses confessional barriers. "We cannot be satisfied with
an evolution towards an institutional parallelism. The institutions must
tend towards the advent of a single *episcopē* in the one church. Our full
communion depends on it."[71]

161. Each particular church is the church in its fullness. This is why we cannot have two ecclesiologies, one for the local church, and another for the
universal church. To consider the local church as a mere fragment of the
universal church and the universal church as a pyramid where the structure of the base is reproduced at the summit would make no sense. It is in
communion with all the others that each local church is the church in its
fullness. This communion calls for a communal, collegial, and personal
ministry of communion.

162. This effort of clarification and proposal seeks ways to develop structures of communion in our churches with realism and imagination according to the three communal, collegial, and personal perspectives whose
merits we all have come to recognize. We intend to pursue this effort in fidelity to our ecclesial traditions submitted to the authority of the Word of
God, loyal to our companions on the road, attentive to what the brothers
and sisters with whom we are not yet in full communion say and live, and
above all with an attitude of listening to what the Spirit is saying to the
churches today.

A Final Wish

163. Must we await the hoped-for moment of full communion before de-
siring the convocation of an assembly where the qualified representatives
of the Catholic Church and the churches belonging to the World Council
of Churches could meet? Such a gathering would undoubtedly not be
given the name of council. Nonetheless, according to the tradition of the
universal church, which confirms that a conciliar assembly constitutes a
"privileged form of the ministry of communion" (no. 147), we believe that
with the aid of the Holy Spirit, such an initiative would not only be beneficial for ecumenical progress, but would be in conformity to the will of Jesus Christ for the unity of his church.

71. Dombes, "The Episcopal Ministry," no. 77.

164. The program for such an assembly would take into account the numerous works, inquiries, and agreements that have already been undertaken and brought to a conclusion in different regions and at various levels. By gathering them together and in conferring its seal upon them, this assembly would recognize a certain number of milestones and allow us to clearly establish the progress realized to date.

165. Our study of the ministry of communion in the universal church draws a spiritual and pastoral portrait of the Bishop of Rome such that, if he were to convoke such an assembly together with the World Council of Churches, he would be faithful to his ministry as a servant of unity. If such a call were to receive a hearing, we bless the Lord.

> *The skeptical world, and also millions of members of our churches, will not take us really seriously until the World Council of Churches and the Catholic Church speak and act together in the name of Christ, to bring new hope to a world threatened by absurdity, self-destruction, violence, and poverty.*

> W. A. Visser 't Hooft
> *SOEPI*, no. 26, 12 August 1985

For the Conversion of the Churches (1991)

—⊷⟨⟩⊶—

Introduction

1. In February 1937 the Abbé Paul Couturier, supported by the Abbé Laurent Rémillieux, founded the Groupe des Dombes together with Rev. Richard Bäumlin. The aim was to set up a cell for prayer and doctrinal work among Roman Catholics and Protestants. Thus the Groupe des Dombes received its distinctive vocation: to look in prayer and dialogue for paths of convergence that would enable our churches to be reconciled with each other and arrive at unity in faith.

2. During its fifty years of existence, the Group has made an experiment in common life, listening to each other and sharing doctrinal and pastoral concerns, seeking to open itself to the best of its ability to the inspiration of the Holy Spirit. The requirement of conversion, which was already present in the Abbé Couturier's spiritual purpose, was not only a hope or a hypothesis but was becoming an experienced reality and a movement of the spirit and the heart that was leading us to new discoveries. At the same time we were becoming aware that the conversion of the churches that are at present divided is an urgent necessity of the Christian faith.

3. Three major stages in the life of our Group have revealed the progress of the attitude of conversion. In an initial stage the Group lived in a situation of face-to-face encounter, accepting in mutual goodwill one another's wit-

ness to the faith. We were thus led to walk side by side, which made it possible to work out a joint comment on some points of our doctrinal controversies.[1] Thus the very development of this conversion dynamic has enabled us to set out together whole chapters of ecumenical theology testifying to growing doctrinal reconciliation.[2] In this way we have experienced a real "ecumenical communion."

4. It is because we have experienced the fruitfulness of the act of conversion, like many other ecumenical groups, that we have been anxious to include it in our documents and let our readers share it. And so we have regularly created our documents on the basis of patterns of doctrinal conversion. As we wanted to embody — to incarnate — the results of our convergences in the life of the churches, we have often ended our documents with invitations for the conversion of our respective churches.

5. At the end of this half-century our Group has felt the need and necessity to reflect on the theological foundations of the experience of conversion. At the same time several churches were raising with us this crucial question: Would the step of conversion you are proposing not tend to the impoverishment, even loss, of our respective confessional identities? In experiencing this conversion can the churches be faithful to the faith they have inherited? We have been deeply aware of this important concern, and the question has been at the center of our work on this new document.

6. But to speak of conversion at once causes resistance. Some kinds of resistance are due to problems of conscience, because of the necessary faithfulness to the confession of faith that each of us has received from our churches. Others are spontaneous, very human instances of psychological reluctance, caused by fear of losing our familiar religious landmarks. All of us are more inclined to look for the conversion of others than to work on our own.

---

1. See the series of theses prepared by the Group from 1956 to 1970 in *Pour la communion des Églises: L'apport du Groupe des Dombes* (Paris: Centurion, 1988), pp. 11-34.

2. See the five documents produced from 1971 to 1985 (included in this volume): "Towards a Common Eucharistic Faith," "Towards a Reconciliation of Ministries," "The Episcopal Ministry," "The Holy Spirit, the Church, and the Sacraments," and "The Ministry of Communion in the Universal Church." Original French versions in *Pour la communion des Églises.*

7. What, then, is our Group's function? It certainly does not involve authority. The Groupe des Dombes, aware of its private nature, knows that its work has only the value that the churches are willing to grant it.

Our role is rather in the nature of witnessing, summoning, and exhorting. In committing ourselves to the path of conversion and reconciliation we hope to encourage those who read our documents and their churches to contribute to this genuine process of "spiritual emulation," which, together with missionary urgency, lies behind the whole contemporary ecumenical movement.

8. We must begin by stating the conviction that was the object of our discovery and underlies all the proposals that follow. Far from excluding each other, identity and conversion call for each other: there is no Christian identity without conversion; conversion is constitutive of the church; our confessions do not merit the name of Christian unless they open up to the demand for conversion.

*   *   *

9. We will develop our argument as follows:

First of all we shall clarify some basic terms: Christian, ecclesial, and confessional identities; Christian, ecclesial, and confessional conversions. We shall thus suggest a certain linguistic convention necessary to make clear what we have in mind.

Second, some historical soundings will correspond to four aims:

- to show that the church throughout its existence has known movements of reform and conversion that really are part of its self-awareness;
- to record the benefits from these conversions as well as the failures, mistakes, or instances of inflexibility they may have occasioned;
- to facilitate a common reading of our history, which is necessary to heal the wounds of our common and divided past;
- to discover in this way the road to conversion, which can result in full visible communion.

We have always been conscious of the need to be guided by the witness of Scripture. That is why the hymn addressed to the Philippians appears as the epigraph to our document. The very nature of our work, however, made us decide to appeal formally to Scripture only *at a third stage,* in the shape of a theological rereading and a process of verification. These will enable us to make the point that the requirement of a conversion that is necessary for identity finds its roots, as well as its models and norm, in God's self-revelation in the life of his people.

A fourth and last stage will bring out some key points of the conversion (*metanoia*) that awaits the churches today.

PART I
Identity and Conversion: Clues for a Terminology

I. Some Paradoxes on Identity in General

10. Anthropologically speaking, an identity is a living reality: it is a concrete expression of continuity and change. On the one hand, our identity always has to do with our origins. Our identity card or passport carries the name and surname we have received from our parents. Our birth certificate defines us as the son or daughter of such and such a person. Thus identity refers back to a history that precedes us; it makes us what we are in advance of ourselves. It also initiates a continuity through time: we live out our personal identity by taking on our original identity and all the determinants that accompany it, about which we can do nothing.

This continuity, moreover, does not have the static, fixed nature of something that is there once and for all. We have to live on this foundation imposed on us, and we progressively build an identity of our own that transforms our original identity even while respecting it. The harmony in our identity depends on how we manage to incorporate in dynamic unity those elements that have been imposed and those that depend on our freedom.

11. What is true of the individual person applies in a certain way to collective and social identities. In our day we have witnessed a certain disquiet in regard to collective identities. In this unsettled world, where the markers of personal existence and the contexts of social existence are constantly called into question, many no longer know where they are or who they really are. It is possible to speak of an identity crisis in a certain number of social or religious activities. Many react to this crisis by relating once again to the original elements of identity. Genealogical research, requests for regional

and cultural identities, returning to traditional customs, etc. — which are necessary to allow individuals and groups to relate to their history and express what they are — can become regressive if they arise out of the desire for a nostalgic restoration of the past. Thus we are living in a time of vigorous reaffirmation of threatened identities, with all that is positive and negative involved in that. This phenomenon may also assume the significance of a necessary transitional element within a process of healthy adaptation to the modern age.[3]

12. A collective identity is always a paradoxical phenomenon. In fact it embraces a tension between the effort of unification, integration, harmonization, and social interaction (the quest for cohesion among the group members) on the one hand and the effort to differentiate and demonstrate uniqueness on the other hand. The group marks itself out by differentiating itself from the other groups or even by opposing them; in trying to be different it is itself. But this group must also become part of a much larger totality in order to be recognized by the other groups. Such mutual recognition is a necessary element in establishing an identity.

The quest for identity takes place in a journey that never reaches its destination, for this destination is confused with the ideal that the group's aspirations are constantly aiming to achieve. An identity that comes to a halt or becomes rigid is corrupted and ultimately lost. A living identity is never in fact perfected: it is always under construction. Only the future will disclose our identity conclusively.

13. The phenomenon of a quest for the security of our identity is also manifested in the religious sphere. Here the tendency is revealed by a renewal of "integrisms" or fundamentalisms — Muslim, Jewish, and Christian. Christian fundamentalism is spread among the different confessions: Catholic, Protestant, and Orthodox. These forms of fundamentalism have in common a rejection of the ecumenical movement, for that movement seems to represent a fundamental danger to a confessional identity that aims at being hardline and undiluted. The typical feature of all forms of fundamentalism is their clinging to the values and customs of the past, without distinguishing the essential from the secondary. Everything is equally sacralized and absolute; and sometimes the most exterior

---

3. Cf. Marcel Gauchet, *Le désenchantement du monde, une histoire politique de la religion* (Paris: Gallimard, 1985).

aspects, which are inherently also the most transient (dress, details of ritual, etc.), become the symbol of affirming an intransigent and even sectarian identity.

14. This is the standpoint from which we wish to propose a reflection that will define as clearly as possible what we understand by the different expressions of Christian, ecclesial, and confessional identities. It is our conviction here that *conversion is an essential constituent of an identity that seeks to remain alive and, quite plainly, faithful to itself.* For this reason we want to deal with Christian, ecclesial, and confessional conversions as being all part of the same process.

Our reflection may consequently take on the appearance of a kind of lexicon. But attention to the words will not make us forget either the down-to-earth realities we have in view — which differ from one confession to another — or the ecumenical problems this kind of perspective raises.

II. Christian, Ecclesial, and Confessional Identities

a) Christian Identity

15. At first sight it seems difficult to distinguish Christian identity from ecclesial identity. These two expressions really apply to the same concrete reality. But they do so from two different perspectives that deserve special reflection.

16. The term "Christian" expresses the relation that unites the believer to the person of Christ. Thus Christian identity is constituted by an existential confession of faith in relation to Christ, which is enshrined in the trinitarian confession and professed in the church.[4]

17. A supplementary way to express Christian identity is to state the "Christian differentia," i.e., what makes Christianity essentially different

---

4. This Christian identity may be defined in terms of the minimum required to merit the name of Christian. This was how the "basis" of the WCC was worked out, in a formula that was initially christological, then formally trinitarian in order to define which religious groups might or might not become members of the World Council of *Christian* Churches; see no. 130.

from other religions. The difference consists in God's fatherly initiative in communicating himself to human beings by sending his Son Jesus Christ and bestowing his Holy Spirit. Thus the gospel mystery of Jesus, which we contemplate in his human life, his passion, and the Easter event of his resurrection, is part and parcel of the difference.

18. This identity may be understood more comprehensively on the basis of the *symbolum,* creed, or confession of faith expressed in the sacramental celebrations of the church and elaborated in a body of doctrine that concerns not only salvation-history but also the church. We then come up against the delicate question of the "hierarchy of truths."[5] The ecumenical problem arises immediately, for the confessions do not all have the same way of looking at what belongs to full Christian identity.

19. Existentially, Christian identity is not static but dynamic. It is a shifting of the center, an exodus, a transition, a paschal movement. Christian identity is always a Christian becoming. It is an opening up to an eschatological beyond which ceaselessly draws it forward and prevents it from turning in on itself. Thus it is a radical opening up to others beyond all the walls of separation. In its very essence it therefore contradicts the fixed or intransigent need for a secure identity. The existence in the church of the living tradition, which is creative in its very faithfulness, has illustrated this constantly through the centuries.

20. Christian identity does not deny differences. It does not set itself up against others. It respects the identity of others and places its own specific difference in the service of a universal communion.

21. In fact Christian identity is not only dialogue or relationship, it is also service, *diakonia.* Its primary point of reference is the Servant Christ — he who washed the feet of his disciples. Christian identity is operative in acts of service. It is displayed in kenosis ("renunciation" and "self-emptying" — "Seek first the kingdom of God and his righteousness" [Matt. 6:33]), and — we might add — Christian identity will be yours as well.

---

5. Second Vatican Council, Decree on Ecumenism *(Unitatis Redintegratio),* no. 11.

b) Ecclesial Identity

22. While the doctrine about the church is not the ultimate truth of Christianity, nevertheless the church of Jesus Christ has something to do with Christian identity. The fact of the church and the belonging to it of each Christian are aspects of that identity.

This reflection makes it possible to distinguish (without separation) between Christian identity and ecclesial identity. For the church, seen simultaneously as a mystery and a community *(societas)*, awareness of its identity is an awareness that here and now in the midst of the world, in its local congregations, it is the church founded by and on Jesus Christ, who died and rose again. By reason of the gift of the Spirit it is like the irreversible and unfailing presence of the gift God has given of himself to human beings in Jesus Christ. Even if this belief is still the subject of ecumenical debate, it is present in every church.

23. Ecclesial identity is also an eschatological gift. While prior to us as a gift, it is one for which we have to be continually asking. Ecclesial identity thus necessarily sets up a tension between the now, the present, and the future, the goal. No confessional church can be identified as it stands with the church of Jesus Christ. In this sense ecclesial identity is the very goal of the ecumenical movement: "May the church be fully the church!"

24. Putting it differently, ecclesial identity is in labor for catholicity. Every church must become more "catholic" in the original sense of the term: full and universal.[6] The catholicity of all the churches is a wounded catholicity. Thus ecclesial identity opens up a large area for conversion.

25. Moreover, if we take into account the idea of the *ecclesia semper reformanda* ("the church is always to be reformed"),[7] we must acknowledge that the church is the place of an encounter where God's faithfulness and human unfaithfulness cannot be disentangled. This situation creates a certain gap, even a conflict, between ecclesial identity as it is experienced and Christian identity as it is proclaimed. Without the church ever getting out of reach of the promises of salvation, it is vulnerable to the givens of psycho-sociology. It can experience distortions, by-products of its real

6. Cf. no. 204.
7. On the origin of this expression, see no. 117.

identity (partisan forms, a superiority complex, collective sin, etc.). It can always — as a body and in each of its members — become obscurantist and even contradict the Christian message of which it is the bearer. There we have an area open for conversion. Ecclesial identity must always place itself in the service of Christian identity.

c) Confessional Identity

26. The distinction between ecclesial and confessional identity is not universally accepted. The different churches spontaneously claim that their confessional identity is ecclesial identity, "full stop." Thus the *Roman Catholic Church* has never understood or defined itself theologically as a confession. It sees itself as that in which the one church of Christ "subsists";[8] it defines itself as the "communion" of that church. It can therefore accept being regarded as one Christian confession among others only from a historical and sociological point of view (in particular from the political standpoint since the sixteenth century).

27. Likewise the *Orthodox Church* claims in its inmost conviction and ecclesial consciousness to be the custodian of and witness to the faith and tradition of the one, holy, catholic, and apostolic church. It considers itself as filling a central place in the world of today for matters relating to the progress of Christian unity. It rejects the idea of the equality of confessions, and what it equates with "confessional readjustment" cannot in its view constitute the unity of the church. In its view, God calls all Christians to the unity of the faith as this is experienced in the mystery and tradition that is within the Orthodox Church.[9]

28. On the side of the churches of the *Reformation,* the term "confession" has a much stronger weight than just a confessional "denomination." "Confession" designates not only a Christian community that presents itself with its own original characteristics among others, but also and especially the confession of faith that seeks to define its ecclesial and Christian

8. Second Vatican Council, Dogmatic Constitution on the Church *(Lumen Gentium),* no. 8.

9. Cf. the report of the third pan-Orthodox pre-conciliar conference in Chambésy (October-November 1986), "L'Église orthodoxe et mouvement œcuménique," *Istina* 32 (1987): 397-400.

identity and expresses itself in a body of "confessional" documents. "Confession" here is therefore the yardstick of a "confessing church" because it refers us to the one subject and object of faith: Jesus Christ. Thus it has normative value. That which is "confessional" in this theological sense then becomes the yardstick for ecclesial and Christian conversion.

29. Confessional identity lies in a specific historically, culturally, and doctrinally located way of living out ecclesial identity and Christian identity. It is the typical "profile" of a group of churches, the common way in which these churches understand their spiritual specificity. Even if this profile undergoes changes in the course of history, a confessional constant remains that resists differences in time and place.

This identity is not only defined by theological characteristics and the marks of ecclesial structure; it also has to do with liturgical life, expressions of personal devotion, and moral stances. Each confessional identity gives special prominence to certain specific aspects of the gospel message and of the "common life" of Christians.

30. To be genuine in Christian terms, a confessional identity must include fullness and universality. These two words must be understood in the sense of the calling, the mission, and the inheritance received from the faith. For each confession is immersed in a tradition that goes beyond its own confessional tradition.

31. But we cannot forget that confessional identities crystallized in history as a result of the occurrence of divisions. Each of the parties doubtless thought it could justify its position for reasons of faith and faithfulness to the original Christian message. Because of this it stressed certain positive elements. But the emergence of these new identities gave rise to certain manifestations of rejection of and aggressiveness towards the way other Christians were living out their Christian and ecclesial identities. These rejections contributed to a certain extent to giving the new identities their public image; and in polemical contexts they reappear to the point of sometimes seeming more crucial than aspects that are properly those of the gospel. The defense of confessional identities has caused wounds, as on living tissue, which are not characteristic of the confession itself, still less of Christianity.

32. The words we use tell us about this reality by distinguishing between "confessional allegiance" [confessionalité] and "confessionalism." Confes-

sional allegiance is the recognition of belonging to a historic church. Ecumenical dialogue requires that the partners should be truly rooted in their own confessions. And it is a good thing that Christians should be grateful for their specific spiritual inheritance and should wish to share it with the members of other confessions in order to enrich the exchanges among different types of Christians. Confessionalism is the hardening of confessional identity into an attitude of self-justification. Confessionalism, also called "denominationalism," withdraws into itself and rejects real confrontation with other confessions or denominations. Without going to this extreme, each, even in ecumenical dialogue, is tempted to safeguard its own identity jealously and to be little open to the share of truth present in its partner.

33. In the history of the ecumenical movement, confessional or denominational identity has sometimes been harshly criticized. Since the Edinburgh missionary conference of 1910, the churches of the third world have vigorously challenged all the "isms" to which Christianity has afforded passage. At the Madras conference in 1938 one delegate declared: "We, the members of the young churches, have no need of your *damnations,* I mean *denominations.*" In 1943 the Archbishop of Canterbury William Temple said: "What is needed is that each of our existing Christian denominations should die in order to rise again in a more splendid form." At the youth conference in Lausanne in 1960, Reformed theologian Johannes Hoekendijk took up the same theme: "There will be no unity until we are ready to die as Reformed, Lutheran, Orthodox in the expectant hope of a resurrection in the presence of Christ, and his one church."

34. Thus confessional identity, even more than ecclesial identity, seems to be mixed. It is a complex of very positive elements and of others that are really negative and marked by sin. In extreme instances, absolutizing the latter features may extend to a contradiction of Christian identity. We know the temptation in some French circles at the beginning of this century that could be summed up in the formula, "Just because we are Catholics does not necessarily mean we are Christians."[10] We may think too of certain socio-political confrontations (Northern Ireland, for example)

---

10. Recall, for example, the tendency of Charles Maurras to contrast Christianity and Catholicism, cf. *Le chemin de paradis, contes philosophiques* (Paris: Flammarion, 1920), pp. xxvii and xxviii.

where confessional identity is used as a powerful emotive lever at the risk of ending up by quite simply contradicting Christian identity and gospel love.

35. Confessional identity must be Christian identity: as such it remains faithful to its truth only insofar as it converts constantly to the gospel. This conversion to the gospel must first of all affect each person's own way of understanding the gospel and living it out. It is also an invitation to take up a different stance towards other confessional groups: not to condemn them, but to treat them as brothers and sisters, to hope for them and in them, to seek mutual understanding, peace, and full communion.

This does not mean an insipid irenicism, for one of the gospel's requirements for Christian fraternity is for fraternal correction (cf. Matt. 18:15).

III. Christian, Ecclesial, and Confessional Conversion

36. In its previous documents the Groupe des Dombes, since 1969, has grouped these three conversions under the term *metanoia*.

In 1976 the document on *The Episcopal Ministry* pointed out that *metanoia* is "a New Testament term currently translated by 'conversion' or 'repentance'. We use it to indicate a change affecting not just interior dispositions and personal behavior, but also the manner in which ecclesial institutions function, and even, if necessary, their structure."[11]

37. The commentary in the document of 1971, *Towards a Common Eucharistic Faith*, already noted in this regard that:

This is for us . . . a step that is at once difficult, demanding and hazardous:

- difficult, because it goes against our natural tendency to defend and justify our own church in any doctrinal discussion;
- demanding, because it is called for by the Holy Spirit and at the same time in full solidarity with our respective churches;
- hazardous, lastly, like every act of faith, which can never escape the snares of the devil, who is always clever at distorting into more or less

11. Dombes, "The Episcopal Ministry," note 1.

masochistic and sterile self-criticism what needs to remain a vigilant combat fought in faith and a plea for mercy fraught with hope.[12]

38. In our documents prior to 1985 we still did not distinguish clearly between ecclesial conversion and confessional conversion. It now seems necessary to deal with three types of conversion: Christian conversion, ecclesial conversion, and confessional conversion. This will be the aim of the following analyses.

a) Christian Conversion

39. Christian identity rests on a basic conversion: "The kingdom of God has come near; repent, and believe in the good news" (Mark 1:15). This conversion is required by the coming and the resurrection of Jesus Christ. Its absolute nature opens onto a process that is never accomplished fully in this world. This conversion to faith is initiated and celebrated in baptism. Thus it includes an "already there" but also a "not yet." It is a grace that opens onto a task. It leads into an existence that must undergo a continual conversion. That conversion is a struggle conducted in grace against all forms of sin, personal and collective. It is celebrated in the proclamation of the Word, and in the sacramental act of reconciliation, as it likewise is in the sacrament of the eucharist.

40. Conversion can take on very diverse forms: a sudden intervention of something new and unheard-of, a slow and continuous progression, the crossing of a series of thresholds. It directly concerns the personality of each believer who is becoming what he or she already is.

b) Ecclesial Conversion

41. Ecclesial conversion has the same content as Christian conversion, but it concerns church members whether collectively or as an institution, as members of the same communion of faith and sharing certain sinful attitudes. Ecclesial conversion is the constant effort of the church community as such to strive towards its Christian identity.

---

12. Dombes, "Pour une réconciliation du ministère: Commentaire," in *Pour la communion des Églises,* p. 70.

42. This effort of the *ecclesia semper reformanda* can experience some moments of decisive significance — *kairoi*. The history of the church has known some of these moments, even if they have not been free from excesses; among them, monasticism in the ancient church, movements for reform in the Middle Ages, the Protestant and Catholic reformations in the sixteenth century, different "awakenings" or revivals emerging from the Reformation churches in the nineteenth century, the profession of faith of the *Bekennendekirche* ("Confessing Church") at Barmen in 1934, the *aggiornamento* or "renewal" desired at Vatican II by John XXIII.

43. Ecclesial conversion is a constituent element of ecclesial identity. When fully and universally achieved, each confessional group will be the church in full recognition of the ecclesial character of the others. There will no longer be partial, incomplete ecclesiality for any, either in its own environment or in that of the others. In particular that means the achievement and recognition of the identity of the church's "structure" in all the confessions. This therefore presupposes general doctrinal agreement on the "structure" of the church (as distinct from the different "organizations," but underlying them and realized in them).[13]

44. This effort at conversion is experienced today in churches that are still confessionally divided. It therefore calls for the effort of confessional conversion, which constitutes one aspect of it. Just as certainly we can imagine the churches helping each other in a common struggle against all the forms of sin that affect them all in their manner of bearing witness to the gospel.[14]

c) Confessional Conversion

45. Confessional conversion relates to the specifically ecumenical efforts achieved by the still-divided churches in trying to regain full communion. It thus represents a particular aspect of ecclesial conversion in the situation of division.

13. Cf. the comments on the difference between "structure" and "organization" in "Le ministère épiscopal: commentaire," in *Pour la communion des Églises*, p. 114.
14. We recognize that the identity and conversion of the Christian churches cannot be isolated from their relation to the mystery of Israel, but this question goes beyond the scope of the present work, which could not have dealt with it as fully as it deserves.

46. Our confessional identities are an inheritance within which we have to apply a discernment based on the gospel in order to gather together all the positive values in the support of the rich diversity of forms in the church and abandon their sinful dimension. They have to be converted. How could our converted identities — which still contain legitimate diversities — *not* lead us to full communion? For confessional identities become a gracious gift from God for the whole church from the moment they enter the common quest for a fullness of truth and faithfulness that transcends them all.

47. All conversions go through the stage of confessing guilt. Our confessions have to "make confession," to move forward to admitting their limitations and inadequacies, even sins. Each confessional family has to acknowledge that there are elements of Christian tradition that it is incapable, at least for the moment, of receiving and incorporating into its own existence.

48. Confessional conversion for its part too is a constituent element of real confessional identity. This requirement of conversion is therefore an invitation to our confessional identities to open up to each other and let themselves be penetrated by the values that the others bear. In particular, each confession must ask itself if its judgment of the others is really founded on the gospel.

49. This presupposes that each confession will acknowledge that there is in itself matter for conversion, for genuine progress in faithfulness to its Christian and ecclesial identity, whether in the sphere of the language of faith or ecclesial structure or in the existential implementation of Christian reality. These conversions will not be symmetrical, because the deficiencies that affect the different churches are not the same.

50. No conversion can be pre-programmed. While it is urgent that each Christian confession should hear this call to conversion, the conversion itself will come unexpectedly. In the strict sense of the term there is no self-conversion; we receive conversion as a grace.

51. Confessional conversion is first of all conversion to the God of Jesus Christ and consequently a fraternal reconciliation among the churches as they seek full communion and full mutual ecclesial recognition — not to

the detriment of confessional identity, but for purification and deepening in line with the gospel.

52. It is along this line that the Groupe des Dombes, in all its documents, has sought to speak about confessional conversion (which it has sometimes also called ecclesial conversion).[15]

d) Balance-Sheet

53. We firmly believe that we can speak of identity and conversion only within a clearly stated linguistic convention. We therefore now summarize the terms we are using.

54. By *Christian identity* we mean one's belonging to Christ, which is founded on the gift of baptism and lived out with a faith nourished by the Word of God — the word that is proclaimed and the eucharistic word. This belonging equally concerns each individual and the church as the people of God.

By *ecclesial identity* we mean the belonging or participation of an individual or of a confessional church in the one, holy, "catholic,"[16] and apostolic church.

By *confessional identity* we mean belonging to a confessional church that comes from a specific cultural and historical context, containing its own spiritual and doctrinal profile, which distinguishes it from other churches.

55. By *Christian conversion* we mean the response of faith to the call that comes to us from God through Christ. This response takes place in a movement [or process] of constant conversion.

By *ecclesial conversion* we mean the effort required from the whole church and from all the churches for them to be renewed and become more capable of fulfilling their mission in accordance with the motto *ecclesia semper reformanda*.

By *confessional conversion* we understand the ecumenical effort by which a Christian confession cleanses and enriches its own inheritance with the aim of rediscovering full communion with other confessions.

15. Cf. no 38.
16. Cf. nos. 24 and 196.

PART II

Examples from History

Introduction

56. To advance our reflection it seemed good to collect historical evidence. This cannot be a matter of going systematically through history, but of taking soundings from some particularly significant records. We shall consider certain notable instances where we see identities being affirmed and efforts at conversion lived out in very diverse situations. Among these conversions some have been successful experiments that have proved fruitful for the unity of the church. Others have produced mixed effects, leaving a gap between the initial project and its reception. Still others, just because of the ambiguities that governed them, have kept alive or even increased the lack of understanding between churches. Whatever the outcome of each of them, these events are for us a mine of learning material, provided they are subjected to a discriminating analysis that is as close to the gospel as possible.

  We shall also collect the testimony of certain great church leaders whose experience may be regarded as typical today. Finally, we shall show how certain themes in the church's reflections on doctrine, from antiquity to our own day, give rise to a "converted" reinterpretation.

I. The Early Church and the Medieval Church

a) Three Examples of Conversion (metanoia) in the Early Church (fourth to fifth centuries)

57. Shortly after the Council of Nicea (325), difficult discussions led Athanasius of Alexandria to recognize as being within the faith of the church those who were uncertain about using a word that was not in Scripture (*homoousios* — consubstantial) to refer to the full divinity of Christ. This was to let it be understood that the ecumenical council had not gone beyond the scriptural evidence to canonize its own terminology.

58. A few decades later, between 370 and 379, Basil of Caesarea was bold enough to defend the divinity of the Holy Spirit but without saying that the Holy Spirit was God. In so doing he judged that abruptly to proclaim

the divinity of the Spirit risked dividing the church and thus grieving the Paraclete himself. It was necessary to avoid the catastrophe of a profession of faith that would end up dividing the church.[17]

59. Following the Council of Ephesus (431), Cyril of Alexandria, realizing that his attitudes had led to a general excommunication, did not hesitate to recognize as perfectly orthodox a theological expression of faith in Christ — that of the bishops of the region of Antioch — to which he had till then turned a deaf ear, thus clearing of any suspicion of heresy their remarkable insistence on the man Jesus in whom the Word dwells as in its temple.[18]

60. Perhaps it needed centuries for the churches to appreciate these three spiritual, theological, and pastoral acts. At all events, encounters of church leaders in the last few years have turned them to good account. Thus, to show just how far one had to go in making sacrifices for the unity of Christians, Paul VI affirmed in dialogue with Athenagoras I on 25 July 1967 that

> love must help us as it helped Hilary and Athanasius to recognize the identity of faith beyond the differences of vocabulary when serious divergences were dividing the Christian episcopate. Did not St Basil himself in his pastoral love defend the true faith in the Holy Spirit by avoiding the use of certain words which, however exact they might be, could turn out to be a stumbling-block for part of the Christian people? And did not St Cyril of Alexandria in 433 agree to set aside the fine theology that was his in order to make peace with John of Antioch, after he was sure that, beyond the different expressions, their faith was identical?[19]

61. The pope's final sentence was echoed on 20 June 1989 by Metropolitan Damaskinos of Switzerland addressing the Coptic Patriarch of Alexandria,

---

17. The Nicene-Constantinopolitan Creed maintains the same discretion as St. Basil regarding the divinity of the Holy Spirit: "We believe in the Holy Spirit, the Lord, the Giver of life, who proceeds from the Father, who, with the Father and the Son, is worshiped and glorified, who has spoken through the prophets."

18. Following the same example in regard to those who rejected the terminology of Chalcedon in the other direction, Paul VI and John Paul II signed with the leaders of pre-Chalcedonian churches christological confessions of faith that do not use the formula of the two natures of Christ. They thus recognize the full orthodoxy of a Christology couched in Monophysite terminology (cf. *Doc. Cath.* 1633 [1973]: 515, and 1880 [1984]: 825).

19. *Doc Cath.* 1499 (1967): 1382.

Shenouda III, in the commission for dialogue between the Orthodox Church and the pre-Chalcedonian oriental churches:

> You have referred to the theology — which we share — of Cyril of Alexandria regarding "one nature of God the Incarnate Word." Our desire and prayer is that his humility and high sense of responsibility may be an example to us. For he did not insist on the priority of his own theology — admirable as it was — in the hope of reconciling himself with John of Antioch in 433, after he had been convinced that, beyond the differences, their faith was the same.[20]

62. These three examples represent an astonishing conversion *(metanoia)*. Besides the fact that they concern bishops whose purpose was the commitment of their community and the communion of the churches, and that what was at issue was the actual expression of the faith in theology and not the kind of free and non-threatening questions raised by a Gregory of Nazianzus,[21] we are in the presence here of the very rule of faith, its solemn creedal expression and its apostolic foundation. What was explicitly at issue in these three instances was the Nicene faith — in the first and third cases the very way in which its terminology about Christ was understood, and in the second the appropriate way of understanding faith in the Spirit.

63. What we are saying is that the church, in its quest for unity, must be open to a renunciation that is not a desertion or a denial or a betrayal but does not limit itself to sacrificing prejudices, habits, or strong emotions. One would have to speak of a conversion of the spirit and not only of the heart. To understand that the theology by which the confessional church to which we belong is not the only one capable of expressing the Christian mystery, even on essentials (Cyril); to know how to be silent or rather how to say what is essential at the appropriate moment, even if not explicitly, so that unity may be upheld or created (Basil); to say that even the best and most carefully chosen words must be the objects of understanding, not veneration, and that they are subject to variation and must therefore be translated both into other languages and into other terminology (Hilary and Athanasius): such would be the conversion of the churches today if they wish to be faithful to the faith in its earliest stages.

20. Quoted in *Istina* 34 (1990): 228.
21. Oration 21, 10; *S.C.* no. 350, *Discours théologiques*, pp. 95-99.

b) The "Conversions" of St. Augustine (354-430)

64. In tackling Augustine's spiritual pilgrimage we are changing the ground a bit. Here it is no longer a matter of ecclesial conversions and decisions but of the personal development of a human being. However, the career of Augustine takes on an ecclesial value, and in the Western church it constituted an exemplary point of reference (even if it included some shadowy elements). In fact, Augustine initiated a new way of undergoing the conversions to which the Christian faith invites us. We shall find these aspects also in many other witnesses of Christianity, especially Luther.

65. The spiritual pilgrimage that led Augustine from unbelief to faith (and we do indeed say from unbelief to faith, not from paganism to the church) is a *conversion to God and to the Christ* of orthodoxy.[22] We see him, a young schoolboy at Madaurus, gradually distancing himself from the faith of his early childhood. We find him again at Thagaste where his year of idleness does not guide him towards God. At Carthage he leads the life of a student for whom spiritual questions hardly arise.

Suddenly he finds philosophy in reading Cicero's *Hortensius*. In it he discovers the vanity of human success and the fundamental importance of the quest for wisdom. "But this book altered my affections, and turned my prayers to Thyself, O Lord; and made me have other purposes and desires . . . and I . . . began now to arise, that I might return to Thee."[23]

66. That search for God was to continue through Manichaeism, the encounter with neo-Platonism, and the preaching of Ambrose. Then Augustine discovered Scripture and the meekness of Christ the mediator who is able to free him from the weight of his sin. Gradually his intellectual doubts dissolve, and he comes to the well-known scene in the Milan garden where his conversion crystallizes. Through a passage of the apostle Paul (Rom. 13:13ff.) he sees the last obstacles fall away. Having become free in order to live in chastity he converted to the God revealed in Scripture:

22. Because Augustine, who from birth was marked with the sign of the cross and tasted of the salt of wisdom (cf. *Confessions* [London: Dent, 1946], I, 11, 17), kept the name of Christ his Savior in his inmost self (cf. *Confessions*, III, 4, 8). But on the eve of his baptism he was unable to have even an inkling of what the mystery of the Logos made flesh contained (cf. VII, 19, 25).

23. *Confessions*, III, 4, 7, p. 36.

"For Thou convertedst me unto Thyself, so that I sought neither wife, nor any hope of this world, standing in that rule of faith. . . ."[24]

But Augustine did not leave it at that. At Cassiciacum he led the studious life of a monk. His writings from that period reveal his state of mind: first and foremost he is a philosopher, but a Christian philosopher. His conversion to the God of Jesus Christ was consolidated, as the *Soliloquia* testify.

67. When we look at this pilgrimage we see that first of all it was a conversion to God: this is the dominant feature of that period in Augustine's life: "And Thou surpassingly art the Self-same, Who *art not changed*; and in Thee is rest which forgetteth all toil, for there is none other with Thee, nor are we to seek those many other things which are not what Thou art: but Thou, Lord, *alone* hast *made me dwell in hope*."[25] There too, however, we find an ecclesial aspect of conversion. The church is present through Monica and the education she has given her son, through the Christian community which intervenes to try to bring Augustine back to the faith, through Ambrose and his preaching, through the meeting with Victorinus. This conversion to God is accompanied *sotto voce* by the motif of a conversion to the catholic and universal church.

68. Moreover, when Augustine was converted, it was not only to the catholic church in the sense of universal, but also to the catholic church in the sense of orthodox. "But somewhat later, I confess, did I learn, how in that saying, *The word was made flesh*, the catholic truth is distinguished from the falsehood of Photinus. For the rejection of heretics makes the tenets of Thy church and sound doctrine to stand out more clearly."[26] In this way the confessional aspect is certainly present in Augustine's pilgrimage, not primarily in the form of a "confessional conversion" as defined earlier, but rather in the form of conversion to orthodoxy. Thus in this first part of Augustine's life, which led him to baptism in Milan in 387, conversion to God, to the church, and to orthodoxy overlap, but with conversion to the God of Jesus Christ predominating: "So I was confounded, and converted: and I joyed, O my God, that the One Only Church, the body of Thine Only Son (wherein the name of Christ had been put upon me as an infant), had no taste for infantile conceits. . . ."[27]

24. *Confessions*, VIII, 12, 30, pp. 171f.
25. *Confessions*, IX, 4, 11, p. 183.
26. *Confessions*, VII, 19, 25, p. 142.
27. *Confessions*, VI, 4, 5, pp. 99f.

69. The second part of Augustine's life, leading from his baptism to the episcopate, is very specially the time of his conversion to the church. That conversion begins with baptism, which brings him into the church. Back in Thagaste in Africa, he lives in community with his friends, this time in a genuinely Christian community. He is increasingly interested in ecclesiastical questions: he is called by the people of God to the priesthood and begins his ministry in the congregation of Hippo. His activities and his theological reflection then give him the opportunity to stress the need for an *ecclesial conversion*.

70. A third period in Augustine's life, that of his episcopate, is marked more by his conversion to orthodoxy. One need only think of the struggles against Donatism and Pelagianism. But the aspect of *confessional conversion* also appears in this same context. In telling the faithful of the "catholic" church that the Donatists are their brothers and that their baptism is that of Christ, Augustine is a genuine ancestor of the conversion of the churches to Christian unity. When he tells Pelagius that by crowning our merits God is crowning his own gifts, Augustine is indicating to the whole church that in its essence it derives from that good pleasure of God which is called mercy.

71. Nevertheless we can trace in this period the presence of two other conversions. *The City of God* is the best witness to that persistence of conversion to God and ecclesial conversion. Augustine opposes polytheism and reaffirms the monotheism of the biblical revelation. In face of the community's perturbation about the future he affirms the enduring nature of the City of God, which continues through the ages to arrive at the kingdom. This time again the three motifs are mixed and interwoven, even if conversion to orthodox catholicity takes first place: "So why, O heretic, do you set aside the question to be debated in order to attack a man? . . . Am I the catholic church? . . . It is enough that I am in it . . . the church known throughout the whole universe is to be found where I was baptized."[28]

72. We draw a double lesson from Augustine's pilgrimage. On the one hand it was the conversion of the church that enabled him to say: "Thou madest us for thyself, and our heart is restless, until it repose in Thee."[29] Augustine

28. On Psalm 36, sermon 3, 19-20; PL, 36, cols. 394-95.
29. *Confessions*, I, 1, 1, p. l.

was converted thanks to a bishop who was faithful to the Nicene faith, in a church renewed by the preaching of the Word. ". . . Thy wonderful works most fully attested . . . wrought in the true faith and the church catholic."[30]

Let us remember on the other hand that his personal conversions gave rise to a dynamic of renewal for the ancient churches of the East and the West[31] and exercised a crucial influence on the Latin Church of the following centuries, and especially on the Protestant Reformers. One could even say of him, fittingly enough, that — like the empire of Charlemagne — he had been somewhat partitioned by his heirs!

c) Identity without Conversion: Theocratic Hardening and the Breach between East and West (ninth to fourteenth centuries)

73. From the ninth to the fourteenth century the assertion of the confessional identities of the East and West increased continually and hardened into differentiation. On each side withdrawal into its own identity and the polemical atmosphere finally called in question the ecclesial character of the other, despite the continuance of many acts of communion and certain sincere quests for unity. In this context evidences of concern for conversion are few in number, fragile, and casual.

74. Both theologically and politically the Gregorian reform at the close of the eleventh century consolidated the Roman identity and its claim to ecclesial primacy. Stimulated by the reforming monastic orders of the twelfth century (for example, that of Bernard de Clairvaux), the reform remedied the anarchy of feudal pluralism in Western Christendom, attacked corrupt *mores* among the clergy, and freed the churches from dependence on the temporal power of the princes. But it did not put an end to the ambiguity represented by the temporal power of the papacy, and its effect was the development of an increasingly authoritarian Roman centralism.

75. The result was the excessive politicizing of the Roman hierarchy and the infiltration of the people of God by streams of lay piety that genuinely cared about reform but were increasingly uncontrolled. The requirement

---

30. *Confessions,* VIII, 6, 14, p. 160.

31. Augustine was the only bishop personally invited by the emperor to the Council of Ephesus, but he died in 430 before it began.

of theocratic uniformity meant that some of these lay movements were rejected by the Roman identity (such as the Waldensians of Lyons and the Lollards in England); others were tolerated (such as the Beguines) or brought into line (like the Franciscan movement, which, however, lost its lay character).

76. With the evolution of papal authority the Latin Church entered the path of legalism and clericalization. Its confrontations with temporal powers led it to see itself too as a power. The papacy was seen as one power alongside the others. The ecclesiology of a vertical catholicity prevailed over that of a horizontal catholicity of the whole Christian people, clergy and laity. The awareness of unity, far from being consolidated by this development, lost what little confidence it had gained in the high Middle Ages under the efforts of the evangelizing monks.

77. The rift between Rome and Constantinople in 1054 — prepared for by a slow, mutual drifting apart of East and West, and aggravated by the excesses of certain crusades — was one of the effects of the Roman claim to a form of ecclesial primacy that was envisaged as a direct authoritarian government of the whole church. Rome affirmed its own identity in an exclusive and intransigent manner; it succumbed to the temptation to make the Roman sacramental obedience the unique and decisive criterion for belonging to the church. Sometimes it seemed that everything was as it should be in the East except obedience to the Roman church; sometimes Rome seemed to think that the Eastern church, separated from it, was no longer the church.[32]

78. The authority of the Roman pontiff was asserted as the principle for the church as the body of Christ. Monarchical in its nature, the Roman identity defined itself as the head, the mother, the pivot, the fountainhead, the foundation of every church. At the beginning of the thirteenth century the Bishop of Rome, having been the "Vicar of Peter," became the "Vicar of Christ." No local congregation could find its ecclesial identity save in relation to the Roman identity because of the institution [of the church] made in the person of Peter.[33] Later attempts at reconciliation, such as those at

32. Cf. Y.-M. Congar, *L'Église de saint Augustin à l'époque moderne* (Paris: Cerf, 1970), pp. 87, 96f.
33. Congar, *L'Église de saint Augustine*, p. 96.

Lyons in 1274 and in Florence in 1439, failed because of the atmosphere thus created between the churches of the East and of the West.

79. In this situation of a breakdown in relations, voices were nevertheless raised in favor of a conversion of the medieval church. In the fourteenth century the desertion of the episcopal see at Rome in the period of the Avignon popes and the struggle between two or even three popes at the time of the great Western schism raised doubts about the genuine ecclesiality of the Roman identity. Great mystics like Mechthild of Magdeburg (c. 1207/10-1282/94), Meister Eckhart (c. 1260-1327), and Catherine of Siena (c. 1347-80) called the papacy and the whole people of the church to ecclesial conversion. Anti-authoritarian ecclesiologies like those of John Wycliffe (c. 1330-84) and Jan Hus (1370-1415) called for such a conversion in reaction against the Roman confessional identity. The question of reform *(causa reformationis)* became a conciliar matter but was constantly put off during the whole fifteenth century and neutralized by the continual rivalry between the authority of the pope and the authority of councils.

80. The church at the close of the Middle Ages became immobilized in that struggle, in which the claims of the Roman identity paralyzed every effort at genuine ecclesial conversion. Bogged down in the abuses of its clergy, incapable of adequately meeting the spiritual needs of *devotio moderna* — which emphasized divine initiative, individual piety, and withdrawal from the world — and concerned to protect its political powers, the Roman church built up internal tensions that were to undermine its unity a century later. Incapable of calling its confessional identity into question, it could no longer prevent the breakup of Western Christendom into separate, diverging churches.

81. Confronted with these new forms of Christianity in the West, the churches of the Byzantine Empire, aware of their continuance in orthodoxy, seem not to have questioned their own identity with the church of the time of the apostles and the fathers. They retained the pride of being the first churches, since the gospel was written in their language and they had welcomed the Savior's message earlier than the others. Hence their lack of interest in and suspicion of what was happening in the world of the so-called Holy Roman Empire and the realms of the barbarians.

82. In the East the major problem was still to protect the Byzantine Empire, where the emperor played an eminent role in the life of the church. Since Constantine, the fate of the church and of the Empire were linked *de facto* and *de jure*. Their relations were understood in terms of the theory of the "symphony [harmony] of temporal and spiritual power" — contrary to the Western theory of the "two swords." Such a situation, extending through the centuries, kept alive the confusions between the two spheres, and continued to contribute to a certain historical immobility and withdrawal into their own identity.

83. For instance, while the origins of the iconoclastic heresy did indeed have a religious basis, its consequences were as political as they were religious. It was as much a state matter as a church matter. In these circumstances religious "reform" depended as much on the emperor as on the patriarch, if not more. Here the reform was always already effected, but unlike the Western reforms, it was made directly at the top by the emperor together with the patriarch. An identity without fissure was consolidated, but it did not open itself up to conversion.

84. Moreover, the ecclesiology of communion, unilaterally understood, was so perfectly orthodox as to be unassailable, but it became so abstract that it no longer had much to do with reality. A gulf was created between the vagaries of history and the theology that was enunciated. The great danger of this state of affairs is to shut oneself up in a theology that is so perfect at the level of language that it makes the idea of ecclesial and confessional conversion difficult. But this rejection of conversion now contradicts the great Orthodox tradition itself, which has always stressed the solidarity of orthodoxy and orthopraxis.

85. Our reading of these five centuries may seem harsh. Of course that period is not limited to what we have said about it. There were a number of personal conversions, and movements of evangelism and spirituality blossomed, especially the Franciscans and Dominicans in the West and hesychasm in the East. Church institutions as such, however, lacked an attitude of conversion during this period. Consequently the best efforts of conversion were condemned to be bogged down. The continual deterioration of the situation was responsible for the explosions and divisions of the sixteenth century.

d) Balance-Sheet

86. The history of the early and medieval church enables us to verify the functioning of the categories of *Christian, ecclesial,* and *confessional* conversion and identity that were identified, and distinguished from each other, in the section titled "Clues for a Terminology." It testifies to genuine conversion experiences that can inspire us even today. It also reveals that in some instances a hardening in relation to identity clearly hindered or excluded the fundamental movement of conversion.

87. The various types of conversion may appear simultaneously and then bear witness fully to conversion in terms of the gospel. Often, too, one of the three dimensions has a dominant position for a time, but in such a way that the two other dimensions are also present and discernible.

II. The Church at the Beginning of the Modern Age

a) The Protestant Reformation

Two Calls for Ecclesial Conversion

88. In his spiritual pilgrimage, the vigor of his theological thought, and the passion of his reforming activity, Martin Luther (1483-1546) incontestably represents an essential element in this great movement for conversion that appeared in the sixteenth century. He underwent "a crucial experience, a sudden illumination, a liberating discovery, a new understanding of the righteousness of God."[34] The debate that set him in opposition to the Roman authority and led to his excommunication related to fundamental problems of the faith like justification; but in the light of recent historiography one may wonder whether "the real breach is located in relation not to soteriology but to ecclesiology."[35] The ecclesiological consequences of Luther's challenge were not slow to appear, as the great treatises of 1520 attest (cf. "Address to the Christian Nobility of the German Nation" or "A Prelude Concerning the Babylonian Captivity of the Church").

---

34. Marc Lienhard, *Martin Luther, un temps, une vie, un message* (Geneva: Labor et Fides / Paris: Centurion, 1983), pp. 383, 388.

35. Lienhard, *Martin Luther,* p. 394.

Caught in that tension between the demands of the gospel on the one hand and his concern for the church and its authority on the other, Luther dedicated his "Freedom of a Christian" to Pope Leo X in October 1520, addressing an urgent appeal to him for ecclesial conversion:

I have . . . turned my heart away from Your Holiness so little that I have constantly formed all the best of wishes for you and for your Holy See. With what zeal have I not prayed for that and with what groans have I not asked God for them to be granted! . . . In fact, allow me to tell you straightforwardly that I am not aware of having spoken of you other than in the most exalted and best of terms on every occasion when I have had to mention you. If I had acted otherwise I could only thoroughly disapprove of myself. . . . It is true that your fame . . . is too renowned and august, not to mention your life, which is without blemish, to be called in question in any way and by anyone, even the most highly placed. . . .

On the other hand, I have constantly and violently attacked impious doctrines and have been not a little scathing towards my opponents, not because of their bad behavior but because of their impiety (their opposition to the gospel). . . . For the rest, I have not entered into argument with anyone regarding their conduct. It is simply a question of the word of truth. On any other point I am happy to yield to anyone you wish, but the word I neither can nor desire to renounce or deny. . . . There is no one for whom that is not clearer than daylight: the Roman church, formerly holy among all the churches, has become a den of thieves, overflowing with license, a house in which debauchery flaunts itself more than anywhere else. . . . Is it not true that under our vast heavens there is nothing more corrupt, more pestilential or abhorrent than the Roman Curia? . . . I was so far removed from anger against your person that I hoped to win your favor and stand by your side for your salvation by attacking your prison, not to say your hell, with all my strength. . . . Moreover, I cannot tolerate that the Word of God should be subjected to the laws of our interpretations, for what matters is that the word should not be bound — the word which teaches in perfect freedom. . . . Beware, therefore, Leo, my Father, of paying heed to the sirens who make you something more than an ordinary man — almost a god . . . , you are the servant of those who serve and no one in the world is in a more pitiable and dangerous situation. Do not let yourself be seduced by those who make you the master of the world and who do not allow that anyone can be a Christian without your approval. . . . Those who recognize the interpretation of Scripture as being solely your responsibility are in error. They are only seeking to install all their impieties in the church under the guarantee of your name.[36]

89. Echoing that appeal by Luther is another one, equally urgent, which came from Pope Adrian VI, successor of Leo X. The statement he told his legate Chieregati to make to the delegates of the imperial Diet meeting in Nuremberg in 1523 is inspired by the same concern for ecclesial conversion:

We freely acknowledge that God has permitted this persecution of the church because of human sins, and especially those of the priests and prelates; for it is certain that the hand of God is not shortened, that he could save us, but that sin separates us from him and prevents him from listening to us. Holy Scripture teaches us throughout that the faults of the people have their origin in the faults of the clergy. . . . We know that, even in the Holy See, for years many abominations were committed: abuse of holy things, transgression of the commandments, so that everything has become a scandal. We need not wonder that sickness has come down from the heads to the members, from the popes to the prelates. All of us, prelates and clerics, have turned aside from the path of righteousness. It is long enough since anyone has done what is good; this is why we must all glorify God and humble ourselves before him; each of us must examine how he has fallen, and examine himself more strictly than God will examine him in the day of his wrath. Consequently . . . we shall devote ourselves wholly to making a start by improving the Roman Curia from which all the evil has perhaps come; from it will come the cure, as from it came the sickness. We consider ourselves committed all the more to do so as the whole world is hungry for such a reform.[37]

36. *Reformation Writings of Martin Luther,* vol. 1 (London: Lutterworth, 1952). Translation here by J. Greig.

37. Cf. Louis Pastor, *Histoire des papes,* IX (1913), pp. 102f.; *Histoire des conciles œcuméniques,* vol. 10: *Latran V et Trente,* 1 (Paris: Orante, 1975), pp. 168f. Pope John Paul II adopted the words of Pope Adrian VI in his speech to the Lutheran bishops of Denmark on 6 June 1989, *Doc. Cath.* 1988 (1989): 689.

Ecclesial Identity and the Emergence of the Confessional Churches

90. The appeals of Luther and Adrian VI, issued in the early years of the divisive sixteenth-century reforms, fell on deaf ears. From 1530 — the Protestants were obliged by the emperor to submit confessions of faith to the Diet of Augsburg — interchurch dialogue on unity foundered on the question of confessional identity. This was affirmed and defended on the Protestant side, as if ecclesial conversion must necessarily take the form of adherence by the entire Western church to the identity set forth by the Protestant Reformation in its confessions of faith. This is illustrated, for instance, in the church of Strasbourg which, having changed to Reformation worship in 1529, demanded four years later that every citizen should adhere to the confession of faith adopted by the city. Of the three types of conversion — Christian, ecclesial, and confessional — it was the third that became the criterion for the other two.

91. Nevertheless, at the very period of the Protestant Reformation there were colloquia on unity — notably in 1540-41 at Hagenau, Worms, and Regensburg — in an attempt to prevent the Western church, which was organically one, from breaking up into mutually hostile confessional churches. These colloquies took place at the instigation not of the church authorities but of Emperor Charles V. Both the Roman authorities and those of the newly reformed communities sought to oppose these discussions on unity. In fact, Charles V, against the advice of both the pope and Luther, wanted to test the possibility of subjecting confessional identities, which were tending to gain the upper hand, to an effort at reconversion to ecclesial unity. There were some political motives for restoring preeminence to ecclesial identity over the emerging plurality of confessional churches. This ecclesiastical policy of Charles V was a failure. The dynamic that fostered confessional pluralism plunged into crisis the principle of Christendom epitomized by the *corpus christianum*. The decline of the awareness of Christendom was at once the cause and the effect of the emergence of hostile confessional pluralism.

92. In this new situation of the church, the Protestant Reformers emphasized in their ecclesiology the distinction — but not the separation — between the church invisible (the church as the body of Christ) and the visible church (the human institution). The former was seen as the real ecclesial community in Christ, which was known to him alone; the latter as

178

the organized, established community of Christians. It was possible to belong to the one without necessarily belonging to the other. This distinction made it possible to deny the church in the Roman obedience the genuineness of its ecclesial identity and its claim to be the one church. The "papist" church of the medieval period was denounced in its organic and historical reality as the false church, the church of the antichrist. The church of the Protestant Reformation could thus justify its own claim to full ecclesial status despite the breach initiated by the excommunications that came from the traditional church.[38]

93. The Protestant Reformers credited the church they had reformed with full ecclesial identity. When they claimed this for their churches alone, expecting that the whole Western church would reform itself according to the same criteria, the dialogue on unity became sterile, for the Roman church did the same over against them. Nevertheless, this claim to be fully the church compelled the Protestant Reformers who laid special stress on ecclesiology — such as Martin Bucer, Philip Melanchthon, and John Calvin — to return emphatically to the "marks" of genuine ecclesiality: unity, holiness, catholicity, and apostolicity. Thus distancing themselves from spiritualizing tendencies, they were compelled to set up new ecclesial institutions corresponding to the theological standards of their confessions of faith.[39]

94. These same Reformers entered into dialogue with the theologians of the Roman church. We find them at the colloquies on unity of 1540-41. For the Protestant Reformers there could not be several churches of Jesus Christ; however, differences of opinion and practice were possible without the unity of the faith being broken.[40] Thus they affirmed that unity of ecclesial identity was possible in confessional pluralism.

---

38. Certain Protestant Reformers such as Bucer and Calvin took into their ecclesiology some surprising themes, including "Mother church" and "*extra ecclesiam nulla salus*"; cf. Calvin, *Institutes of the Christian Religion,* IV, 1, 7.

39. Note, for example, how Martin Bucer refers emphatically to Ephesians 5 in order to call the church to a permanent conversion, so that it may become the body of Christ "without spot or wrinkle." Here Bucer goes beyond the initial ecclesiological concern of Luther who, in the situation of anti-Roman polemics of 1520, reduced the church to the gathering of believers *hic et nunc* to listen to the preached Word and the celebration of the sacraments as the "visible" Word. In his ecclesiology Bucer sought to locate himself in the tradition of the fathers.

40. Calvin, *Institutes,* IV, 1, 12.

Luther, Bucer, and Melanchthon recognized in the Roman church of their day, and of previous centuries, its share of ecclesiality even at the worst moments of the medieval abuses. Nevertheless, neither the churches that emerged from the Protestant Reformation nor the Roman church were able alone to claim to be the church in its fullness. Conversion of their ecclesial identity was becoming necessary for each of the churches that had become confessional churches, including the Roman church, if it did not wish its ecclesial identity to lose the "mark" of unity. Nevertheless, and despite this openness to unity, these Protestant Reformers were convinced that the conversion of the whole church (Roman and Protestant) to ecclesial identity would lead it to the fundamental principles propounded by them.[41]

95. The Protestant Reformers, and after them the Protestant theologians who were concerned about unity, called for a general council as a final court of appeal and authoritative doctrinal guide on unity.[42] They saw in such a body a possibility to rediscover the ecclesial unity that was in process of breaking up. Thus their ecclesiology fell into the conciliarist line of the fifteenth and sixteenth centuries. Their ecclesiological motives, however, came up against the opposition of the popes of their day and were blocked by the political motives of Charles V, who also called for such a council. The failure to convene such a council at the beginning of the Protestant reforming movement destroyed the chances for a conversion of the church to unity at the Council of Trent.

b) The Catholic Reform

96. The Catholic reform[43] was not a *creatio ex nihilo*. In recent years historians have clearly shown that the reforms of the sixteenth century had

41. With the Catholic theologian Johann Gropper, Bucer drew up the famous "Book of Ratisbon," which presented possible points of agreement for a theological consensus to be discussed at the consultation on unity in Regensburg.

42. Such as the Czech theologian John Amos Comenius (1592-1670), who was still demanding such a council to bring Christians back to unity. Cf. *Ausgewählte Werke* (Hildesheim / New York: Georg Olms, 1977), vol. 3, p. 46.

43. Contemporary historiographers talk about the "(Protestant) Reformation" and the "Catholic reform" following on it and in reaction to it. The Catholic reform developed polemical elements that historians refer to as the "Counter-Reformation."

been preceded by many spiritual currents, such as *devotio moderna*. More-over, the Catholic reformation in the proper sense of the term is not reduc-ible to the dogmatic texts of the Council of Trent (1545-63). The disciplin-ary decrees for the reform of the clergy had a crucial influence and were the channel for a spiritual current that stemmed from a genuinely mystical inspiration.[44]

97. Another caveat is also essential: the Council of Trent should not be confused with Tridentinism.[45] The council was a reaction, often oversensi-tive though well considered, within a Western church that was becoming aware of a division whose effects it had not yet evaluated. Tridentinism, by contrast, was both a systematic organization of doctrine carried out on the basis of the council's documents, regarded as almost self-sufficient, and the establishment of institutions that would leave a considerable mark on Roman Catholicism.

98. *Mutatis mutandis*, the Catholic reformation was to experience the same problem as the Protestant Reformation. Just as the Protestant "confes-sions" drifted into confessionalism, so, too, the heritage of Trent degener-ated into Tridentinism, with the risk of some potential unfaithfulness to that heritage. The danger was that of confusing a stage on the road with the entire journey.

Christian Identity and Christian Conversion

99. If it is not too pretentious to make an overall judgment on the Council of Trent from the standpoint of Christian identity, it may be thought that we find there a kind of "re-centering" in Christ, the source and cause of sal-vation. Whether the issue is the sacraments, the sources of revelation (Scripture and tradition), or justification and sanctification, we may expect to see a magnification of the work of divine grace. At all events the theses of Trent could not take away from the primacy and gratuitousness of the gift

44. It is noteworthy that at Trent the doctrinal decrees on the one hand and the reform-ing decrees on the other were discussed so much in parallel that when the council ended in 1563 the conciliar decrees had established a new framework for the activities of the Catholic clergy. See N. S. Davidson, *La Contre-Réforme* (Paris: Cerf, 1989), pp. 41ff.

45. This point is underlined by M. D. Chenu and G. Alberigo; cf. the latter's "Du concile de Trente au tridentinisme," *Irenikon* 54, no. 2 (1981): 192-210.

of God. We are thus confronted with a christological theocentrism, which certainly leaves little room for the Holy Spirit. Following a certain Thomist inspiration, linked to a pastoral concern for the transformation of Christians, the council affirms that the individual must cooperate with God in the process of justification and sanctification. That cooperation may be demanded by God because it is given by his grace. The primary initiative is wholly God's, while human beings are given the initiative of letting themselves be transformed by him.

100. From that starting point it is possible to state that the Council of Trent, especially in its first period (1546-47), wanted a more spiritual church, a less ritualistic and less legalistic Christianity, which would allow the believer to enter more fully into the mystery of salvation. The text on the catechumen's progress to baptism, in the decree on justification, is all the more exemplary in this respect, coming as it does from a period that hardly knew anything but infant baptism.[46]

We may thus speak positively of Christian conversion at the Council of Trent, a conversion that affected not only the moral behavior of church members but also their profound adherence to the mystery of the faith.

101. It remains true that doctrinally this conversion also had negative effects. For, insofar as the true interpretation of the gospel is at stake, Trent, in reaction to the Protestant Reformation, overemphasized the institutional church. This subsequently caused some confusion between obedience to the faith and submission to the authorities. A typical Roman Catholic dogmatic sensitivity began to develop, leading by a consistent logic to Vatican I.

Ecclesial Identity and Ecclesial Conversion

102. The Council of Trent did not consider ecclesiology to be its theme. The reason for this is evident, given the historical context: the Protestant Reformers were basically attacking the doctrine of justification and the

---

46. "Human beings are disposed towards justice itself, when, being urged on and aided by divine grace, and with the faith they hear preached being formed in them, they turn freely towards God . . . ; when, understanding that they are sinners, . . . they arise to hope, trusting that God will be favorable to them because of Christ; when they begin to love him as the fountainhead of all justice . . . ; when, finally, they propose to receive baptism, to begin a new life and to keep the divine commandments" (Sixth Session, Decree on Justification, chap. 6).

sacraments. It might even be said that Trent ignored ecclesiology and was not responsible for the ecclesiology that found its spokesperson in Cardinal Bellarmine, which was a defense and illustration of the church as an institution.[47]

103. In the realm of ecclesiology the Council of Trent appears to be affected by a double handicap:

By default: it says nothing about the church as a mystery. It was necessary to await the twentieth century and Vatican II for the mystical current in ecclesiology to resurface in official documents. The christocentric ecclesiology of the Epistle to the Ephesians does not shine through in the work of Trent. Likewise, we are far removed from the ecclesiology of the Greek fathers, in which the Logos sanctifies a united and regenerated human nature.

104. *By excess:* by this we mean a view according to which God seems to act "directly" in the church. The council lacked a sense of ecclesial "mediations" through which the mediation of the sole Mediator is in fact disclosed and implemented. The distance between Christ and the church is not pronounced, and still less the distance between the church and the kingdom of God as found in the gospels.

105. What conversion did the Council of Trent cause from the perspective of the church?

On the positive side the church felt more linked to Christ and recognized that it should be more obedient to him. For the church, as the living instrument of Jesus, must not get in his way with practices contrary to the gospel. On this point some isolated voices in the church have been able humbly to ask forgiveness.[48]

---

47. Bellarmine defined the church as "the assembly of human beings bound together by profession of the same Christian faith and communion in the same sacraments, under the government of legitimate pastors and chiefly of the one vicar of Christ on earth, the Roman pontiff. In order to be in some measure part of the true church, . . . no inward virtue is in our view required, but only the outward profession of the faith and the fellowship of the sacraments, which is something accessible to our senses. In fact the church is an assembly as visible and palpable as are the assemblies of the Roman people or the kingdom of France or the Republic of Venice" (quoted by Congar, *L'Église de saint Augustin,* pp. 372f.).

48. We cited earlier (no. 89) the confession by Pope Adrian VI. In 1546 Cardinal Reginald Pole, the papal legate for the first phase of the Council of Trent, likewise declared: "We are all to a great extent responsible for the misfortune that has struck us — the rise of

106. On the negative side the absence of ecclesiology had the predictable consequence of considerably strengthening the institution as such. Confronted with the Protestants who challenged it, the council placed such a high value on the institution that it was later virtually equated with the mystery of the church. That equation is all the more regrettable because it linked up with another equation that would mark Catholic theological teaching to a great extent in the following centuries: the identification of Catholic doctrine with the sum of the refutations of Protestant theses at the Council of Trent.[49] But a collection of counter-propositions does not constitute a balanced doctrinal synthesis. "Bellarminism" would not really be overcome until Vatican II.

Confessional Identity and Confessional Conversion

107. The confessional identity of Catholicism emerged at that time even though Catholic theology had always abhorred the idea of regarding Catholicism as a "confession." Politically it was indeed to be regarded as such. Of course this was more a result than a deliberate choice. But at the start of the Council of Trent Catholics had not yet become aware of the incurable ecclesial division with the Protestants.

108. Subsequently the established church of the period realized it was confronted for the first time with an insurmountable "heretical" problem that was bringing authentic ecclesial bodies into existence. This was something wholly different from the separation from the Eastern church, which had been seen as a "schism." Hence direct opposition to the theses of the Protestant Reformers (often reduced to statements completely divorced from their context, as in the canons pronouncing anathemas) constituted "Ca-

---

heresy and the collapse of Christian morality — for we have not been capable of tilling the field that was entrusted to us. If we do not repent, God will not speak his word to us" (quoted by Davidson, *La Contre-Réforme*, p. 41).

49. For instance, in regard to eucharistic doctrine the Council of Trent dealt with only three disputed questions: the real presence and transubstantiation, the legitimacy of communion in one kind, and the eucharist as a sacrifice. Clearly eucharistic theology of the period said more than that. A similar point may be made regarding the relation of the priest to the eucharist. To answer the challenges of the Protestant Reformers on the ministerial priesthood, the dogmatic texts of Trent consider the priest as above all a "sacrificer." Here Trent must be corrected by Trent itself, for the disciplinary decrees place enormous stress on the responsibility of the priest and the bishop in relation to the Word (cf. A. Duval, *Des sacrements au concile de Trente* [Paris: Cerf, 1985]).

tholicism" and gave it a confessional inflexibility. The worldwide spread of this situation, which was still very European, was to take place through the expansion of the Western churches in the Americas, in Africa, and, in a more limited way, in Asia.

109. While the differences between Protestants and Catholics ought to have retained their specific form, their serious nature, and their challenge, by about a century after the Council of Trent they boiled down to a popular simplification that has had free rein up to our own day. For instance, if the Catholic confession of faith should normally attest to the real presence of Christ in the eucharist, the role of Mary in the economy of salvation, and the pope's ministry of unity, the result is that the Protestant is "identified" as one who does not "believe" in the real presence or the Holy Virgin or the pope.[50] Forgotten are the Protestants' faith in Christ as the one Savior, their love and knowledge of the Word of God, and the positive value of the Lord's Supper which they celebrate.

The understanding which the Catholic Church has of itself is accompanied by an "integralism" that tends to deny that aspects of the Christian faith are obscured or minimized in it. This simplification is also expressed in the "diptychs": Protestants believe in the Word, Catholics in the sacrament; Protestants in Scripture, Catholics in tradition; Protestants are saved subjectively by faith, Catholics objectively through the efficacy of the sacrament, and so on. Through these caricatures, Catholicism has forged a practical confessional identity in which polemics has extended statements of faith beyond their real meaning and devalued the identity of other Christians.

110. Were there any positive aspects in this identification of confessional type? The impact of the Tridentine conciliar decrees on church discipline, the abundant fruit of the establishment of seminaries, and the mystical and apostolic movement of what was to be called the French School of spirituality demonstrate beyond any doubt that Catholicism had implemented its reformation. Three points emphasize this: everything relating to catechesis and catechisms (some of which adopted the structure of the Protestant catechisms); the organization of ministerial training for genuine preaching of

50. We deliberately use the word "believe" with all three objects, though the meaning becomes more analogical from one to the next. This is the well-known theme of the "three white things" (the host, the immaculate robe of the Virgin, and the pope's soutane), lavishly embroidered by many preachers.

the Word; the obligation laid on bishops and parish priests to be "resident," which means that every pastor must be present with his flock.

111. The negative aspects of this confessional identification are familiar enough. Tridentinism, sometimes going beyond its own intentions, reinforced ecclesiastical centralism; it caused the loss of what was to be valued in a moderate Gallicanism; and finally it brought about a regrettable identification of catholicity with Romanism. Catholicism in the "modern" sense of the term was born, no longer as an essential description of Christianity itself but as one of the great Christian denominations that continued to be separated from each other.

c) From Confessions of Faith to Confessionalism (seventeenth and eighteenth centuries)

112. The Protestant and Catholic reformations, despite their aspects of confessional polemics, were both inspired by the desire for ecclesial conversion. Luther's personal experience may illustrate this: it was sustained by a threefold conversion — Christian, ecclesial, and confessional — comparable with what we set out above in relation to St. Augustine. In the historical situations brought about by Luther's movement, however, misunderstandings and rejections led to a distortion of the reforming dynamic. Preeminence was given to confessional identity, which became the point of reference for ecclesial identity, the one or the other then serving as the criterion for Christian identity. This inversion of priorities distorted the possibilities of conversion in the two reformations. Each side wanted to lead the entire Empire or the whole kingdom of France to the same confessional identity, which would be normative for ecclesial identity. The latter became in turn the ultimate yardstick for the Christian identity of each of its members. The threefold conversion was caught in a trap, because any conversion could only end up in one confession or another.

113. The formula *cuius regio, eius religio* ("a person's religion is that of his country"),[51] which had been applied since the Peace of Augsburg in 1555 and confirmed in the treaties of Westphalia in 1648, illustrates the divisive

---

51. This formula meant that the confession of the prince (or any other civil authority) had the force of an obligation for all the subjects of the same territory, on pain of exile.

principle of territorial confessional churches and the reversal of the priorities among the three conversions. This political principle froze the situation of the confessional churches — and historically the Roman church is to be thought of as such from that moment. Confessional identity, having become a yardstick for ecclesial identity, could no longer be challenged, as each confession regarded itself as the only bearer of the characteristic "marks" of full ecclesiality — of the fullness of the church. An ecclesial conversion could be regarded only as a denial (of one's ecclesiality as a confession), or even as treason.

114. Thus from the end of the sixteenth century until the eighteenth century the encounters of the confessional churches that emerged from the two reformations became confrontations, wars of religion, and incurable divisions. The dialogue for unity could only be confined to a few conversations between individuals, always doomed to failure in a climate dominated by controversies.[52]

115. There were nevertheless some encounters, consultations, and efforts at unity throughout that period. Thus in France in the seventeenth century, Gallicanism drove certain Catholic and Protestant theologians to the "unionist" reconciliation, in which unity had to be achieved to Rome's disadvantage. In Germany the Lutheran Georg Calixtus (1586-1656) called for a consensus based on the confessions of faith of the ecumenical councils of the ancient church and the tradition of the fathers. He rejected doctrinal intolerance and commended a more irenical dialogue that would recognize members of the different confessional churches as "true Christians."[53] This effort at unity made itself evident even in the Orthodox Church

---

52. The correspondence between Bossuet and Leibniz at the end of the sixteenth century on the role of the Council of Trent for Christian unity is one example; another is the exchange in France between Catholic and Protestant theologians on the eucharist (such as P. Noüet and Nicole with Pastor Jean-Claude). Conversion of one group to the church was then seen by the others as an individual conversion, in particular on the part of princes, whose conversion implied that of their subjects. Cf. H. Jedin, ed., *Handbuck zur Kirchengeschichte*, vol. 5 (Freiburg in Breisgau: Herder, 1965), pp. 555-70.

53. The well-known motto *in necessariis unitas, in non necessariis libertas, in utriusque caritas* (unity on what is necessary, freedom on what is not necessary, charity in everything), often wrongly attributed to St. Augustine, probably comes from the Augsburg theologian, Rupert Meldenius, in a book written around 1626: *Paraenesis pro pace Ecclesiae ad theologos Augustanae confessionis*; cf. *Realenzyklopädie für protestantische Theologie und Kirche*, XII (Leipzig: J. C. Hinrichs'sche Buchhandlung, 1903), pp. 550-52.

where Patriarch Cyril Lukaris (1572-1638) attempted a reconciliation of Orthodoxy and Calvinism, which proved abortive.[54] In England, to combat the successive persecutions of non-conformist Protestants or Catholics, some Anglican theologians sought to convince the other confessional churches of the need for a "middle way."

116. Following the Thirty Years' War (1618-48), voices were raised in favor of going back to Christian conversion as the priority and yardstick for ecclesial and confessional conversions — in other words, a return to this order of priorities: Christian conversion, ecclesial conversion, confessional conversion. These voices came from movements challenging the divided state of the church: for instance from pietism, through its initiator, the Alsatian Philipp Jakob Spener (1635-1705), or from missionary universalism, through the Czech Jan Amos Comenius (1592-1670).

117. Disappointed at the inability of the confessional churches to find their path of ecclesial conversion towards unity, Protestant theologians like Spener, Comenius, and others put forward an ecumenical plan for missionary universalism. This leap beyond confessional particularism was to be a return towards the very meaning of the churches: to be at the service of the whole of humanity. This ecclesial conversion, they thought, would be the new reformation of all the confessional churches. *Reformatio vera in unitatem reducit* — genuine reformation leads back to unity — wrote Comenius.[55] A *reformatio* of this kind would proceed by way of the conversion of theological discussion to the primary mission of the church.[56] These "irenicals" for unity considered that the reform of the church had not been completed,[57] and that confessional identity was not the end-result but a stage along the way to full and shared ecclesiality.

54. Cf. M. Carbonnier-Burkard, "Une liaison gréco-réformée au XVIme siècle," in *Foi et vie* 3-4 (July 1990), special issue: "Constantinople aux portes de l'Europe," pp. 67-77.

55. "We are all cosmopolitans, citizens of the same world and, I would add, of the same church." "After such great horrors [those of the Thirty Years' War] the time has come to contemplate the conversion of the hearts of all people. . . . You Christians, the people beloved of God, your constant arguments on philosophy, theology and politics prove that you are unaware of your salvation. Oh, the opinions dividing us are countless. Hate and the disorder that are the product of these are endless and beyond measure. . . . This is not God's will; the right way is not to combat discord by discord but to consolidate everything that can be united by unity." Comenius, *Ausgewählte Werke*, pp. 25-29 and 115 (212).

56. Comenius, *Ausgewählte Werke*, pp. 77 (17); 80f. (26); 93 (36).

57. Contrary to the commonly accepted view, the expression *ecclesia semper reformanda*

118. These calls for ecclesial conversion and for restoring the true priority among the three conversions did not succeed in making themselves sufficiently heard. In the eighteenth century and under the influence of the Enlightenment the principle of religious *tolerance,* rather than *unity,* became the criterion for the co-existence, side by side, of the confessional churches. Unity was only restored by the confessional churches as a "mark" of ecclesial and Christian conversion, from the nineteenth century onwards, under the pressure and fear of materialism and secularism, which made them gradually doubt their respective and separate claims to full and sufficient ecclesiality. That was how the way opened up for the contemporary ecumenical movement.

d) Balance-Sheet

119. When the confessional churches, as they were produced historically by the divisive reforms of the sixteenth century, each claim full correspondence between their confessional identity and ecclesial identity, they render their confessional situation inflexible. Faithfulness to ecclesial identity is then inevitably confused with faithfulness to doctrinal formulas and confessional practices. Any ecclesial conversion that challenges confessional inviolability, even on grounds of unity, is then regarded as a denial of ecclesiality itself.

120. Conversion is then limited to individual conversion, the only remaining locus for change. In a historical situation of this kind, only personal Christian identity remains open to a process of transformation.

121. The era of confessionalism, in which the churches equate their confessional identity with full and sufficient ecclesial identity, illustrates the risk that such ecclesiology poses to any possibility of conversion. Turning upside down the priorities among the three conversions causes and consolidates ecclesial division. Confusing confessional identities, *plural,* with ecclesial identity can neither express nor produce unity unless we consider

---

seems not to go back to the sixteenth-century Protestant Reformers but to the Pietist Jodocus van Lodenstein (1620-77), who used it around 1675; cf. E. Mülhaupt, "Immer währende Reformation?," in *Luther im 20. Jahrhundert, Aufsätze* (Göttingen: Vandenhoeck & Ruprecht, 1982), p. 267.

unity to be a reductionist uniformity or separated but tolerant side-by-side existence.

122. If conversion to unity is essential to ecclesial identity — and it is so, according to the confessions of faith of all the churches — it calls for reversing and transcending historical positions that, on this point at least, are considered to be erroneous and sinful. *Divisive confessional pluralism can only be provisional; it calls for conversion to a confessional pluralism compatible with ecclesial unity.* This development implies the acknowledgment that the church in its separate confessional forms is marked by sin. Ecclesial conversion to unity calls for such an admission on the part of the confessional churches, which makes it possible to emerge from the confessionalist status quo. In fact as soon as Christians recognize that their confessional church lacks ecclesiality because of division, the process of ecclesial and confessional conversion to full catholicity becomes possible once again.

123. For contemporary Protestant ecclesiology, this turn-about means rediscovering that the visible church is not only a sinful historical community, but is also intended by Christ as the *one* and *holy* church. The tradition of the churches of the Protestant Reformation may find among its own Reformers of the sixteenth century the theological elements necessary for the rediscovery of these two "marks" of the church. Unity and holiness are not only the characteristics of the church invisible, but are also to be lived out in the historical and confessional reality of the visible church.

124. For Catholic ecclesiology this turn-about means rediscovering the initial inspiration of the Catholic reformation, beyond its later debasements in the form of "Tridentinism." It consists in recognizing that the church is not just a hierarchical structure and an institution, but is in its essence a *mystery:* the gift of Christ through whom salvation comes to us. It implies that the consistency of modes of behavior and practices with the gospel message is not just something to be affirmed verbally. It calls us to go beyond too narrow or exclusive a sense of "catholicity" and "apostolicity," which must above all be measured against this mystery of the church which Christ intended to be *one* and *holy.* All who bear the name of Christians are called to live in unity and holiness.

III. The Ecumenical Movement: A Movement of Conversion

a) Conversion at the Origin of the Ecumenical Movement

125. The ecumenical movement born in the nineteenth century does not represent a completely new beginning. It has its roots, since the schism between the East and West and the split in the Western church in the sixteenth century, in the hearts of Christians of different confessions. These people were filled with the concern for reconciliation and had already become aware of the conversions that would have to be effected in order to rediscover full communion. In this connection we may mention the fraternal dialogues between Anselm of Havelberg and Nicetas of Constantinople on the procession of the Holy Spirit and on the papacy (twelfth century). The second Council of Lyons (1274) and the Council of Florence (1438-45) were convened out of the desire to reunify and reconcile East and West.[58] Their failure in history cannot make us forget the legitimacy of their purpose or the spirit of conversion that inspired some of their supporters.

126. In the West, even before the break was completed, there were the efforts of the Colloquia of Hagenau, Worms, Regensburg (1540-41),[59] and Poissy (1561), during which leading Catholics and Protestants were in dialogue with each other. Even at the Council of Trent, in its second period (1551-52) there were negotiations to enable Protestant envoys to come and take part in the work of the council. Reasons of theology, religious politics, and simply politics as such prevented the realization of this project. At the time the dynamic of separation on both sides was stronger than that of reconciliation — all the more reason not to forget the efforts that bore witness to an attitude of conversion at that time.

127. The birth of ecumenism, in the modern sense of the quest for full communion among churches, was due to a series of missionary initiatives, awakenings, and militant student movements eager to "win the world for Christ," which evolved in the Reformation churches. This evangelical and missionary concern drew attention to the scandal of division among Christians and the need for their conversion to unity. The spiritual motivation of the project made itself evident in the establishment of an initial form of a

58. Cf. no. 78.
59. Cf. no. 91.

global week of prayer for unity. In this movement the role of pioneers who belonged to a variety of confessions was crucial.[60] The personal conversion of some individuals progressively encouraged that of church groups and, later, confessions. Like conversion to the faith, conversion to full communion has developed through the contagion of witness and example.

128. The end of the nineteenth century saw the creation of the great world confessional alliances.[61] This movement of the Reformation churches towards a wider communion was the fruit of a conversion of the regional or national churches, which thus abandoned an isolation that was contrary to the gospel.

129. Crucial reconciliations between the confessional churches marked the first half of the twentieth century. After the Edinburgh missionary conference (1910) and the First World War, the Malines conversations (1921-26), and the conferences in Stockholm (1925) and Lausanne (1927), among others, called the churches to repentance and conversion. Christian youth organizations provided new leaders for the movement. Among the latter, Dietrich Bonhoeffer (1906-45) condemned theologically superficial ecumenism and called for a more profound approach and for the spirit of conversion.[62]

130. The Second World War created an even greater awareness of ecumenical urgency for all the churches. In 1948 the process came to a climax with the establishment of the World Council of Churches, which took on the task, according to the terms of its "basis," of working in the service of that "fellowship of churches which confess the Lord Jesus Christ as God and Savior according to the Scriptures, and therefore seek to fulfill together their common calling to the glory of the one God, Father, Son and Holy Spirit." The ultimate aim of the World Council of Churches is certainly the conversion of all the member churches, even if some of its constitutional provisions may well appear to favor the status quo.

60. To mention only a few names from the nineteenth century and beginning of the twentieth: Jean-Frédéric Oberlin, Tommy Fallot, Pusey, Charles Wood, Lord Halifax, John R. Mott, Marc Boegner, W. A. Visser 't Hooft. We may remember also the part played in the ecumenical movement since 1942 by the Taizé community.

61. Dombes, "The Ministry of Communion in the Universal Church," no. 81.

62. Cf. E. Bethge, *Dietrich Bonhoeffer: Theologian, Christian, Contemporary* (London: Collins, 1970), pp. 181ff.

131. In the nineteenth century the Roman Catholic Church remained officially outside this great movement, despite more frequent meetings between Catholics and Protestants in the field. Some interventions by Pope Leo XIII, however, inspired by the theology of "return" ("unionism") but imbued with a spirit of genuine charity, did discreetly open up the path.

132. In the first part of the twentieth century the official attitude of the Roman Catholic Church was that of isolation and then a hardening in regard to ecumenism. Nevertheless some of the great pioneers of the movement of Christians towards unity were among the members of that church.[63] Thanks to a number of providential encounters, all of them had had a personal experience of conversion to Christian unity. Their witness and activities had prepared the ground for the conversion of the Catholic Church, especially with the development of the Week of Prayer for Christian Unity observed in January each year.

133. It was necessary to wait for the convening of the Second Vatican Council to see the emergence of the official and institutional conversion of the Roman Catholic Church to the dynamic of ecumenism. Here again, at the origin of this conversion, was that of a man, Angelo Roncalli. During his various incumbencies as a nuncio he had met Orthodox Christians and had long engaged in reflection with Dom Lambert Beauduin, exiled at the time from his monastery. Having become pope as John XXIII, he included in the agenda of the council a primary concern for the unity of all Christians. Despite the great authority of his office, it remained a question whether the council would enter into this point of view and bring to life the changes proposed to it. Many bishops were uncertain about the stance their colleagues would take. When the first vote was taken on how the council should proceed, there was surprise. "When the bishops saw that they were in agreement," wrote Father Congar, "the Catholic church converted to ecumenism in a few minutes or at most a few hours."[64] In fact the adoption, almost unanimously, of the Decree on Ecumenism took place only three years later. This thunderbolt of grace, this *kairos,* had brought with it a dynamic impetus for confessional con-

63. The names of some who are no longer with us are well known: Abbé Fernand Portal, Cardinal Mercier, Dom Lambert Beauduin, Abbé Metzger, Abbé Paul Couturier, Father Maurice Villain.

64. Y. Congar, *Essais œcuméniques* (Paris: Centurion, 1984), p.35; cf. H. Roux, *De la désunion vers la communion* (Paris: Centurion, 1978), pp. 215-47.

version, liberating the Catholic Church from all its previous fears. It was a conversion that had been prepared by decades of unpretentious work and fervent prayer.

134. Conversion is not simply at the source of the ecumenical movement. It represents its constantly underlying motivation. When conversion flags, the ecumenical movement stagnates or even goes into reverse. All the Christian confessions and all the Christians in each of them have to keep moving forward in the attitude of conversion. The forms of resistance to the ecumenical movement and to the confessional conversion it calls for are many: a preference for the more comfortable status quo, a fear of losing one's confessional identity, and, above all, indifference on the part of the majority. Non-doctrinal factors are still important: the old clichés and fears continually reappear while the gap separating theologians undertaking research, church officials, and the majority of the Christian people becomes more pronounced. These attitudes often express a false idea both of unity and of truth, of identity and conversion.

b) Conversion Underway

135. Ecumenical conversion is underway in the church, by three converging routes: symbolic gestures, documents on doctrinal dialogue, and finally, acts or decisions that commit the churches.

Symbolic Gestures

136. The scope of symbolic gestures is wide because of the representative value of those who make them, and because they express visibly and emotively the evolving conversion. Who could remain unmoved by the pilgrimage of Pope Paul VI and the Patriarch Athenagoras to the land of Jesus in January 1964, which culminated in their fraternal embrace of reconciliation? Does that event not take us back to the brotherly extension of "the right hand of fellowship" between Paul and Peter "as a sign of communion" in that same Jerusalem (Gal. 2:9)? In 1975, Pope Paul VI made the unheard-of and astonishing gesture of kneeling before Metropolitan Meliton, the envoy of Patriarch Dimitrios, to kiss his feet. Considering the Vatican protocol — not so long ago — requiring those favored with an audience to kiss the feet of the pope (which almost caused the meeting be-

tween the Orthodox Patriarch Joseph II and Pope Eugene IV to fall through on the eve of the Council of Florence), how can we fail to rejoice that so ambiguous a gesture of homage to authority should be reversed and suddenly find its evangelical meaning, that of Jesus washing the feet of his disciples and inviting them to wash each other's feet?

137. Among symbolic gestures we may also recall the confession by Paul VI at the beginning of his pontificate, addressed to all the "separated" Christians:

> If we are in any way to blame for that separation, we humbly beg God's forgiveness and ask pardon too of our brethren who feel themselves to have been injured by us. For our part, we willingly forgive the injuries which the Catholic Church has suffered, and forget the grief endured during the long series of dissensions and separations. May the heavenly Father deign to hear our prayers and grant us true brotherly peace.[65]

138. The major meetings between church leaders are also symbolic gestures of conversion and reconciliation. The decision of Michael Ramsey, Archbishop of Canterbury, to go to the Vatican to meet Paul VI (1966) is one of these. On that occasion the pope presented him with his pastoral ring. Likewise the visit of Pope Paul VI to the World Council of Churches in Geneva (1969), followed by the invitation to John Paul II by the WCC (1984) and the latter's visit to the Lutheran church in Rome (1983) on the occasion of the 500th anniversary of the birth of Luther. And how many more! In a category of its own, which is not part of the ecumenical process in the strict sense, the Assisi encounter (1986), in which the representatives of the great religions of humanity met together to pray for peace in the world, was also a common gesture of conversion. For Christians also have to experience together a conversion to charity and respect towards their brothers and sisters who are believers of other faiths.

139. Symbolic gestures do not take place only at the top. And even these were made possible thanks only to the numerous gestures of conversion that Christians who are still separated had made at the grassroots. Usually

---

65. In his address at the opening of the second session of Vatican II, 29 September 1963, Xavier Rynne, *The Second Session: The Debates and Decrees of Vatican Council II* (London: Faber & Faber, 1963), p. 358.

these latter gestures have value only for those who experience them. Thus it is impossible to list them here, whether they were made by individuals, local congregations, or regional leaders.

140. In May 1989 the European Ecumenical Assembly in Basel on Justice, Peace, and the Integrity of Creation represented a symbolic communal event. Convened jointly by the Conference of European Churches (CEC) and the Council of European Catholic Bishops (CCEE), it enabled Christians, both lay and ordained, from practically all the churches of Western and Eastern Europe to live, pray, celebrate, and enter into dialogue together for the first time. With the passage of time this event appears, because of its exceptional atmosphere of freedom and loving fellowship, like a prefiguring of the great movement of liberation of the peoples of Eastern Europe that began at the end of 1989.

141. These symbolic gestures, which are the product of a conversion, become in turn generators of the spirit of conversion. They encourage and embolden Christians of every confession to be involved in a similar process. As such, these gestures are indispensable for the dynamics of unity.

Doctrinal Dialogues

142. The merit of the Commission on Faith and Order, and then of the World Council of Churches, is to have paved the way for a multilateral doctrinal dialogue among the different Christian confessions. A period of slow maturing was needed before it was possible to publish significant documents — especially the convergence document on *Baptism, Eucharist and Ministry* adopted in 1982 at Lima and submitted to all the churches as a call for their conversion.

143. On the Roman Catholic side, the conversion to ecumenism of Vatican II was not implemented only in the drafting of the decree on "the restoration of unity among all Christians" — the Decree on Ecumenism *(Unitatis Redintegratio)*. It was a continual concern in the drafting of all the council's documents. While the observers from the other churches did not take part officially in the discussion, they were regularly consulted and were able to give their reactions to the different drafts. The editing commissions always took full account of what they said. From this standpoint, the texts of Vatican II are already the products of an initial doctrinal dia-

logue. The conversion which led to a full recognition that the "separated brethren" were Christians opened the way to another conversion, that of the understanding. It made possible a new era in theological reflection, in which the spirit of controversy yielded place to kindly consideration of the doctrinal position of the partner. Whereas once each tried to show the others that they were wrong, from then on they have tried to go along with the share of truth of which his brother or sister is the bearer.

144. The documents of Vatican II represented only a beginning for the Roman Catholic Church. After the council it set up a large number of bilateral commissions with different Christian alliances or confessions. This long-term dialogue is still going on. The Catholic Church also takes part in the multilateral work of Faith and Order. Some confessions have also organized bilateral dialogues (Lutheran-Reformed, Anglican-Orthodox, Lutheran-Orthodox, etc.). These encounters, patiently repeated, have woven new links of esteem and friendship among the participants, and generally take place in an atmosphere of common concern and prayer. The spiritual conversion of each person grows in them and finds its fruitfulness in the doctrinal conversion that makes it possible to sweep away certain points of contention that have no real basis, and to see the real points of dispute in a new light. Considerable doctrinal convergence has already been achieved in the areas of salvation and justification by faith, the church and ministries, baptism and eucharist. In the vast common enterprise of doctrinal ecumenical dialogue the Groupe des Dombes tries to play its part by living on the basis of the dynamic of conversion that is part of the grace of its foundation.

Acts and Decisions Taken

145. Among the decisions taken, the first to be mentioned must be the lifting of the excommunications between Rome and Constantinople effected in 1965 by Paul VI and Athenagoras. The Leuenberg Agreement (1973) between Lutheran and Reformed churches of Europe also includes a removal of anathemas, as does the document resulting from the Lutheran-Mennonite dialogue of 1980 in France.

The work of the joint German commission on the mutual condemnations by Catholic and Reformation churches in the sixteenth century leads one to observe that most of these condemnations no longer apply to the partners in their present situation. The reasons of yesterday can no longer justify such anathemas today.[66] Mutual lifting of the condemnations of the past would be a far-reaching gesture of ecclesial conversion in which the partners' confessional identities would no longer be defined as in opposition to each other.

146. The recognition of the ecclesial nature of another confession is also a decision for conversion. Thus the Catholic Church no longer talks of "heretics" and "schismatics" but of "separated brethren." It no longer considers that in the communities that have separated from it there are only "vestiges of the church": it talks of "churches" or "ecclesial communities" (Vatican II). The Extraordinary Roman Synod of 1985 spoke of an "ecumenical communion of churches." Pope John Paul II spoke of "Christian churches" when he traveled to the Lutheran countries of Scandinavia (1989).

147. Among the acts in the process of ecumenical conversion it is important to stress the role of the reception of the documents of ecumenical agreement or convergence. Here the term is not taken in its canonical but in its theological sense: it is a question of the welcome given in practice to these documents in the thought and life of the members of each church. The preface to *Baptism, Eucharist and Ministry* put it this way: "As concrete evidence of their ecumenical commitment, the churches are being asked to enable the widest possible involvement of the whole people of God at all levels of church life in the spiritual process of receiving this text."

148. It is not simply a question of receiving a written document. Long ago St. Francis de Sales used to recall the difference between musical notation and music that is sung. The text that is received must be able to represent a genuine "score," making it possible to sing the libretto or play the piece on every level of the church's life. Only the responsible authorities can take official ("canonical") decisions to receive a document. But they can do nothing so long as a de facto reception has not taken place among the whole membership of the churches. The process of reception is in this case a conversion process.

149. The increase in the number of councils of Christian churches in the world, including in those countries with a Catholic majority such as

---

66. Cf. the results of the work of the joint Protestant-Catholic commission formed in Germany after John Paul II's 1980 visit there, *The Condemnations of the Reformation Era: Do They Still Divide?* (Minneapolis: Fortress, 1990).

France (in 1987), is also an act of conversion and the crossing of a threshold towards mutual recognition.

150. Parallel to the stances and actions that have just been recalled, the development of research in the biblical sciences[67] and the collaboration of Christians of different confessions in the movements of social Christianity[68] have stimulated ecumenical dialogue and the spirit of conversion. Thus we arrive at a fair number of expressions of unity: the celebration of the Week of Prayer in January, social welfare initiatives, joint chaplaincies (in hospitals, prisons, the military, and among confessionally mixed families, etc.), ecumenical translations of the Bible, pulpit exchanges, the invitation of observers to the deliberative bodies of each church, etc.

c) Balance-Sheet

151. Throughout our century the ecumenical movement has been and remains characterized by the problem of the compatibility of identity with conversion.

152. This long progression of confessional conversions aimed at leading the church towards unity is far from complete. It has to focus on many points of doctrinal controversy that remain unresolved. Today the question of "models of unity" is already being raised. A variety of scenarios have been proposed under various labels: "organic unity," "conciliar fellowship," "ecclesial communion," "reconciled diversity," and so on, which moreover have some similarities to each other. At the heart of this reflection we find once again the whole dialectic of identity and conversion.

153. For our part, on the basis of the analyses we have just carried out, we see the ecumenical movement as a great process of conversion and reconciliation of our diversities in the quest for communion among confessional identities that, once cleansed of their unevangelical or sinful elements, can receive each other, become complementary, and enrich each

67. Such as the creation of dialogue and research forums like the Society for New Testament Studies (SNTS) in 1938.

68. We may recall here the Rev. Wilfred Monod and the Lutheran Archbishop Nathan Söderblom, whose social commitment in the name of the gospel was accompanied by an indisputable ecumenical openness.

other. Difference is legitimate within *koinonia* (communion). Thus the churches are invited to arrive at a common recognition of what distinguishes legitimate differences from separative divergences.[69] Confessional identities are not to be abandoned, but to be transformed. Such a vision aims at always linking the concern of unity with that of mission. It is received as faithfulness to the Spirit who leads us forward.

154. This set of soundings, made in an ecumenical spirit, has taken only some aspects of church history into account. But the intention was to respond to the appeal made on the one hand by Lukas Vischer and on the other by Pope John Paul II, that the history of disunity be studied in a spirit of confessional conversion and contribute to the cleansing of our memories:

> We need a new awareness of the past. Despite the ecumenical movement we still tell the history of the church in terms of the criteria that come from our own traditions. Is it possible to understand and write the history of the church in a way which enables all the churches to recognize themselves in it? . . . We can only live in one and the same tradition if we succeed in verifying its existence through the centuries in a common presentation of the history of the church. The history of the other churches must begin to form part of our own history.[70]

> The fact that we have different ways of judging the complex events of past history and the differences that continue to exist in some central questions of our faith must not divide us permanently. Above all, the memory of past events must not limit the freedom of our present efforts aimed at repairing the damage caused by these events. The purging of memory is a prime element in ecumenical progress. It involves frank recognition of the wrongs done to each other, and of the mistakes made in the way we have reacted towards each other, while we all intended to make the church more faithful to the will of its Lord. Perhaps the day will come, and I hope it will be soon, when the Catholics and Protestants of Switzerland will be in a position to write the history of this troubled and complex era with the objectivity that is conferred by profound fraternal love. Such an achievement will

---

69. Cf. the Joint Catholic-Protestant Committee in France, *Consensus œcuménique et différence fondamentale* (Paris: Centurion, 1987).

70. Lukas Vischer, "Œcuménisme — chemin de l'histoire," *Unité des chrétiens* 51 (July 1983): 9.

make it possible to entrust the past unreservedly to the mercy of God and, "straining towards what lies ahead" (cf. Phil. 3:13), to be in all freedom to make it more in conformity with his will, which is that his people will have but one heart and one soul (cf. Acts 4:24, 32) to unite in the proclamation and "praise of his glorious grace" (cf. Eph. 1:6). In fact, for each Christian there must be that deep and continuous conversion of the heart, and for each community there must be a constant effort to renew itself in a more profound faithfulness. I am convinced that the foundations necessary for personal and communal ecumenical commitment lie there.[71]

PART III
The Witness of Scripture

155. Inasmuch as the whole of Scripture witnesses to the centrality of conversion, it was neither possible nor desirable to undertake an overall review of the scriptural evidence. We thought it more fruitful to verify by a number of soundings whether there is a good foundation for our basic intuition that the call for a conversion inherent in identity has its roots and justification in Scripture.

Without misjudging the historical distance and the difference in situations, which forbid us any specious harmonizing, the similarities that can be pinpointed are appeals that have binding force for us, rather than just being encouraging signs.

I. Repentance and Conversion

156. In this work the Groupe des Dombes uses the terms "conversion" and "metanoia" as equivalents.[72] This usage brings into the term "conversion" the elements of meaning that derive from two families of Greek words: *epistrephein* and *metanoein*.

Metanoein and its derivatives and the Hebrew root they usually translate in the Greek Old Testament mean "renounce" or "repent." The New

71. John Paul II, speech to the Federation of Swiss Protestant Churches, June 1984, *Doc. Cath.* 1878 (1984): 726.

72. In this section we always translate *metanoia* by "repentance" and *epistrephein* by "convert."

Testament limited the scope of the meaning of *metanoia* to the act of renouncing a way of thinking or acting regarded as bad. In the New Testament it is people who can repent, while in the Old Testament God himself also repents (Gen. 6:6f.; Jer. 18:8-10; Jonah 3:9).

In the New Testament *epistrephein* and its derivatives and the Hebrew root they generally translate in the Greek Old Testament mean "come back," "return," "turn to," "be converted," and are used in both the secular and the religious fields.

157. Repentance does not come of itself. It is the response to a call (Matt. 3:2; Mark 1:15; Acts 2:38). In Matthew and Mark that call is the first word uttered by Jesus (Matt. 4:17; Mark 1:15). Repentance is the act of human beings who respond to that call, but it is also a gift of God (Jer. 31:18; Acts 5:31; 11:18). In the book of Jeremiah the two actions are linked: human repentance can take place only thanks to God's action.

158. Repentance and conversion are linked twice in the New Testament: "Repent therefore and turn to God so that your sins may be wiped out" (Acts 3:19); and the nations have to "repent and turn to God and do deeds consistent with repentance" (Acts 26:20). It is a way of saying the same thing twice but with a nuance: conversion depends on repentance. Repentance indicates the decision, conversion its implementation.

The two terms are applied to the Jews (Acts 3:19 and 26:20) and to the gentiles (Acts 26:20). They are used for initial conversion to God and for the ongoing conversions of believers.

The subject of conversion may be individual (Jer. 15:19; Luke 22:32) or collective (Jer. 3:10; Acts 9:35). The same is true of repentance; it is individual (Jer. 8:6; Luke 15:7) or collective (Jer. 31:19; Acts 2:16).

II. Identity and Identities

159. While the vocabulary of repentance and conversion occurs in Scripture, the word "identity" does not appear there. But its reality is present.

On the one hand, identity is essentially a name given when one is addressed: it is a calling, and often a promise. It becomes effectual when what lies in the name is brought into play. This is true both for individuals and for groups: John means "the Lord is gracious"; Jesus means "the Lord saves"; Israel means "the one who fought with God," which is said of Jacob and of the people (Gen. 32:28); church means "that which is addressed and called"; Christians are those who appeal to the authority of Christ (Acts 11:26).

160. Name and identity are linked to the point that a change of name means a change of identity. Abram becomes Abraham; "Not my people" becomes "My people" (Hos. 1–2; cf. 1 Pet. 2:10; Rom. 9:25); Simon becomes Peter. Likewise the Christian is given a new identity as one who bears the name of Christ. This existence can be defined only in terms of one's total dependence on Christ (cf. Gal. 2:19f.).

161. Moreover, identity is also defined by recognition of the call of God. Individuals or groups acknowledge their identity by confessing God. Confession is correlative to calling (Pss. 95:7; 100:3; Rom. 10:9-13).

Confession of faith is at the same time an invitation for everyone to acknowledge God and live out the identity of believers. This invitation goes out to the ends of the earth (Pss. 96:1-3; 148; Acts 1:8).

162. Within the church there are groups with different identities, such as Jewish Christians and Gentile Christians. In Ephesians 2–3, the author, a Christian of Jewish origin, addresses Christians of gentile origin as the "nations." Even as Christians, the latter keep their cultural identity and do not have to be circumcised and live as Jews. Those people who belong to the "nations," once they have become believers, are fellow-heirs and form one body with the Jewish Christians: "the Gentiles have become fellow heirs, members of the same body, and sharers in the promise in Christ Jesus through the gospel" (Eph. 3:6). Ecclesial unity respects the identity of the existing groups. Through reconciliation with God the difference is no longer divisive, and reconciliation is also achieved between believers of different origins:

> For he [Jesus] is our peace; in his flesh he has made both groups into one and has broken down the dividing wall, that is, the hostility between us. He has abolished the law with its commandments and ordinances, that he might create in himself one new humanity in place of the two, thus making peace, and might reconcile both groups to God in one body through the cross, thus putting to death that hostility through it. (Eph. 2:14-16)

This mutual recognition is a constitutive element of the church.

163. This way of being in the church is in tension with another that can be identified in Acts 15. According to this passage certain Jewish Christians wanted to compel Gentile Christians to be circumcised and to live in accordance with Jewish regulations. This requirement was a challenge to the identity of the Gentile Christians. What made it possible to resolve the conflict was recognition of what God had done (Acts 15:8-10) and a rereading of Scripture (vv. 15-17). Gentile Christians were recognized as believers, respect being paid to their origin. The Jewish Christians abandoned imposing their requirements on them, and Gentile Christians, for their part, gave up practices that were offensive to the identity of the Jewish Christians. The identity of each was converted through these acts of renunciation. Christians of Jewish origin gave up identifying the gospel with their demands, which were only a particular way of living out the gospel. Gentile Christians gave up what could seem to be idolatry (eating "food sacrificed to idols"), discovering that freedom does not happen without limitations. Freedom and obedience then both appeared in their gospel genuineness. The basic identity grounded in the gospel shone through their respective conversions.

III. Identity, Renunciation, and Conversion

a) The Example of Christ

164. Such acts of renunciation are in line with Christ's own experience. In him the loving freedom of God underwent its "conversion"; that is, God's turning towards human beings in accordance with what the hymn in Philippians 2:6-11 proclaims:

> [Jesus Christ] who, though he was in the form of God,
> did not regard equality with God
> as something to be exploited,
> but emptied himself,
> taking the form of a slave,
> being born in human likeness.
> And being found in human form,
> he humbled himself
> and became obedient to the point of death —
> even death on a cross.

Therefore God also highly exalted him
and gave him the name
that is above every name,
so that at the name of Jesus
every knee should bend,
in heaven and on earth and under the earth,
and every tongue should confess
that Jesus Christ is Lord,
to the glory of God the Father.

165. Jesus Christ renounced the prerogatives that were by nature his. He who was in the form of God freely took the form of a slave. A threefold self-abasement reveals this: becoming a man among human beings, making himself their servant to the end, giving himself up wholly to his God and Father, even to the cross. That gesture was a submission to the will of God, a renunciation of every claim to autonomy, trusting the Other and the others, and giving himself to him and them. Thus Jesus made manifest the different nature of the love of God, going so far as to undergo the "humiliation" of the cross so that God's identity might be revealed and exalted.

His attitude is the very opposite of humanity's initial attitude in their sinful desire for a spurious identity — "you will be like God [or gods]" (Gen. 3:5) — based on absorption or exclusion, fusion or schism, delusion and falsehood. Adam was laying claim to an identity without renunciation and without conversion to God.

166. Through this renunciation God granted to Jesus passage from death to life and allowed him to receive his full identity as Lord, signified in "the name that is above every name," confessed by the whole universe "to the glory of God the Father." God turned him who had turned towards humanity in self-denial back towards himself in glory. Thus Jesus completed the full cycle of identity through renunciation, a pilgrimage that it then becomes important for the ecclesial community to make its own (Phil. 2:1-5). For this gift and this turning — "conversion" — by God to human beings, achieved in the kenosis of the man Jesus, make possible and already bring about the conversion of human beings from pride and their renunciation of every claim to make themselves, by themselves, the image of God.

167. This turning of God towards human beings shows up in those manifold gestures of turning by Jesus towards those whom he encountered, in

which a bodily movement expresses the gesture of acceptance or calling, of love or forgiveness. Jesus turns towards the disciples of John who seek him (John 1:38), towards the woman with the hemorrhage (Matt. 9:21f.), towards those who have the blessing of seeing his ministry (Luke 10:23), towards the crowds who follow him (Luke 14:25), towards Peter, who has just denied him, to fix his gaze on him (Luke 22:61), towards the "daughters of Jerusalem" on the road to Calvary (23:28). This movement of turning calls for reciprocity. Mary Magdalene, for her part, turns twice towards her master to recognize him (John 20:14-16).

168. This process of renunciation is set in a faithfulness that defines the contours of it. Far from giving up his filial relation to the Father, which made him what he is, Jesus displayed it in its primordial truth and made it a reality as a man by his earthly pilgrimage.

Likewise Christians may renounce some elements of their identity they consider important, but not those that are at the heart of their confession of faith. There are some instances where renunciation would be suicidal. "By this you know the Spirit of God," says the first epistle of John. "Every spirit that confesses that Jesus Christ has come in the flesh is from God, and every spirit that does not confess Jesus is not from God. And this is the spirit of anti-christ" (4:2-3). One cannot renounce the Spirit through whom Christ is confessed in fullness. The confession of faith not only brings together the elements in Christian identity but also defines its boundaries (cf. also Gal. 1:8f.; 1 Cor. 12:3).

b) The Biblical Images of Conversion

169. If renunciation is not the loss of identity, neither is the process of repentance and conversion. On the contrary, it is the renewal and indeed the transfiguration of identity. This may be illustrated from the many passages in the Bible that are in effect parables of conversion.

170. Joshua 24 tells us of an event of conversion, even if the specific vocabulary of conversion is not used. Israel is called upon to renounce idols and choose the Lord: "Now therefore revere the Lord and serve him in sincerity and in faithfulness; put away the gods that your ancestors served beyond the river and in Egypt, and serve the Lord" (v. 14). In making that choice Israel reveals itself as the people of God, led by him from the start (vv. 2-13

and 16-18). It can lay hold of its past and open itself to the future. Its full identity is thus accessible to it.

171. In 2 Kings conversion is presented as a return of the people and its religious institutions to God in accordance with the Law: "Before him [Josiah] there was no king like him, who turned to the Lord with all his heart, with all his soul, and with all his might, according to all the law of Moses" (23:25). By renouncing the idolatry revealed by the Law the people rediscover that which constitutes their identity, that is, their bond with God who gave them birth and to whom they belong. Observance of the Law is the reference by which they can identify their divergences and their fidelities, and reappropriate their identity as the people of the covenant (cf. also vv. 1-3). This passage also shows the role that can be played by a few officials — the high priest Hilkiah, the secretary Shaphan, Huldah the prophetess, and King Josiah in the conversion of an entire people and its institutions (see the whole of 2 Kings 22–23).

172. Among the parables of forgiveness in Luke's Gospel (Luke 15) that of the Prodigal Son can be read as a story of a lost and rediscovered identity. The younger son claims the rights of his identity as a son by asking for his inheritance. In the process he loses it: in the "distant country" he is no longer anyone's son and he becomes the starving slave of a foreigner. When hunger makes him "come to himself," he realizes that he has lost everything, and his desire is to find at least the identity of a well-treated worker. Thus his repentance takes shape in the turn-about that makes him go back along the entire road that had separated him from his father. The moment of his confession is the moment when his father begets him afresh, treating him as his son who has come back to life, and giving a feast in his honor. The lost identity has been found again.

The older son who stayed at home has to all appearances retained his identity as a son. But for him it has become a right to be claimed. By refusing to recognize his brother in the man whom his father has welcomed back as his son, he in turn loses his own identity as a son. But once again the father goes out from the house: just as he had gone to meet his younger son he comes out to beg the elder to convert to a genuine filial attitude by recognizing in turn as his brother the one whom he calls "your son."

173. In Revelation, a church is called to repentance through the angel who represents it: "Repent then. If not, I will come to you soon and make war

against them with the sword of my mouth. Let anyone who has an ear listen to what the Spirit is saying to the churches. To everyone who conquers I will give some of the hidden manna, and I will give a white stone, and on the white stone is written a new name that no one knows except the one who receives it" (Rev. 2:16f.). Confession of faith does not exempt the church from continually repenting by returning to its attachment to Christ. Repentance leads the church also to its final confessing identity, given symbolically to "everyone who conquers" in the stone on which is written the name that is confessed (v. 17).

c) The Strength and Weakness of Identities

174. According to Matthew 16:18 Jesus said to Peter: "You are Peter, and on this rock I will build my church." He had given Simon the name of his new identity; he had indicated his unique role in the founding of the church. Such was his grace, such was his "strong point." But immediately afterwards Jesus treats him as Satan, the tempter, because Peter opposes the announcement of the passion. Whatever meaning our churches may give to the authority conferred on Peter, we observe that this same Peter, appointed as the foundation of the church, behaves like a tempter towards his Lord. Thus Peter's new identity, which is his strength, leaves him vulnerable to weakness. This is why Jesus speaks to him again, indicating that his thoughts are not the thoughts of God, and calls on him to come after him and follow him.

We may say that what is called for from Peter is a conversion. Insofar as we recognize that this passage relates not only to Peter but also to the life of the church, can we dismiss the warning that is part of it?

175. Likewise in Matthew 18:20, Jesus says that "where two or three are gathered in my name, I am there among them." This saying is given special status in some churches to the point of being sufficient authority in their eyes for their ecclesial identity.

But this is to forget that fraternal communion is not established without conflict, reconciliation, and regulation. It isolates the saying from the verses preceding it, which invite us to listen to the church and which define its authority: "If another member of the church sins against you, go and point out the fault when the two of you are alone. If the member listens to you, you have regained that one. But if you are not listened to, take one or two others along with you, so that every word may be confirmed by the evidence of two or three witnesses. If the member refuses to listen to them, tell it to the church; and if the offender refuses to listen even to the church, let such a one be to you as a Gentile and a tax collector. Truly I tell you, whatever you bind on earth will be bound in heaven, and whatever you loose on earth will be loosed in heaven" (Matt. 18:15-18). If we find a basis for ecclesial identity in the saying in Matthew 18:20, can we forget the institutional context in which it is included?

176. Likewise Paul was the object of an exceptional calling. The Risen Christ had appeared to him; he had had the privilege of visions and revelations; he had been "caught up to the third heaven." His being called was the basis of his identity as an apostle. But he knew the risk of pride that is attached to all these gifts. Thus he rejoiced in experiencing weakness and the thorn in his flesh (2 Cor. 12:7). Hence he did not dare boast except in his weaknesses. That experience had already enabled him to warn the Corinthians that "if you think you are standing, watch out that you do not fall" (1 Cor. 10:12).

177. *Thus the strongest point in our identity is also that which is most vulnerable to temptation. We can live truly in accordance with our identity only in a continual process of conversion.* In pursuing our research, these passages from Scripture have been an illumination for us.

d) Balance-Sheet

178. This brief biblical survey has progressively interrelated identity and conversion and verified in its own way that conversion is the very opposite of a loss of identity. As people of God, body of Christ, and temple of the Spirit, the church is invited to repentance as that which will lead it to its final identity. Knowing how difficult it is for Christians to understand that conversion is not only something done by each member of the church but by communities as such, we are thus helped by Scripture to grasp the depth of this conversion to which we are called in Jesus' words to Peter: "When you grow old, you will stretch out your hands, and someone else will . . . take you where you do not wish to go" (John 21:18).

PART IV
Final Recommendations

179. In this final part of our work we shall try to define, from three different but converging points of view, the positive developments that progress in confessional conversion demands of our churches. We shall begin with a spiritual setting by reflecting on the four marks of the church; we shall then ask for a conscientious examination of our respective temptations; finally, we shall propose a few more specific and practical points.

I. The Four Marks of the Church: An Invitation to Conversion

180. We should like to suggest a rereading of the four marks of the church that are intrinsic to the faith of Nicea, as expressed in the Nicene-Constantinopolitan creed: *one, holy, catholic, apostolic.*

181. An initial comment is essential: only "one" and "holy" are scriptural expressions. "Catholic" and "apostolic" are derivative marks, whereas *unam sanctam* is a kind of definition of the church in line with Scripture.

182. There is a profusion of biblical passages: unity founded on Christ, the one foundation (1 Cor. 3:10-13); the unity of the Spirit in a diversity of gifts (1 Cor. 12); one body in Christ (Rom. 12:3-8); one shepherd and one flock (John 10:16); one as the Father and the Son are one (John 17:20-26); thanks to the unity of the Spirit in the bond of peace, just as there is "one Lord, one faith, one baptism, one God and Father of all" (Eph. 4:1-6).

183. A passage from Ephesians is also crucial for defining the holiness of the church: "Christ loved the church and gave himself up for her, in order to make her holy by cleansing her with the washing of water by the word, so as to present the church to himself in splendor, without a spot or wrinkle or anything of the kind — yes, so that she may be holy and without blemish" (Eph. 5:25-27).

184. Now — this is a second comment — patristic reflections on the holiness of the church revolve around this passage from Ephesians. They express a marveling certainty: the holiness of him who alone is holy is communicated through the Son and in the Spirit. That is why the community

of sinners is the body of Christ and frail flesh is the temple of the Spirit. That is why there is the communication of holy things — or, better, of the holy mysteries. That is why describing the church as *unam sanctam* means defining it as the communion of saints.[73]

185. We know that no Christian confession professing the Nicene faith can consider this combined mark of unity and holiness as devoid of all meaning. Undoubtedly there are diverging interpretations of it — according to Christian confessions, in the course of history, also within each confession.[74] But when we take another look at history we discover that the debate on the holiness of the church has been the bearer of hope — and hope of conversion — far less than the debate on its unity.

186. On the eve of Vatican II the Catholic interpretation of the unity of the church which could be regarded as classical was that of Möhler: spiritual, mystical, and doctrinal unity is expressed in organic unity.[75] This may be interpreted thus: the church in its spiritual unity is Christ in his mystical body, which is also a body of doctrine. Organic unity is Christ in his ministerial and sacramental priesthood, which is fulfilled in the episcopate and through the primacy of the pope.

187. This pattern was not challenged by Vatican II. But it was transformed by the theme of the people of God. The strength of this people does not lie in its gatheredness but in its being called or, rather, in the one who calls them. The church is that people whom God calls through the grace of his Son and whom he gathers in the freedom of the Spirit. Thus the Spirit has priority over the church, which obliges the church to acknowledge the Spirit's initiative and thus not to set its own bounds.[76] Consequently the

73. The most concise statement of this unity-holiness of the church is undoubtedly Cyprian's formula, adopted in *Lumen Gentium*: "a people brought into unity from the unity of the Father, the Son and the Holy Spirit" (Cyprian, *De Oratione Domini,* 23; *Lumen Gentium,* 4).

74. Recall some of the reasons for reticence about the holiness of the church: Is the holiness of Christ, the pattern, not incommunicable and moreover just a little discouraging? Does not this affirmation of holiness turn into worship of the saints and does it not set up the church as a judge of holiness? Is the holiness of the church not solely eschatological?

75. Cf. Möhler (1796-1838), *Die Einheit in der Kirche.*

76. Cf. Acts 10:47: "Can anyone withhold the water for baptizing these people who have received the Holy Spirit just as we have?" If Irenaeus wrote: "Where the church is, there is the Spirit of God," he also added: "And where the Spirit of God is, there is the church and every

ancient formula *extra ecclesiam nulla salus* — no salvation outside the church[77] — acquires a meaning that is no longer the marking out of a limit but the recognition of a wholly spiritual criterion: there is no salvation, save in communion, and there is no other boundary than the communion of saints. One might equally hazard this description of the church: it is a general summons to humanity for communion with Christ.

188. If the Roman Catholic Church maintains that it is the body of Christ, and if it is convinced that the one church is inalienably present within it,[78] that claim must bring about a deep and unceasing conversion. In fact, neither incorporation in the church (the fact that one professes the faith, participates in the sacraments, and obeys its ministers) nor the membership in the church of all who bear the fine name of Christians has any meaning if the motivation and dynamic do not come from the church's evangelical and missionary orientation. Without that orientation the unity of the church would be a delusion.

189. Second, the statement that the church is completely holy in its head, Christ, and that no unworthiness in its ministers is an obstacle to the transmission of that holiness, must not be used to conceal the faults that we should undoubtedly have the courage to call sins of the church. Likewise — and there we come to the third mark of the church — catholicity is sometimes understood too much as a universal expansion of the church of Rome, whereas it is in fact that church which has a duty to be faithful to its charism of being catholic. The churches dispersed everywhere are Roman only through the bond of communion with the first of the apostolic churches, that of Peter and Paul. Finally, apostolicity, which is organic continuity with the apostles, takes on its full meaning only through life lived in accordance with the gospel and the preaching of the Word.

190. On the Protestant side, while the Reformers and some of their successors maintained the ecumenical creeds and thus the marks of the church, one often sees in practice that unity is regarded as an aggregate of diversi-

---

grace. . . . And the Spirit is the truth" (*Adversus omnes haereses*, III, 24, 1). In other words, the church is that which the Holy Spirit guides into all truth. This priority of the Spirit over the church was reaffirmed by the sixteenth-century Protestant Reformers.

77. Origen, "On Joshua," *Homilies*, 3, 5; *S.C.* no. 71, p. 143; Cyprian, *Letter*, 73, 21, 2.

78. *Lumen Gentium*, 8: "Haec ecclesia . . . subsistit in Ecclesia catholica. . . ." ("This church . . . subsists in the Catholic Church. . . .")

ties that at best tolerate each other, each jealous of its autonomy and its customs; that the *holiness* of the church no longer depends on the holiness of Christ, its head, but on the members' purity of doctrine or life; that *catholicity* has been divested of its dimension of fullness and become nothing more than universality in space, the very use of the term "catholic" being generally rejected; that *apostolicity* consists in a claim to affirm, think, and act as the apostles would have done, with hardly any remaining link to the tradition that guarantees their succession.

191. For this reason we may hope for the following type of theological and spiritual conversion in the interpretation of the four marks of the church:

The Christian confessions must give up the idea of *unity* as uniformity or as a federation; of *holiness* as a canonization of devotion to the ecclesial *res publica* or contrariwise as praise of virtues that are only private; of *catholicity* as a universalism conquering or holding on to conquered territories; of *apostolicity* as a literal return to origins or repetition of beginnings.

192. These temptations must be resisted so that the churches may open themselves up to:

- unity as a challenge to all uniformity and all disparity, in the name of a christological and trinitarian confession;
- holiness as the obedience of faith, faithfulness to the gospel, and listening to the Spirit;
- catholicity as the possibility offered to all persons, whoever and wherever they are, to venture towards truth in its fullness;
- apostolicity as viewing from afar the shore of the kingdom, which the episcopal overseer[79] is pointing out to us and which the beloved disciple was the first to recognize (John 21:7).

193. Thus the God who is greater than our hearts (1 John 3:20), the Christ of mercy,[80] and the Spirit who is well pleased where truth is a sweet savor[81] will be confessed as the one thing of which there is need (Luke 10:42) by the one church.[82]

---

79. On the clear understanding that the term "episcopal overseer" here covers several forms — bishops, presidents, synods; cf. our document "The Episcopal Ministry."

80. Cf. Hosea 6:6; Matthew 12:7; Irenaeus, *Adversus omnes haereses*, IV, 17, 4.

81. Augustine, *Confessions*, IV, 12, 18.

82. Cf. the reading of Song of Solomon 6:9 by Cyprian in *Letter*, 69, 2, 1.

II. Our Respective Temptations

194. As we come to the end of our investigations and of what we have learned, our impression is that the twofold concern with conversion and identity enables us to avoid two false paths in which a quest for unity may go astray:

- The path of one church being absorbed by another. This was long the only path conceivable on all sides, and for some it remains so; one thinks only about one's own identity and sacrifices that of the other.
- The path of the status quo. This is the recent temptation of churches that are content with the state of separation, or of vague relations that are no longer regarded as divisive: it is thought possible to retain the identities of all peaceably, in an existence where there is no conversion.

195. As the witness of Scripture has led us to say, the strongest point in identity is also the one most vulnerable to temptation. The only way to live in truth in line with one's identity is in a constant movement of conversion.

Catholics and Protestants could no doubt agree on the affirmation that the charism which makes one church take seriously the exercise of authority in the name of the Lord may lead to an abuse and perversion of authority, and that the charism in some other churches which esteems life in Christian freedom may give rise to a perversion of liberty.

In fact, "the inalienable share of truth"[83] that is present in each church is always liable to be the point of its own perversion. We are thus invited to ask ourselves about where the identity and at the same time the temptation of each church takes root. Ecumenical dialogue has enabled us to discover these places on the basis of the questions we have asked each other.

196. Thus the question for Catholics relates to the understanding and use of authority in their church, which display an excessive concern to provide institutional guarantees at the expense of the freedom of the Spirit.

Likewise the question for Protestants relates to the understanding and use of freedom in their churches at the risk of confusing all the confessional options with the revelation of the Spirit.

---

83. Cf. the Joint Catholic-Protestant Committee in France, *Consensus œcuménique et différence fondamentale*, no. 17, p. 25.

197. The balance between the personal, collegial, and community dimensions in the exercise of the ministry within our churches is also threatened, as our previous writings have shown, particularly regarding *episcopē*.[84] Among Catholics the personal dimension is the strong point, but it may overlook the necessary complementarity of the collegial and community dimensions, and thus even be perverted. The Reformation churches face a similar danger, some of them granting high status to the collegial aspect (the presbyterian-synodal system), others to the community aspect (the congregationalist system).

198. Regarding the work of the Spirit, it is conceived by Catholics as an irrevocable gift, at the risk of thinking that it excludes all error, while for the churches of the Protestant Reformation it is understood as a promise, at the risk of thinking that it removes all constraint and all security.

199. In general terms Catholicism is so concerned about fullness that it tends to add and include even impurities and syncretism, while the Protestants are so concerned about obedience to Scripture that they tend to cut down and suppress, at the risk of falling into purism and abstraction.

200. Finally — and this is an urgent problem — the development of science and technology raises new ethical questions for Christianity.

The Catholic Church answers these by referring to a doctrine of creation and through the voice of the magisterium, at the risk of sacralizing a concept of natural law disrespectful of the ultimate rights of the individual conscience.

Protestants appeal essentially to the diversity of scriptural witness and to personal responsibility, at the risk of removing all value from the texts as normative and leaving the individual conscience to its own devices.[85]

201. These are some of the questions where it seems that our strong points show themselves to be also the bearers of perversion. Thus we have to ask each other about what we have just called "the inalienable share of truth" of each of our churches. We cannot ignore each other or exclude each

84. Dombes, "The Ministry of Communion in the Universal Church," no. 9; and "The Episcopal Ministry," nos. 42-44.

85. Cf. Joint Catholic-Protestant Committee in France, "Catholiques et protestants face à la morale dans une société laïque," *Doc. Cath.* 1995 (1989): 1072f.

other: on the contrary we are called to encounter each other and correct each other fraternally so that the gospel may not be proclaimed by conflicting voices.

III. Towards Mutual Emulation in Conversion

202. In the field of ecclesiology and the sacraments the Groupe des Dombes has in its previous documents voiced many calls for conversion, which were addressed to each church by its own members.

We do not wish now to repeat the contents of these appeals, but all of us are concerned to tell our churches that the translation of these appeals into practice is a matter of urgency.

We are so bold as to indicate together as Catholics and Protestants some points at which each of our churches must go through a transition in the process of conversion that must lead us to full communion. Finally we shall express a call for a new stage of conversion that concerns them all alike.

a) A Call Addressed to the Churches of the Reformation

203. Are the churches of the Protestant Reformation drawing all the consequences of their conviction that they belong to the one church of God instituted by Christ? The key terms — *sola scriptura, sola fide, sola gratia* — can open no door other than that of the *sola ecclesia,* which remains the one and only church in its various traditions.

204. That one church is indubitably a eucharistic church, that is, a church of praise and of thanksgiving. The eucharist is not in itself an article of faith, but in St. Irenaeus's words it is faith itself *in compendio* — in a nutshell.[86] Consequently the celebration of the Word and the Lord's Supper together, the essential act of Christian worship, must be regular and frequent.

205. To stress this character of unity and universality, is it not essential that the term "catholic" be given fresh treatment in the churches of the Protestant Reformation? Unhappily, each confession has arrogated to itself traditional designations that belong to the whole church as a distinctive la-

---

86. Irenaeus, *Adversus omnes haereses,* III, 16, 7.

bel: but it is the whole church that is catholic, just as the church in its entirety is evangelical, orthodox, and called upon to reform itself. This primordial designation, which speaks of the fullness of Christianity[87] at the same time as its universality, must be recognized in each individual church[88] and cannot be removed from our common history. These divided churches of today are all of them together heirs of the church of the fathers and of the medieval church with its riches and its woes.

206. The churches of the Protestant Reformation rightly claim that apostolic succession is fidelity to the faith of the apostles. Ought they not to listen to the appeal that the Catholic and Orthodox churches address to them regarding the visible continuity that brings ministers into the continuum of the ministry of the apostles?

207. The churches of the Protestant Reformation rightly stress the reality of the priesthood of all who have been baptized. Should they not also recognize the special gift God has given to his church in the persons of the ministers of the Word and sacraments, the *episcopē* and diaconate, in line with the structure of the church instituted by Christ?[89]

208. The Reformation churches cannot forget that the church has to be constantly reformed. Thus they will honor the name by which they are known only if they seek still today to undergo a confessional conversion that snatches them out of the danger of folding themselves up in their own identity.

b) A Call Addressed to the Roman Catholic Church

209. Will the Roman Catholic Church allow itself to be questioned by the fundamental conviction of the Protestant Reformers that salvation is first

---

87. "Religion must be sought among those alone whom we call catholic — that is, orthodox — Christians. They preserve the integrity which they follow in uprightness," Augustine, *De vera religione*, 5, 9; PL, 34, 127.

88. The letter from the church of Smyrna to the church of Philomelium reporting the martyrdom of Polycarp is of course crucial on this matter. Polycarp in particular is described there as bishop of the catholic church of Smyrna (16, 2; S.C., no. 10, p. 265).

89. We understand these words in accordance with the statements in our previous documents, "Towards a Reconciliation of Ministries" and "The Episcopal Ministry."

of all a free gift of God offered to everyone and that this grace, received from the Father's mercy, made effectual through the unique sacrifice of the Son on the cross, and lived in faith under the influence of the Holy Spirit, is not in the power of any person or of any human authority?

210. The church, which is at once the body of Christ and a visible institution marked by sin, is faithful to its mission only when it recognizes this order of priority, which subordinates it to the free sovereignty of its Lord through the work of the Holy Spirit.

211. If the Roman Catholic Church sees itself as the sacrament of the mediation of Christ, while priding itself in the mystery of its origin, will it nevertheless accept, as a human and historical reality, that it recognize itself as an imperfect, sinful sacrament that contributes to division? In this historical situation of sin, which places it in a fellowship of repentance with the other churches, should the Roman Catholic Church not advance in its recognition of other ecclesial loci in which the unique mediation of Christ is exercised, in the indisputable but impalpable conjunction of the church as the mystery of the body of Christ and the church as a human community? This progress would lead it to understand and affirm with greater humility what it confesses about itself when it says that the true church of Christ "subsists" in the Roman Catholic Church.

212. If each confessional church, and therefore also the Roman Catholic Church which emerged from the Catholic reformation of the sixteenth century, bears its share of sinful responsibility in the divisions from which the ecclesial body of Christ is suffering, has not the church of Rome also in its historical nature lost ecclesial fullness on account of the schisms of the eleventh and sixteenth centuries?

213. The Roman Catholic Church has the fraternal duty to ask the other churches about their ecclesial authenticity; and this inquiry must relate to the faithfulness of these churches to the gospel of Christ, the confessions of faith of the ancient church, and the apostolicity of their ministry. But should it not acknowledge that apostolicity, prior to being the expression of a historical continuity, consists first in faithfulness to Christ, the foundation of every ministry, a faithfulness experienced according to Scripture in the diversity of forms and communities of the apostolic age?

214. By respecting that priority and by calling on the churches that arose out of the Protestant Reformation to reexamine their ecclesiality, the Roman Catholic Church could ask them unambiguously about the faithfulness of their ministry to the apostolic tradition. While noting the break in historical continuity made in the sixteenth century, could it not nevertheless recognize the apostolicity of the ministry in the churches that came into being as a result of the Protestant Reformation as well founded? The path would then perhaps be opened up for a shared conversion to full ecclesial communion, in mutual recognition of the apostolic basis of the ministries on the one hand, and in the non-divisive diversity of expressions of the faith and church practice on the other.

c) A Call Addressed to All Our Churches

215. Progress in confessional conversion of the still-divided churches calls now for decisions that will have both real and symbolic value. We mention only a few particularly significant examples.

216. Has the time not come to propose to all Christians a common version of the traditional creeds in languages in which they are not yet available? Achieving this presupposes the effective desire to solve the few problems on which this common version has so far come to grief.

217. The mutual excommunications between Rome and Constantinople have been lifted. Has the moment not come to act in the same way on a large number of anathemas the churches pronounced on each other in the sixteenth century? Their removal, celebrated liturgically by the leadership in the churches, would show that these anathemas of the past no longer affect the partners of today. It would make it possible to show that a good many points no longer constitute a problem. Following the examples culled from the ancient church, it would demonstrate that the difference between doctrinal terminologies is compatible with unanimity in the faith.

218. Recent ecumenical research has made it possible to define more appropriately the differences that remain within the ecumenical consensus on our ecclesiologies. Has the moment not come to work together at discerning what is a legitimate difference compatible with unity and what is a

divisive divergence that must be overcome? Each church would then take the decisions necessary to overcome these divergences.

219. In the field of the doctrine of the faith, many dialogues, multilateral and bilateral, have been undertaken in the last twenty-five years. Even if they still need to be continued, has not the time come not only to draw up a balance-sheet on them but to bring them to a conclusion, that is, to raise their status, whenever possible, from that of documents of interconfessional commissions to the level of new expressions of the faith, which would be authoritative, even if still limited and incomplete, and to draw from them all the consequences for the life of the churches?

220. The progress that has been made towards unity invites our churches not only to pursue resolutely the doctrinal dialogue in which they are already involved, but also to ask each other about the actual behavior of Christian congregations. It is imperative to recognize that some gestures of reconciliation, the principle of which has been accepted in theory, have still not been put into practice. Even where some elements of agreement have been achieved, they do not always give rise to the ecclesial and confessional practices that would be appropriate to them.

221. Many words have been said and many documents written; but too often actions are slow to follow, and this situation becomes worse as the years go on. May our congregations and communities have the courage to confront their practice with the convictions that have already been approved by the ecumenical movement. May they progress as their conversions progress and at the appropriate time celebrate acts of reconciliation that will be symbols of the thresholds that have been crossed. In this way confessional conversion will serve ecclesial conversion and enable the church to give a credible witness to its conversion to Christ.

Appendix: Some Simple Suggestions for Catechesis Where There Is Conversion

Has the day not come when a papist hand might slip the following into Protestant catechism books so that it might be received with a catholic heart?

1. Members of the Roman church, that is, Christians who belong to that church which was founded by the chief of the apostles and the apostle to the Gentiles, make the sign of the cross of Christ.

In so doing they are not indicating or asking that everyone should do what they do. They are simply confessing that salvation through the cross is given to us in the name of the Father and of the Son and of the Holy Spirit.

2. Members of the Roman church apply to Mary the apostle's words: "What do you have that you have not received?" (1 Cor. 4:7). True, they say this using the words of the angel and of Mary's relative Elizabeth: "Greetings, favored one! The Lord is with you. . . . Blessed are you among women and blessed is the fruit of your womb" (Luke 1:28, 42). They consider that what more is said to or about Mary comes not from the Evil One but from the tradition of the church, in a sort of reading of the Scriptures that begins when one closes one's eyes: "Holy Mary, Mother of God, pray for us. . . ." Those who pray in this way sometimes forget to do so in secret, but the Lord's Prayer is their daily bread which they share with all their brothers and sisters.

3. Members of the Roman church celebrate the Lord's Supper just as we do. They do not yet celebrate it with us but we can celebrate it with them. On seeing it done, the desire should grow in us for that blessed day when there will only be one bread for the many that we are, and one cup of blessing that we shall all bless. We can also consider the respect with which they surround the consecrated bread and wine as a sign of the loving faith of the church of God for its Lord offered in communion.

4. Members of the Roman church are never without an entourage of people whom they consider as their spiritual leaders, giving one of them the name of pope. We must learn, and perhaps remind our brothers and sisters, that these people are all bishops, the first among them being the Bishop of Rome. In saying this, members of the Roman church affirm that these people have the mission of keeping the churches in continuity with the apostles and in faithfulness to the Scriptures. We must consider them as being for our brothers and sisters what our pastors are for us: representatives of God to his church and not creations of the church.

5. Like us, members of the Roman church must be continually converted. They have a great reverence for those who have received the grace to re-

spond "to the end" to this call to "repent and believe in the good news." They think of them as saints, and in worship they thank God for having made of these sinners creatures saved by Christ, intercessors and examples. We may not share this view, and may even ask our brothers and sisters to be faithful to the *Tu solus sanctus* ("you alone are holy") of their own liturgy. But we must never forget that members of the Roman church invoke on our behalf the saint whose name we bear.

6. Because of all this, we must consider members of the Roman church as our brothers and sisters in Christ. We must also recognize that for them this fraternal relation is a desire to do everything so that their own church may not be an obstacle to the practice of that relationship. On the contrary, members of the Roman church expect from that church that its recourse to Peter and Paul will mean the withering away of its Roman-ness for the sake of the apostolic vitality of the holy church of God dwelling at Rome.

*　　*　　*

Has the day not come when a Huguenot hand might slip the following into the catechism books of the Roman Catholic Church so that it may be received with an evangelical heart?

1. Protestant Christians, members of a church derived from the Reformation of the sixteenth century, do not think that the church began at that moment, but receive the faith of the fathers and councils gratefully, in solidarity with the ancient church and as a beneficiary of it.

2. Protestant Christians, with the assurance that the Word of God preserves the church which keeps that Word, nevertheless think that the living and genuine tradition of this church must be subordinated to the sole standard of Scripture.

3. Protestant Christians, when they confess their faith, not only with the traditional creeds but also with the confessional texts of the sixteenth century — such as the Augsburg Confession, the Confession of La Rochelle, or others — consider that it is the confession of faith that gives the church its structure.

4. Protestant Christians, finally, when they confess the one universal church beyond the visible and institutional forms taken by the historical churches, do not resign themselves to these divisions. In their quest for ecclesial unity in Jesus Christ, they recognize that this diversity is nevertheless not an irreversible obstacle to the realization of unity, and that in a non-divisive plurality, following the example of that of the ecclesial communities in the New Testament, the quest and hope for the kingdom and the righteousness of God may be made manifest.

*   *   *

Fr Jean-Noël Aletti
Rev François Altermath
Fr Joseph de Baciocchi
Fr René Beaupère
Rev André Benoit
Rev Alain Blancy
Rev Marc Chambron
Fr Bruno Chenu
Fr Marc Clément
Fr Robert Clément
Fr Irénée-Henri Dalmais
Fr Henri Denis
Fr Michel Fédou
Rev Flemming Fleinert-Jensen
Rev Michel Freychet
Rev Daniel Fricker
Fr Paul Gay
Fr Claude Gerest
Fr René Girault

Fr Étienne Goutagny
Fr Pierre Gressot
Rev Godfried Hamann
Fr Joseph Hoffmann
Fr Maurice Jourjon
Rev Guy Lasserre
Rev Michel Leplay
Rev Louis Lévrier
Fr Robert Liotard
Rev Alain Martin
Rev Alain Massini
Rev Willy-René Nussbaum
Rev Jacques-Noël Pérès
Fr Bernard Sesboüé
Fr Damien Sicard
Rev Jean-Marc Viollet
Fr Pierre Vuichard
Rev Gaston Westphal